Naked Savages

NAKED SAVAGES

By
Dale M. Brumfield

HJH Media Richmond, Virginia

Copyright © 2019 by Dale M. Brumfield

This book is a work of fiction. Any references to real events, real people, real places, languages or cultures are used fictitiously. Other names, characters, events and places are products of the author's imagination, and any resemblance to actual places, events or persons, living or dead, is coincidental.

All rights reserved. No part of this publication may be reproduced, distributed or transmitted in any form or by any means, without prior written permission except brief passages for review purposes.

HJH Media
Richmond, Virginia
For media inquiries please email HJHmedia@mail.com

Cover design and illustration by Hunter Brumfield.

Naked Savages/ Dale M. Brumfield -- 1st ed. 2019

ISBN-13: 978-0-578-44055-2 (paperback)

ISBN-13: 978-0-578-44057-6 (electronic)

NAKED SAVAGES

By
Dale M. Brumfield

HJH Media Richmond, Virginia

Copyright © 2019 by Dale M. Brumfield

This book is a work of fiction. Any references to real events, real people, real places, languages or cultures are used fictitiously. Other names, characters, events and places are products of the author's imagination, and any resemblance to actual places, events or persons, living or dead, is coincidental.

All rights reserved. No part of this publication may be reproduced, distributed or transmitted in any form or by any means, without prior written permission except brief passages for review purposes.

HJH Media
Richmond, Virginia
For media inquiries please email HJHmedia@mail.com

Cover design and illustration by Hunter Brumfield.

Naked Savages/ Dale M. Brumfield -- 1st ed. 2019

ISBN-13: 978-0-578-44055-2 (paperback)

ISBN-13: 978-0-578-44057-6 (electronic)

By Dale M. Brumfield

Memoir

Three Buck Naked Commodes: and 18 More Tales from a Small Town

Fiction

Remnants: A Novel about God, Insurance and Quality Floorcoverings

Trapped Under the Pack-Ice (eBook)

Bad Day at the Amusement Park (eBook)

Standers

Non-fiction

Richmond Independent Press: A History of the Underground Zine Scene

Independent Press in D.C. and Virginia: An Underground History

Virginia State Penitentiary: A Notorious History

Anthologies

Richmond Macabre

Richmond Macabre II

Web

http://www.dalebrumfield.net

Staunton News-Leader: https://www.newsleader.com/

https://medium.com/@dalebrumfield

Theme Park Babylon

https://www.instagram.com/brumfield.dale

https://www.facebook.com/dale.brumfield.1

"Complex systems tend to oppose their own intended function."

-variation on LeChatelier's Principle,
as proposed by John Gall in
"Systemantics" (Pocket Books, 1975)

PROLOGUE

"I just had the remote – now where the hell did it go?"

Lying in bed, Wallace Carswell clutched his tightening chest and grimaced while he leaned and frantically felt around the floor by the bed. He had muted Ronald Reagan droning about his upcoming re-election chances before changing the channel and dropping the remote. After briefly closing his eyes, he opened them to see actors Michael J. Fox and Madonna seriously and silently discussing something on a show called Entertainment Tonight while a crawl at the bottom of the screen announced "Hollywood and Screen Actors Guild uniting behind Japanese/American collaboration to help save vanishing Ethiopian tribe." The scroll sent him on a scurry to un-mute – the television break of a lifetime was unfolding right in front of him and he couldn't goddamn hear it.

Beside him, Mary was sleepy and unconcerned. "I don't know Boo Boo, you dropped it after bitching about Reagan ..."

He leaned way over and fumbled around on the floor. "Dropped it where, Mary? For Christ's ..." Spotting a corner of it almost under the bed, Wallace scooped it up, quickly pointed it at the television and restored the volume. It was too late – the segment was over; Fox and Madonna were gone, and the blonde host was talking about yet another seventies metalhead going into rehab for cocaine addiction.

Though disappointed, Wallace managed a brief smile as a somewhat familiar lightning bolt shot from his chest down his left arm. He moaned softly, with some concern but more with a curious sense of satisfaction. His documentary project just got a healthy dose of good national buzz, and the first frame had yet to be shot.

Wallace looked up from his bed in the hotel room that served temporarily as his office (while his regular office building was being fumigated) and saw the low setting sun glinting a dull orange off the fading Sunset Boulevard buildings far off in the background. He took a drag on his high-tar British cigarette that made him feel like a Tinseltown big shot then looked down in a bemused combination of lust and irritation at the beautiful nude woman lying beside his sadly out-of-shape 62-year-old body.

Mary Semper was a bit of a slippery parasite but a damn gorgeous one. Wallace walked into a relationship with her wary it was a tightrope – he of course reveled in her sexual appetites, and her attention was a much-needed boost to his self-confidence, but he knew the real reason she hooked up with him was to enter the film business in more serious behind-the-scene roles with his somewhat modest film production company in the hopes of either taking them all up a notch or (as he suspected) jumping to Paramount or MGM.

Despite putting her on payroll, Mary was a hobby, not a career. Reliance Film Group, Inc. survived, even flourished sometimes, but never made millionaires. He simply had no jobs for her, despite his ambiguous promises to the contrary.

Unfortunately, he inadvertently muddied their already sloppy and opaque relationship even more yesterday, when she overheard him on the phone speaking of an upcoming documentary that he was producing in an eastern African no-man's-land in Ethiopia between the Eritrean border and the Red Sea called the Danakil Desert. Now she wouldn't leave him the hell alone about it, needling him for a production management position. Then, in his clumsy attempts to downplay the project, he complicated the situation even more by trying to sidetrack her with the empty promise of another job – a "much better and higher profile" job – that was "just around the corner."

There was no way Wallace was going to place Mary on the Ethiopian documentary. Her take-charge, micromanaging style would not be a good fit on a multi-cultural, Ethiopian-financed, Japanese-directed project that had suddenly drawn the attention of a handful of Hollywood elites and had to be handled with much delicacy. Mary was a hard worker, for sure, but she had little respect for job titles and defined boundaries. He knew especially that the project's mysterious Ethiopian financial backer, as well as the Tokyo-based film team already signed on to make the film, would never allow the involvement of a pushy, take-charge American woman on their pet project, in any managing capacity especially. Sexist? Sure – but that was the nature of the business.

This documentary project had miraculously fallen into Wallace's lap. His partner, a penny-pinching bean counter named Marvin Waltz, stumbled upon a Tokyo film team that had their original American producer pull out of an impending collaborative project while under investigation by the CIA for accepting bribes from a shadowy group of Eritrean liberationists who had been censured by the UN for human rights violations. Wallace was initially hesitant to sign the Japanese, but they insisted they had this no-fail project, documenting the historical mistreatment of an indigenous Ethiopian culture and people that was sure to be completely annihilated in a projected famine-induced civil war.

Wallace realized that the film would make good money, but even better it would portray him as a selfless humanitarian – a distinction he sorely needed after a misstep two years earlier from which he was still recovering that unfairly pegged him as an old school stereotype. The Japanese even had majority funding secured via their previous producer through that Ethiopian magnate, which certainly sweetened the deal. Wallace's involvement was largely ornamental, more to exploit his plentiful distribution contacts and label the project as an American/Japanese/Ethiopian collaboration, with a potential big payoff and almost no risk. Taking Marvin's advice, he accepted the project.

Then, a miracle occurred: just after accepting the project, news began circulating that musician Bob Geldof was interested in organizing a rock super-group to raise money for a nearby part of that deprived region. Leeching onto and riding the publicity behind Band Aid, and with Geldof's canvassing of musicians and heavy-hitting celebrities at fund-raisers, it suddenly looked like Wallace Carswell's gamble could pay off in an unexpected and most spectacular way.

As if suddenly realizing Wallace was thinking of her, Mary stretched, smiled and ran her finger down the railroad trestle in the center of her partner's almost hairless chest. "It's about time you revealed my surprise, Boo Boo," she said, post-coital sleep still fogging her mouth, "You promised."

Wallace tapped his cigarette on the edge of the ashtray. "Please, Mary, can't we just lie here and not talk about work?" He went out of his way to portray the documentary to her as just another insignificant distribution job – not the millionaire-maker he prayed it would be.

"You need to calm down," Mary more ordered than cooed, a little agitated, walking two fingers up the rippled scar to her bedmate's lips. "Marvin said you were so preoccupied lately with this mysterious African project, so you either have to tell me what it is, or ..."

"Marvin has a big mouth," Wallace snorted, an acidic knot rising in his throat. He briefly looked at the nightstand between the Tylenol and Xanax for his antacid. There was no way he was putting Mary on the project – the Ethiopian and the Japanese would surely reject both of them – but he had to offer her something, and soon; he couldn't keep stringing her along, she was driving him nuts.

He thought fast. "But, well – the thing is, Mary – the surprise is I have a DP job for you. But you have to keep it a secret for now."

Mary sat up in bed, her face first quizzical then opening into a broad smile. "I'm on a shoot? Seriously! Who's directing? What do the financials look like?"

Wallace clutched his chest and tried to roll away. He only had two other films in early development, and one lousy script in turnaround. Christ, he just couldn't keep his mouth shut around her. Projects were few and far between in this crap Reagan economy, and he hated mixing work and play – it never ended well. He was terrible around women, why did he always blab around her? Why was the prospect of being with her so damn appealing he turned into such a prattling lunatic?

He suddenly had an idea – not a good one, but at least a half-baked appeasing notion. He took a final drag on his cigarette before grinding it out in an already overflowing ashtray on the nightstand. There was an anvil on his chest.

"No, no, one thing at a time," he grunted as he picked up and shook an empty Jim Beam bottle then laid it back on the floor. "I'll get Marvin to fax your project over. Mind you, it's all very preliminary, still in fund-raising. I was going to tell you when the details got firmed up. In the meantime, why don't you go shower so we can go get pancakes down at the Toddle House. We'll talk more about it then."

Mary grabbed Wallace's face with both hands and planted a sloppy kiss on his lips before she hopped out of bed and strode nude and confident into the bathroom. "I knew you'd come through, Boo-Boo! I can't wait to hear about it!"

Once the door closed and the shower started Wallace thought for a minute before he picked up the bedside phone and punched a number. On the fourth ring a gruff voice picked up.

"Marvin, it's me," Wallace whispered coarsely, watching the bathroom door. "Did you have that high-dollar VCR recording while Fox and Madonna were both talking about that tribe on Entertainment Tonight a minute ago? ... No? Damn, what'd you even buy it for? Michael J. Fox. The actor. I don't know, I couldn't hear a fucking thing. Well, trust me they were. Yea. When is Kanayama's crew scheduled to start filming anyway? When? June 7th?"

Wallace clutched his chest and moaned as he looked up at his embarrassing and sparsely-filled planning wall calendar over his desk. "It was just that damn sausage roll," he continued. "Yes, they're prescription, and I take them every day. Listen I've decided to send a second unit in a week earlier to do the landscapes and scenery ... the Danakil ... I know it's a change of plan, but they'll be in and out before Kanayama and his guys even show up ... change can sometimes be good, Marvin, sometimes you gotta think on your ... how would I know? You're the fucking genius accountant find a way! Pay them all scale, or better get their Ethiopian investor, what's his name? What? ... Haile-Selassie? ... Seriously? Get him to bankroll them. He's so fucking concerned and apparently he's sitting on a mountain of salt mining cash, it won't break him. Hell, we got to strike now. People – important and influential people – are starting to talk about Ethiopia, the famine and that tribe, and I gotta find something for Mary to do. This solves all of my problems."

Wallace tapped out another cigarette and lit it, the phone cradled under his chin. As another knot of reflux shot up his esophagus, he choked it back down and glanced at the bathroom. The shower was still running.

"I'll leave strict instructions with Mary for them to leave the people the hell alone under penalty of death. Call Kanayama and tell him that a second unit is going in a week early, then his people can do all the heavy lifting once they get there."

"What? Because I'm the producer, that's why ... then they can just get over it. This has to be perfect – if this project saves that tribe we can get an office downtown, Marvin. Especially if Geldof's project comes together, but we gotta beat Geldof to the punch."

Wallace listened to Marvin's question and thought for a second. "... somebody cheap. Hell, a high school student could ... you know what, Tom Desmond's been busting my chops for two years for a directing job. I know he'll work for almost nothing. Put his name on the cover page as a reminder, I'll throw him that bone ... no, he didn't die on the Cavett show ... he had plastic surgery on his face, you can hardly tell ... it's second unit stuff, even he can't fuck up shooting pictures of rocks and sand."

Wallace gasped in pain and grabbed his left arm, letting the receiver fall on the bed. He slowly picked it up and placed it back to his ear. "... I'm here ... fax me over the main project and a dollar figure and I'll pull a second unit outline from it tomorrow. Run a preliminary cost by this Lord God Haile-Selassie. This is a win-win."

Wallace paused. "... Stop it, Marvin, stop it, you won't have to do shit," he continued after another short pause. "Christ, they're going to the armpit of the world – no phones, no fax, no mail, no nothing. Just a radio for safety and medical emergencies. A million degrees in the shade. They film scenery and sunsets for a week, come back suntanned, no one will even know they left. We put Desmond and Mary in charge and forget about it, just get a budget approved. And find a way to keep Madonna on TV talking about those villagers, her mouth is money in the bank."

His chest pain easing, Wallace hung up the phone and fell back on the bed. Inside the bathroom the water turned off.

He may have fallen ass-backwards into a great humanitarian project but he really wanted a true moneymaker. For 25 years his company Reliance Film Group had produced and distributed cookie-cutter theatrical and made-for-TV dramas, straight-to-video sci-fi thrillers and even gay and straight pornos that produced modest profits or broke even at best. He careered financially in 1964 with a film noir potboiler titled Knock Knock, Who's Dead, prompting Hollywood Reporter to describe him simply as a "new up and coming studio." Despite the faint praise, good and some great (but not spectacular) projects materialized.

In 1981 he thought he had a break-out winner when he acquired sole American and European distribution rights to a feature made in the Soviet Union called Scream Your Guts Out. It was a film about two hideously deformed men who kidnapped, graphically tortured and murdered teenagers at an abandoned amusement park who, in defiance of Hollywood standards and practices, went unpunished.

The trouble started almost immediately when the film received a "kiss of box office death" X rating. Reading the report and without even viewing the film, Carswell personally lobbied the ratings board to change the X to an R, which they eventually did after the director – some 26-year-old Russian kid Wallace never heard of – cut 135 instances of the F-word.

Questionable word of mouth and no advance critical reviews dramatically limited the number of theater chains willing to screen

Scream Your Guts Out, so it opened in only 67 mostly independent theaters on a mid-February Tuesday in Kansas, Nebraska and the Oklahoma panhandle.

That public relations disaster was pulled from almost every theater within days. Even most of the scattered masochists who actually paid to see it walked out before the third act. A front page Kansas City Star-Tribune article described reports of degenerates caught masturbating in a few of the near-empty theaters during the more explicit torture scenes; a story that provoked a half-hearted Republican-led senate inquiry into the sorry state of Hollywood standards and the efficacy of the MPAA ratings board – an investigation no one in the film industry welcomed.

Rapidly becoming an industry pariah, Wallace actually considered hiring Tom Desmond to re-cut the godawful movie to atone for the misstep after receiving a letter from him announcing his return to the film industry after a long absence. But honestly he had forgotten about him.

Wallace generated another ton of bad press in late 1982 when it was revealed during the Senate hearings that he asked the young Russian director to only delete the fucks but leave the torture and murders intact for the sake of the R rating. An unrated VHS version got no rental traction because Erols and Hollywood Video stores banned it, but it eventually found an audience with maximum-security prisoners and Liberian warlords. The notoriety caused Reliance to enjoy a brief spike in rentals of their older films but by early 1984 that interest was fading.

After about ten minutes of calm a screaming rocket roared through Wallace's chest. Fumbling for the phone he suddenly froze as the fax machine on the desk beside the bathroom door rang once and pages started appearing in the tray. "Afarkil Documentary," stated the cover page, "Main Project Outline. Top Secret."

Just below the title in sloppy handwriting Marvin had written, "Tom Desmond to direct? Money approved per GH-S. –MW."

The bathroom door opened in a sauna-like cloud and Mary

emerged, wrapped in a fluffy white robe, looking like a Venus with her hair up in a towel and smelling like steamed lavender. Seeing the fax pages spitting from the machine she walked barefoot over to them, never noticing Wallace flat and colorless on the bed. She picked up the curled pages and saw Marvin's note.

"Tom Desmond to direct?" she muttered. "Didn't he die on television?" She then briefly flipped through the pages and then realizing what she was holding her face lit up in delight.

"Holy shit this is the African documentary!" She turned to Wallace. "You're putting me on your African documentary? Seriously? Boo Boo that's the ..."

She paused and looked closely at the unresponsive Wallace. He appeared not to be breathing, and his eyes were open and staring vacantly at nothing. His cigarette had already burned a small hole through the bedspread. The dropped phone receiver beeped impotently on the floor.

"Boo Boo?"

CHAPTER ONE

It was already called "the cruelest place on earth" by National Geographic before Tom Desmond's team even showed up.

The Danakil Depression – in the northeast Ethiopian Afar triangle – was the lowest-lying and hottest basin of the Danakil Desert, and universally recognized for its vicious, almost impossible living conditions. The depression was almost 100 feet below sea level, the temperature averaged around 115 degrees Fahrenheit, May through September, and there was almost no fresh water.

Complicating matters was an oncoming famine and an explosive political crisis raging through Ethiopia, including a civil war against Eritrean and Tigrayan insurgents conducted by Mengistu Haile Mariam, Ethiopia's President, which further isolated this area. Even worse, the desert was regularly patrolled by renegade Ethiopian militia and Oromo marauders, who killed on sight. No one could have picked a worse place, a worse political and cultural climate, nor a worse time of year to make a movie.

Director Tom Desmond and Production Manager Mary Semper stood on a single-lane baked macadam road that dead-ended in the center of a Quonset hut compound that had been used by a United Nations peacekeeping force and weather station in the 1970s, strategically located between Lake Karum to the south and the abandoned settlement of Dalol about an hour to the north.

They had traveled by jostling bus almost twenty hours from Addis Ababa along the sometimes-paved Assab road before getting dropped off after Desmond unexpectedly forked over fifty dollars each to their nine Kalashnikov-armed escorts, provided to them by their main benefactor, the salt mining tycoon Mr. Gabriel Haile-Selassie.

The topography of the Danakil could not have been off half a bubble for hundreds of miles. This area was a gray, salty, nondescript desert, made dazzling white by the blinding, roasting sun. Only scattered patches of scrub, a stand of Baobab trees a few clicks to the south and a few other gnarled trees of unknown species broke the immediate horizon, where cliffs and odd rock formations loomed like squat, fat-bottomed ghosts. Desmond thought there were mountains to the north, even volcanos nearby, but a hazy scan with his binoculars revealed nothing. He actually had no idea how far away they were, or if he even looked in the right direction.

Mary told him on the bumpy flight from London's Heathrow to Addis Ababa, then on the horrific bus ride to the depression with the armed militants, that they landed in this particular basin almost at the peak of the summer, when the outrageous heat seemingly burned straight through clothing. Desmond did not need to be told that – after just a few minutes he felt as if he were cooking in the middle of a giant wok, with the sun reflecting off all sides, concentrating on him, Mary and the compound like a magnifying glass on Japanese beetles.

"This is a harsh and unforgiving environment," he announced as he squinted into the distance. It was a catch-phrase that he adopted as his own and was considering copyrighting.

"Harsh and unforgiving, yeah I heard you the first time," Mary muttered.

As Desmond and Mary walked quickly back from their scouting excursion toward some shade in the compound they kept an eye on the hardscrabble road that wound into its center. The rest of the crew was arriving any minute, and they were anxious to get them to work. The sun did not set until after 8:00 p.m., so there remained several hours of daylight to plan and possibly scout some good establishing shots.

Mary had been in charge of hiring the crew. She told Desmond that two were Reliance Film regulars, a couple she knew from previous jobs and the rest came from a union directory. She also told Desmond she quite frankly was surprised to hear he was directing, as she knew of his previous movies, but like most assumed he had died, since he pretty much disappeared after a legendary taping of an unaired Dick Cavett Show episode in 1971.

While Desmond bemoaned the unpleasant working conditions, he was nonetheless thankful he had finally snagged a directing job after a lost decade of substance abuse, nameless motel rooms, dead-end retail jobs, disability and various forms of rehab that seemed to segue one into another. This was his life since 1971, wondering why he couldn't find the work he really wanted and felt he richly deserved.

According to Mary, Mr. Carswell's accountant partner Marvin Waltz sent them and her hand-picked crew to the Danakil to make a documentary about an indigenous nomadic tribe that once numbered in the thousands but apparently was now reduced down to only a handful of members, due to a convoluted variety of environmental and political reasons he had tried to memorize on the trip. He had been brought on board at the last minute and still had a lot of catching up to do. He found it odd that his job description was so undefined, but was eager nonetheless to put his personal stamp on the project.

As he and Mary walked quickly back to escape the boiling sun and dry wind, Desmond had time once again to reflect on the unfortunate circumstances that brought him to a most regrettable point in his career. He after all, had fourteen years to reflect on the disasters of 1970 and '71.

Tom Desmond was Hollywood's most promising young film director in the 1960s after making two very profitable and critically-acclaimed feature films in a row. Then, an uncompleted third film landed him injured in a hospital, made him the subject of numerous criminal and civil lawsuits, then jobless and untouchable. This led to a cascading series of even more disastrous events that eventually left him an unemployed junkie living in a truck stop.

But then, in the late 1970s, he began straightening out his life and clawing his way back into the Hollywood food chain. Now here he was in 1984, back in the director's chair. It had been a long, torturous road for sure.

The films he had directed back then were still fresh and brand new in his mind: the scripts, the talent, production, every edit, it was all there. His quirky 1966 horror thriller, King Size Peggy, was acknowledged as the best film of the decade for a first-time director. Then in 1968, his surreal comedy, Normal Paul, garnered two academy award nominations for best screenplay and best cinematography.

And before his life and career crashed he had all the trappings that accompanied a burgeoning 1960-era movie-making career: a trophy wife, a beautiful home, two expensive cars, pricey clothes, designer drugs – not to mention the steady stream of invitations to non-descript film festivals in exotic beach-front locales, automatic seats in Hollywood's best restaurants and the constant attention of mealy-mouthed toadies, eager to cater to his every whim.

Desmond managed a smile as he recollected the pitch for his psychosexual horror film, King Size Peggy. It was about a reclusive small town child kidnapper who started seeing an 8-foot tall woman with a plastic head hanging around and protecting the town's children from him. It was a hard sell due to the objectionable subject matter, the point of view and the unorthodox title, but a producer at Culver City Films – riding a wave of mid-sixties art-house movies – finally relented, denoting the film a tax write-off and raising an insulting $1.3 million for a script Desmond budgeted at $5 million. Pissed but eager to "show 'em all," Desmond brought it in for just under $1 million on December 30 to get the write-off, with cash left over to market and promote.

Adeptly handling the unpleasant plot and objectionable characters with remarkable sensitivity, the film was a surprising hit, with critics favorably comparing it to the 1931 Fritz Lang film M and the 1942 Jacques Tourneur classic, Cat People. King Size Peggy eventually made $13 million stateside and an astonishing $21 million in Europe and Japan, placing it a comfortable number 9 on 1966's highest grossing films. Not too shabby for a first-time director who flunked out of Chicago Film School (then avoided going to Vietnam because of a 4-F classification due to a lingering case of childhood depression).

How his artsy-fartsy professors hated him! Their dry ponderings on abstract film theory were almost always drowned out by his strident insistence on "commercial potential." Feature filmmaking, according to him, was about profit margin. Even a cheap, poorly-made film was a success in his eyes if it was profitable

"Desmond!" The same skeptical producer exclaimed with a smile when King Size Peggy recouped a substantial chunk of its production costs on opening weekend, the best Labor Day opening in four years. "Loved the film!"

Desmond looked again at where the clay road blurred into the horizon. No sign of the crew yet. Mary told him Mr. Carswell had challenged them to make a documentary that would be seen by two million people, a challenge he readily accepted before in a fit of bravado upped the ante to five million.

"Maybe I should consider sunscreen," he mumbled out loud, rubbing sand out of his eyes. He felt sand in every orifice since arriving the day before.

Desmond followed up the success of King Size Peggy in early 1968 by again tapping the psychological horror genre, this time turning it upside down into a black comedy titled Normal Paul. The film was an instant hit with both the anti-war and drug crowd, who viewed it as a metaphor for America's role in the Vietnam War, and the cold war clingers, who saw it as a metaphor with America's relationship with the Soviet Union.

Shot in four weeks, and taking place almost exclusively inside a seedy motel room, the main character, a delusional bank auditor named Paul, became convinced someone else was living in his room when he wasn't there. Finding what he believed were clues, and becoming more and more paranoid, he started concocting schemes to catch the person – each more outrageous than the last, going so far as to hire and seal a homeless man inside the heating ducts to catch the interloper, with surprising (and horrifying) results. At the conclusion, audiences were left unsure if there really was an interloper or if Paul imagined the whole episode, but that murkiness drove even more to the theaters.

Critics unanimously raved about the unconventional film (Desmond was especially fond of one who insisted it was "more confounding, more maddening, even more of a psychedelic head trip than Kubrick's 2001: A Space Odyssey but just as genius"), and it established Tom Desmond as one of the decade's most exciting and adventurous new directors.

Desmond knew he somehow struck gold twice with somewhat unusual products, but he was eager to show both were not flukes and that given the chance, he could seamlessly transition into big-budget mainstream features – the kind that made everyone truly rich. So in the summer of 1969, while Neil Armstrong and Buzz Aldrin walked on the moon, he got that opportunity of a lifetime, and dove headlong into what would be his epic undoing; an uncompleted megabudget action thriller called Pyro.

In retrospect he realized many great directors seemed to have one career-killing film: Charlie Chaplin enjoyed two decades of success but his livelihood was derailed by The Great Dictator. Michael Cimino struck gold with The Deer Hunter but flopped badly with Heaven's Gate.

Pyro in turn became Tom Desmond's Great Dictator. A deadly accident on the set, followed by a disastrous taping of a television show that was supposed to atone for that accident, effectively torpedoed his feature filmmaking profession. It was as if his two earlier successes meant nothing, and the very people who praised him earlier stopped returning his calls.

Pyro was a bloated and almost plotless colossus; a Global Studio product comprised of too many meddling hands, a jumbled screenplay, too much money and no clear vision. It was one of those giant publisher's clearing house checks made out to Tom Desmond for $15 million in production alone, not counting marketing, and starring several big period names.

Only one scene was shot: a pyromaniac antagonist machine-gunned an airport control tower crew, then sprayed jellied jet fuel over a runway and ignited it as a passenger plane took off. Desmond thought the sight of a blazing 727 taking off before exploding spectacularly in the night sky was well worth that one scene's stomach-churning cost, which included the three months of both set and location shots, the full-size 727 mockup, models and green screen matte work. He never even got close to filming the climax, which was to feature the napalming of over 100 acres of virgin forest in the Brooks Range of northern Alaska and the bombing of the real-life town of Nunavut, an act that would have surely infuriated every sixties environmentalist north of the equator.

On a personal level, the surprise successes of the modestly-budgeted King Size Peggy and Normal Paul, then coupled with the sudden infusion of a mountain of studio cash for Pyro, transformed Desmond from an idiosyncratic creator of dark psychological minor masterpieces into a self-indulgent, arrogant taskmaster in the mold of the classic despotic directors of Europe's silent era. That reputation, plus the critical fawning and the sudden wealth made his rapidly inflating ego's inevitable entry into the late sixties drug scene far too slippery. He eagerly accepted invitations to every West Hollywood "fruit salad" party, back-slapping with the glitterati while tossing back multiple cocktails and a dizzying selection of pills and capsules from a hand-cut crystal bowl in the center of the room. Lines of freshly-cut cocaine always appeared at midnight at these parties, as did a selection of sugar cubes with the characteristic LSD blue dot, a party favor personally introduced to him by Dr. Timothy Leary at a bash at Dennis Hopper's house.

He pressed flesh at every opening, every festivity and every public event, zonked on a narcotic of some sort, with a flask of premium bourbon in his jacket pocket. He was the life of the party.

Desmond's nocturnal party proclivities boiled over into Pyro during the day, and he became so addled and arrogant he fashioned himself an expert on every nit-picking technical aspect of the filmmaking process. "I probably know more about explosives than any one of you," he repeated often to his explosives experts, who had done it for decades.

But was the accident solely his fault? That depends on which attorney one would ask, or which deposition one chose to read. Maybe he did rush the incendiary technicians; maybe he did insist on a premature take while stone drunk or blitzed on the pharmaceutical of the day, as reported by gossip columnist Rona Barrett.

The obvious answer to him (and the one his lawyers somewhat successfully argued) was the pyrotechnic guy screwed up – after all, he was an import, a Paramount flunky brought in after the previous three had been fired. Out of almost 5,000 explosive squibs it took only a pathetic little single one, badly duct-taped to the padded back of the stunt woman, to misfire, fall and ignite a cordite gel canister too early. The ensuing chain reaction resulted in a fireball that almost consumed the entire set.

"This take is ruined!" Someone told the desperately hungover Desmond he had screamed, perfectly unaware as the firestorm billowed straight toward him, "You people are idiots!"

The stunt woman, a seventeen-year veteran, died of burns suffered in the explosion, as did a 44-year-old male counterpart, another veteran of over a dozen films. Six others suffered second- and third-degree burns and permanent disability, and thousands of dollars of equipment and set was destroyed.

The studio insurance company declared force majeure and filed a $6 million insurance claim to recoup their losses and terminate production. Investors (and friends) ran screaming while the investigators and adjustors rolled in, leaving Global on the hook for millions in off-the-book losses, and Desmond on the hook for almost as much in legal fees after years in and out of a courtroom. All he had for his efforts was rough footage of a flaming passenger plane exploding.

It was also revealed in the trial that producers had recognized that

Desmond had already begun his descent into the maelstrom long before the accident. At the moment of the accident, a Global producer was on his way to the set to replace him with another young director named Sidney Lumet.

Today however, the former celebrated director Tom Desmond was back in the saddle, notified by a woman he never met that he was hired by an accountant he never heard of to make a documentary for a tightfisted production company about a dying civilization in the hottest and most dangerous place on earth with equipment and a crew he barely knew. He didn't even know his own budget.

He learned his lesson and was a new man, however – a caring, empathetic man who fully realized his responsibility to save this society while reviving his own career. It was a challenge he took very seriously. He had a lot to prove on this shoot – saving an entire race of people would demonstrate his atonement for the loss of life on Pyro. And he was determined to not spend one more hour in a courtroom.

Of course, Desmond had many concerns about his first documentary. On location – especially an isolated and inhospitable site like this one – was another world altogether from the closed studio environment he had cut his teeth on almost twenty years earlier. Certainly, there was nothing wrong with making docs – Robert Flaherty's Nanook of the North put the director in the history books. Leni Riefenstahl enjoyed a reputation as a great documentarian of an appalling subject matter. A first-time director named Ken Burns made a great documentary about the Brooklyn Bridge.

Not a natural documentarian like those others, but playing to his strengths, Desmond made the decision to make this documentary like a feature film – a genre in which he felt most comfortable, and where he could better control the production. Creative nonfiction he called it. It was a bold and progressive decision of which he was very proud, and made him feel in charge.

He and Mary had just reached the shade of an awning in the compound when a final scan finally revealed a telltale plume of dust rising from the shimmering horizon, signaling the arrival of the crew.

"About damn time," he whispered as he looked at the rough semicircle of drab, prefab metal buildings arranged around a central parking area that surrounded him. On his left were five dormitories designated male and female, then a single dormitory on his far right for himself. Two of the crew bunkhouses were only one-bunk, two were larger two-bunk versions and the largest one slept four. His house was the largest one bunk house, and was comprised of a single room, with a bed, editing table, desk and dresser and most importantly, a large box fan. It was all very austere, but adequate. He never expected creature comforts out there, and his job was much too important to be concerned with such trivialities.

It was certainly a philosophical switch from his previous pampered life as a features director, but fireballs, deceased personnel, millions in lost funds and a career on the line changes one's priorities.

Directly in front of him beside the bunkhouses stood a catering trailer and a kitchen. A walk-in refrigerator and food storage pantry were behind it. Connected on the left side of the kitchen was an outdoor dining area covered by an awning. An equipment storage trailer and a small windowless room to be used for film editing sat to the left of the catering trailer. There was a full 500-gallon fresh water tank, gas and diesel storage tanks and a propane tank. Several gas generators used for electricity were scattered throughout the compound, including a huge propane generator used solely for the kitchen, food pantry and freezer.

Mary told Desmond that the investor, Gabriel Haile-Selassie, got the compound in livable condition a month earlier for a Danish documentary crew that canceled at the last minute due to concerns over an impending civil war. He had repaired the generators and lights, stocked the pantry and freezers and topped off the water and fuel storage tanks. An older but fully operational front end loader and a bulldozer sat in a parking area, and banks of floodlights on four 20-

foot poles provided light.

"By the way, how was Mr. Carswell when you saw him?" Desmond asked Mary as the gentle roar of the approaching crew grew louder.

"The same," Mary shrugged. "They were putting in a stent. If he comes out of the coma he'll be there probably two months or more. Long after we return from here."

"That's a shame. I would really like him to see the good we're doing here."

Mary glanced toward him out of the corner of her eye before turning back toward the road. "Yea, that's not very likely. Don't get your hopes up."

"And who's the dude who hired me?" Desmond asked.

Mary exhaled in frustration. "Waltz is his name. Marvin Waltz. He's Wallace's VP and accountant, and he's running this project until Wallace gets back. That's like the third time I told you."

Desmond was about to object to Mary's abruptness when the crew arrived in a raucous convoy comprised of a dusty, military-style covered truck, two jeeps and a flat-bed truck loaded down with stuffed wooden crates, suitcases and a fiberglass Porta-john. A new, solid black customized Humvee, provided by Mr. Haile-Selassie and driven by a brunette woman in a cowboy hat led the procession. They pulled slowly into the center of the compound, circling counterclockwise like a wagon train until they all moaned, squealed and groaned to a stop in a parking area near the heavy equipment, raising stagnant clouds of white and gray dust between the clanking hisses of sand-clogged brakes.

Aggravated that his crew was provided vehicles while he and Mary had to take a bus with armed escorts he had to bribe, Desmond still watched excitedly as his crew piled out, most of them whining and griping about the hot, torturous 370 mile trip from Addis Ababa International Airport.

"People! People!" Desmond announced over the din as they stretched and hoisted personal belongings amid the dissipating dust,

"Welcome to the Danakil! Quick meeting over by the storage building right away! All essential staff! Nonessential staff will stow your belongings! Make sure your names are on your bags! Let's move please!" Desmond did not like to trifle with such insignificant activities as unpacking; he had a job to do, and wanted to get right on it.

"Who exactly is considered nonessential?" asked one young man with a buzzed haircut.

"Only those not directly involved in making the film."

"Then I guess that would be me and Eric," the man responded, motioning to a waxed, muscular, handsome young man in a white tank top getting out of the flatbed truck. "I'm base security, and he's construction and props."

"Fine then. Let's go people!" Desmond shouted, keeping his new crew motivated.

"Get the bathroom set up first!" Mary yelled to Eric, the flatbed driver, "The outhouse here is a fucking biohazard."

Eric bowed. "As you wish, madam."

While the irritable, nonessential staff member Eric began untying straps that held the luggage and supplies on the truck, the rest of them made their way under the awning to picnic tables. They were still grouchy because of the ride but their egos seemed sufficiently placated by not having to suffer the indignities of retrieving, carrying and unpacking their own luggage. They gathered around Desmond, getting as comfortable as possible in the minor shade. A few stood, presumably sick of riding. They all held water bottles.

With the crew in place, Desmond approached a podium he set up for every pre-planning meeting – his former good luck charm. He did not conduct his first meeting with the crew of Pyro from his good luck podium and look what happened. He quickly scanned the crowd: he commanded seven film professionals, eight including himself.

Desmond was a prematurely graying man who stood a towering 6'-4" and weighed a sinewy 213 pounds. He was considered handsome and quite dashing some years back, but now was transparently showing every minute of his 42 years, mostly due to a (thankfully) now-resolved love affair with narcotics and alcohol, an ugly divorce and the stress of a career that was stuck in neutral. He preferred black cargo pants, a black long-sleeve safari shirt, black lace-up boots and a black neckerchief that kept the sand out of his shirt. His eyes were irritated red from only 24 hours in the desert, exacerbated by his refusal to wear a hat or sunglasses.

"Welcome to the Danakil Desert, the hottest place on earth," he announced in his best public speaking voice as the attending rabble settled down. "My name is Tom Desmond. I am not dead, despite what some of you may have heard. And let's clear a few more elephants out of the room: my 1966 feature film, King Size Peggy, received critical praise and made a ton of money. My 1968 film, Normal Paul, received even more critical praise, made a ton of money and earned me two Oscar nominations. And you all heard of the accident on the set of my film Pyro, and then my taping of a thankfully unaired Dick Cavett show episode shortly after that. That was all 14 years ago and now ancient history. I want to assure all of you I am clean, sober and back at the top of my form, and I look forward to making this the best project we can."

The crew stared unmoved. Desmond paused and got back on track. "So okay, I'd like to take a few minutes to tell you exactly why you're here, and what I hope to accomplish ..."

"And yes, it is always this damn hot!" Mary suddenly proclaimed from inside the group in response to grumbling of the oppressive heat. Mary had done a little minor acting but mostly worked in casting and wardrobe almost twenty years on about a dozen of adequate, medium- and low-budget films. She never made the tabloid covers, but she enjoyed a steady stream of acting boyfriends, who threw themselves at her. Until, of course, she met Wallace Carswell, his influence and as she guessed his potential moneymaker.

Desmond looked at Mary as she tied her hair back. "Quiet please. Yes, it is always this damn hot," he repeated. "This is a very harsh and unforgiving environment. We are about sixty feet below sea level here, and yesterday it was 107 degrees when we arrived. At night it gets down in the seventies, but during the day your clothes never get wet because your sweat immediately evaporates. You won't realize how much water you are really losing, so drink continuously or you will hallucinate, then your pee will come out in clumps and then you die."

"Anyway," he continued to a crowd obviously repulsed by that last statement judging by their facial expressions, "we are here to document the past and the present to assure the future of the Afarkil tribe. The Afarkils are native to this area, and once contained more than 30,000 members in a society that covered 2,000 square miles across Ethiopia, into parts of Sudan and what is today Djibouti. Today they are confined to one small village a little over a mile from here, and reduced down to their last twelve or so members."

"What happened to these Afarkils?" asked a barrel-chested man in a white chef's uniform.

"Folks please tell us all your name when you speak," Desmond asked. "Some of us have never met."

"Okay. I'm the cook and catering manager," the chef announced, looking around at the assembly. "The name's Bradley but everybody calls me Bruny."

"Thank you Bruny. I don't know the full history of the Afarkils," Desmond continued. "It's very complicated – I know that in 1973 a famine killed something like 80,000 Afarkils, Afar herders and Oromo tenant farmers. Much of their land after that was confiscated under Emperor Haile Selassie. Suffice to say it is the same sad story that happens to most indigenous people – disease, government encroachment, what have you. This weather can't help."

"Actually ... oh, the name's Ricky Vekoma," piped in a pale young man with dirty blonde hair, "and I'm the audio engineer. The Afarkils are considered a clan, not a tribe. Though the term 'tribe' has long been accepted by anthropologists, it now is considered an insulting term, as it implies a second-rate lifestyle that..."

"Let's skip the political correctness and stay on topic for

timeliness sake," Desmond cut in, to Ricky's obvious embarrassment.

"How could anyone consider this a second-rate lifestyle?" Mary announced. "Why it's positively Palm Springs here! Let's fill the pool with Perrier!"

Desmond raised both hands to quiet the chuckling assembly. "I'm sorry, Ricky is it? What were you saying?"

"Oh, I was just saying that like most famines, this one is man-made," Ricky continued, his white film school arms gesturing broadly. "The current crops have failed because of drought, and Ethiopian President Mariam's war against the Eritreans has him bombing trade convoys to disrupt food supply chains, which is cutting off deliveries not just to the Eritreans but to the Afarkils and the Afar farmers to the north. Add to the mix Marxist thugs, territorial salt and uranium miners, machete-wielding civilian militias, AIDS and blight. It's a humanitarian and cultural disaster."

"You seem to be on top of all this," Desmond asked, pointing to the pale young man. "Is it your knowledge of the tribe what got you hired? I'm sorry, the clan?"

"Partly. I did sound for an industrial film on sludge management," Ricky answered. "Mr. Carswell told me one time I made treated sludge sound ... romantic. So I got hired as a sound guy."

"Are we safe here?" Somebody suddenly asked. "I don't like all this talk about bombing and Marxist thugs."

"I don't want any of you worrying about our safety," Desmond continued. "The famine and the fighting occurring right now are miles and miles from here, mostly confined to the Tigray and Wollo areas, in a place called Begemder and one other area I can't recall. So rest assured we are safely outside of the worst areas."

Mary stood, seeming to sense there was unease for their safety. "Mr. Waltz assured me that our benefactor in Addis Ababa is committed 100% to this documentary, and he personally guarantees our safety." There was some relieved murmuring. "We are in a NATO demilitarized no-fly zone, and we have an emergency radio that can get us help within an hour."

Desmond shook his head in agreement. "Thank you Mary. Anyway, our responsibility here is to document the plight of the remaining Afarkils, to show they were once a thriving presence, compared to what they have now become, to raise global awareness of their predicament. It is my understanding many celebrities are coming on board this project, and that discussions are now under way with Bono, Michael J. Fox, Madonna, Cher and maybe some others to appear in the introduction. We need to tell the world the tragic story of the Afarkils, in the hope of reviving my ... reviving the tribe. The clan."

"Why are we responsible for doing this?" cut in a swarthy, New York Sicilian man with a hoop earring in one ear. "Isn't there a huge relief effort underway by some rock stars?"

Desmond thought he recognized the man when he heard his voice. "You're Mickey Donato? You did some art directing for Arthur Penn. Bonnie and Clyde, right? I thought you had retired."

"I thought about retiring," Donato answered as the woman in the cowboy hat beside him leaned into him and whispered something. "Too many greedy ex-wives with their hands out and decent gin is twenty bucks a bottle. It was either be art director here or blow my brains out."

He turned to the woman. "And stop calling me a turd, Schuyler – it's ancient history. Wench."

"Yes, there are some rock stars organizing relief measures for the hardest hit areas of Ethiopia, but it's very preliminary. We are focusing on the effects only on this one clan," Desmond continued. "It is rumored also that there is some kind of a secret maternity hospital hidden around here somewhere never seen by the outside world, and that when the Afarkil women get pregnant they go there for care and to give birth. It would be great to find this hospital and highlight it, because it would certainly give hope to the Afarkil's survival – and for Ethiopia in general – to see healthy babies born, or at least see where they would be born. Anyway, does that answer your question?"

Ricky raised his hand, like he was back in Mr. Wampler's 11th-grade social studies class at Palisades High School. "The rock star benefit is still months away, but there's really no one specifically helping the Afarkil clan, who are in much danger not just from the encroaching famine but from President Mariam's policy of diverting aid to the military," he responded to Donato's question without waiting for acknowledgement from his director. "The United Nations has actually chosen to ignore the extinction of the clan in deference to the Marxist Dergs and their resettlement programs. The standard of living has been tanking here since 1977, when the Dergs' ridiculous agricultural policies took effect, and ... this gets complex, but bear with me a min ..."

"All quite fascinating," Donato interrupted. "What language do these Farkills talk?"

"They are Afarkil," Desmond continued. "Please everyone make sure you get the name right. We cannot take a chance offending them by mispronouncing their name. As for their language ..." He scanned the crowd. "Don't we have a language expert here? What's your name and where are you?"

"That would be me, I have a fluent understanding of their language, Mr. Desmond," admitted a tall, skinny young man standing in the back. "My name is Buddy Bitzer, and they speak what we call a 'clicking' language, a little-known cross between the Chari-Nile and Nilo-Saharan branches. It more closely resembles Khoisan, or even Tigrinya."

"Okay, Buddy's our transla..."

Desmond was suddenly interrupted by an enormous crash across the compound beside the flatbed truck.

Startled, everyone turned to look at the now shirtless, 5%-body fat Eric unloading their gear. Several crates had tumbled off the truck onto the ground, and some had broken open. The ground was littered with dozens of Perrier and Evian water bottles, and the portable toilet lay on top of the mess. Eric looked at the group and shrugged. "Sorry. I'm just nonessential staff, working by myself here."

"None of my film equipment better be in that pile!" Schuyler stood and yelled to him. "We have very limited stock as it is!"

Eric looked at the pile, and started to pick through it. "Seems mostly to be water bottles, cookware, toilet paper and stuff. I don't see any film equipment."

"Thank God. Look. We are most likely this civilization's last chance for survival," Desmond continued, very seriously as Schuyler and everyone turned back to face him. "I speak for me and Mr. Carswell when I say it is critical that I get five million people worldwide to watch this film so we ensure this group's continued existence. The Afarkils have no other way to tell the world they are dying out. Therefore, I expect no less than 110% commitment from each one of you. No slackers or egos will be tolerated. Let me be clear: you will be removed from the set if you do not stay committed to our cause."

"That goes for nonessential personnel as well," Mary announced, her legs crossed and her foot swinging nervously back and forth before she turned to glance at the nonessential guy trying by himself to muscle the portajohn into an upright position. She elbowed Schuyler beside her and whispered something.

"I beg your pardon?" Desmond asked, "Mary? Schuyler is it? I couldn't hear all of that. Could you share with the group?"

Mary laughed. "We were just making our 110% commitment."

"What do you say you and Schuyler here commit to meeting me behind the storage shed after this meeting?" Donato laughingly asked, loud enough for everyone to hear. "I gotta paying job for ya. It's alphabetical – I'm already on the 'B's."

"Why don't you go suck on a breath mint, Donato," Mary blurted, to the enjoyment of the others. "By yourself, as usual."

Schuyler glowered at Donato's sexist remarks. "You're pissing me off already, Donato. Cut it out. I took you out in Montreal, and I have no problem taking you out again."

"You broads don't have a sense of humor anymore." Donato leaned back in his chair. "Fucking women's lib took it all away."

"Okay, you guys that's enough," Desmond admonished, anxious for the meeting to get back on track. "And Schuyler? Introduce yourself and tell everyone what you do."

Schuyler stood again. Desmond smiled; he thought she was a 5'10" cowboy goddess in her boots and hat. "Schuyler Courtland. Camera operator and sometime cinematographer. Pleasure to be here." She sat back down.

"Yo." The other nonessential staff member, the lanky, young man with the buzzed haircut and mirrored sunglasses stood. He was dressed in off-the-shelf camo wear, with a wad of smokeless tobacco in his lower lip. "Mr. Desmond? Everyone? I am in charge of security on this project. You don't need to know my name or anything about me. Just rest easy knowing that security here never sleeps."

"You need a name," Mary interrupted, starting to laugh, "so why don't we call you Buzzcut, after your haircut? That makes sense." The rest of the crew laughed and agreed with Mary's comment. She seemed to be loving controlling the conversation.

The Buzzcut turned and looked at her with a squinted stare. A small smile crossed his thin lips, and it was impossible to tell if he was angry or not. "Okay, you may call me Buzzcut," he said in a soft, ominous voice.

"Okay, people!" Desmond pleaded, trying to distract everyone from their social aberration security guard. "We're thankful for our well-groomed security. We all know we're in good hands."

The crowd began fidgeting and chattering. "I guess we're done. Oh, by the way," Desmond continued in an elevated voice as everyone stood and stretched, "Art director ... who else ... cinematographer, and sound? Stow your gear and meet me back here in two hours. We're going to scout the village while we still got the light."

CHAPTER TWO

"Happy and sad ...?" Desmond squinted at the fading fax pages to the stagnant hum of his box fan. "Facial expressions are multifarious ...? What the hell is this, Japanese ...?"

Desmond was at his desk trying to decipher the project outline Mary got from Carswell when there were two knocks on his door. "Enter."

It was Schuyler. "We have problems with the equipment, Mr. Desmond. That asshole was lying."

Desmond looked up at her. She was a strong, independent woman, who he thought bore a close resemblance to actress Sigourney Weaver in her white muscle shirt, jeans and cowboy boots. She had shoulder-length, curly black hair tied back, square shoulders and amazing triceps.

"Well that didn't take long. What kind of equipment trouble, Schuyler?"

"Well, the brand-new Canon XL2 digital camera works but I can hear something rattling around inside of it and I don't trust it. I tested the Sony Betacam and it's okay."

Ouch. The Canon had been provided by Mr. Haile-Selassie. "We'll just have to shoot it all on tape with the Sony to be on the safe side, then convert it. It won't affect quality that much, right?" This was disappointing, but not the end of the world.

"No, as long as the tapes are okay, but that's not all. I checked the rest of the stuff. That Leica SLR zoom lens won't zoom, all the fluid seems to have leaked from the head of the three-stage tripod, and your Scriptboy timecode clapboard is flashing '12:00' and won't reset..."

Desmond moaned and looked down at the fading fax pages in

front of him. Some of them were already unreadable. That Scriptboy had been a present from his mom to celebrate his return to filmmaking. "Schuyler, can you read Japanese? Japanese that is fading before my eyes?"

"No. Also the 20-inch monitor is shattered, but that high-res 13-inch is okay."

"Goddamn Schuyler, Eric said there was just cookware and toilet paper in the boxes that fell off the truck!" Desmond's blood pressure took a bump. "I'll have a word with him about his carelessness. The heat and the sand are harsh and unforgiving on sophisticated equipment as it is, we can't be throwing it off trucks."

"I told the twerp kid to tell Donato to check his stuff, since so much video gear was busted up," Schuyler continued. "He can't even find some of his lighting equipment, including the Chimera banks, and a few of his stands, clamps and gobos are either missing or damaged."

Desmond looked down and closed his eyes.

He remembered the day like it was yesterday – June 3, 1971. Thirteen years to the day. Looking at the floor, he shifted uncomfortably in his chair. It was his producer's, the studio's and a half-dozen defense attorneys' ideas to appear on Dick Cavett's television show to come clean about the film he had been making and atone for the accident that may very well end his filmmaking career, despite the two moneymakers and his two academy award nominations. They told him this was a "career saver" move but he considered it beneath a director's dignity to stoop to personal appearances to promote their own films, much less to apologize for accidents. That's what marketing and PR firms were for.

Desmond's segment taped right after author Gore Vidal. Seated in the chair occupied only minutes earlier by the temperamental author, Cavett leaned over to him as an assistant clipped a microphone to his collar. "You look nervous, Mr. Desmond. This is just a taping. Try to relax."

Desmond looked back in amazement. Who was this man kidding? How dare he suggest that his appearance on a lame television talk show make him nervous! "I'm counting on not regretting this, Cavett," he scoffed as another young woman gently approached him and asked his permission to apply a little powder on his nose and forehead.

After a couple of minutes, a young television director (Desmond thought he looked like a kid) counted down from five with his right hand then pointed at them as two of the three remote controlled cameras were slowly positioned into place. Dick Cavett perked up and looked into the camera to his right.

"We're back, with film director Tom Desmond. Mr. Desmond has been described as the next Alfred Hitchcock, the heir apparent to a new generation of exceptionally talented and personable young film directors leading the entertainment industry into the 1970s. But a devastating accident on the set of his last film has some critics predicting the demise of this brilliant young filmmaker's career. Mr. Desmond, I appreciate you being on the show. Mr. Desmond? Desmond ..."

"Desmond? Want me to call the buzzcut?" Schuyler continued when he didn't respond to her damaged equipment report, "He probably has his nipple clamps and car battery unpacked by now. If there is a saboteur here I think he can weed him out."

"No, I don't think Eric or anybody on this crew are saboteurs. It had to be an accident," Desmond affirmed, shaking out the memory. "We'll just have to make do. There's no way we can get more equipment out here in time, anyway," he added, trying to be cheerful. "It was all I could do just to get a crappy two-way emergency radio, much less expensive film equipment."

"You know, Schuyler," he continued, standing as she shrugged, "Harlan County USA was shot with an off-the-shelf 16-millimeter camera and a single microphone." He looked at his cluttered desk. "A brilliant crew and a talented director can overcome any shortcomings. The world doesn't care whether our good camera's busted, or my Scriptboy flashes 12:00, or the lighting isn't just right, or I can't read these fucking faxes."

Seemingly surprised at Desmond's cool in the face of adversity, Schuyler turned to leave. "Whatever you say." His eyes absently dropped down to look at her butt. He knew she would be mad if she caught him, too.

Suddenly she turned to face him, and his guilty eyes shot up to meet hers. "And by the way, Donato makes one more sexist crack I will take him out and this time I will not be nearly as forgiving."

"I heard you mention an incident in Montreal?" Desmond asked, suddenly feeling guilty. "What was that about?"

"About four years ago. We were both on that Spottiswoode slasher film shoot, the one with Jamie Lee Curtis," Schuyler recalled. "I listened to his drunken sexist comments for a week, but when he tried to play that retarded game "come in, London" on my nipples through my shirt, I took him down. Broke his finger. It shut him up, though. And Jamie Lee thought it was hysterical."

Desmond only stared at her. "Can you describe the retarded game 'come in, London' so I'll know it if I see it?"

Schuyler rolled her eyes. "I thought all emotionally stunted boys played it. You know, you put your ear up to a woman's chest, then twist her nipples like you are tuning a radio, saying 'come in, London?'"

Never hearing of this game, it was all Desmond could do to keep from bursting out laughing. "I assure you I will speak to Mr. Donato," he promised as Schuyler turned to leave. "But don't let his loutish behavior be a distraction – our priority remains the same, to tell the Afarkil story, and with whatever equipment we have. Saving a tribe from extinction is a grave responsibility and – I mean saving a clan from extinction ..."

Desmond closed his door and stood at his desk. "Come in London ... Christ." He picked up the faxes, flipped through several pages and squinted at it. "... keeps the safety perfectly? What the heck does that even mean?"

There was another knock on the door. "No rest for the weary," Desmond muttered as he turned and opened the door. It was Mary, and she looked hot and pissed.

"What gives with the toilet, Desmond?"

"What do you mean?"

"The toilet doesn't work. It has an out-of-order sign hanging on it."

"How can a porta-john be out of order?"

Exasperated, Mary looked down for a moment, before she suddenly looked back up. "Porta-john? What the hell is a porta-john?"

"It's like a waterless portable bathr ..."

"Waterless?" Mary shot back at him. "Wait – you're telling me our only toilet here is another goddamn outhouse? And out of order as well? Have you seen the other one, the original? It's disgusting – like somebody opened the door and shot it with a shit fire hose."

"It's a chemical toilet, and, well, this is a rather harsh and unforgiving ..."

"A suggestion? You need to dump that harsh and unforgiving bullshit and get the toilet situation settled, like right now," she blurted angrily. "I refuse to use that revolting pit toilet, an outhouse, or the bushes."

"I assure you, Mary, I will get right on it." He peered around the compound for Eric, the nonessential guy and made a mental note to get him to fix it as Mary turned to leave. "Hey Mary."

She stopped and turned. "You ever hear of a game called 'come in, London?'"

"No," she replied. "What is it?"

"Nothing. I heard it was something boys used to do to girls ..."

"You mean the nipple twisting thing? I haven't heard that since I was twelve. But if you're planning to call London, I strongly suggest you use the emergency radio and not someone's tits unless you want a sexual harassment suit. It's in my cabin. Just get the toilet fixed."

Desmond spent another frustrating hour taking notes from the indecipherable project outline that was turning brown and illegible almost before his eyes before deciding it was time to round up his team and go to the village to get some atmosphere and pre-plan shots. As he left his bunkhouse, he was met outside the door by the Buzzcut, standing and holding something behind his back.

"Mr. Desmond," he announced stiffly. "It has been brought to my attention that we have been the victims of sabotage to valuable film equipment." To Desmond's shock he presented an AK-74 assault rifle from behind his back.

"Unless you are convinced it was an inside job, I propose Oromo insurgents got to it just outside Dalol, where we stopped for an hour to eat and get the vehicles serviced. I didn't trust those guys anyway. I will be happy to investigate. Your call, sir."

Schuyler may be right – this guy probably did have nipple clamps and car batteries. "Put that gun away right now!" Desmond ordered, stunned by the security guard's apparent willingness to wander into the desert and hunt down local hooligans by himself. "Mr. Whatever-your-name is, the equipment apparently got broken when it fell off the truck! There is no evidence of sabotage or theft here! And if I see that gun, or any gun again with no good cause, you will be ordered off this set!"

Buzzcut slowly cradled his firearm and looked at Desmond. "I apologize if I alarmed you, sir, but you realize I am licensed for this shoot as armed security due to the location and local unrest. And, for insurance purposes, you cannot throw me off or fire me without a ready replacement."

Desmond raised himself to his full height and met his gaze. It was a power move, the first direct threat to his authority. "No, I cannot," he admitted, his voice shaking. Buzzcut was correct – only Mr. Carswell, Mr. Haile-Selassie or their appointed representative could remove personnel from this shoot, especially security. "But if you pose a threat to this project, in any way, I will file the proper forms to start the appeal for a recommendation to have you removed."

Buzzcut let out a long, very serious deep breath before he

suddenly smiled and extended a hand. "It's a deal! Put 'er there, Mr. Desmond!" Desmond exhaled and tentatively shook Buzzcut's hand as the tension broke. "No hard feelings! Just doin' the job I was hired to do!"

"Just throttle it back a few notches, OK?"

"10-4 sir!"

"By the way, do you know anything about porta-johns? I'm trying to figure out how our only toilet is out of order."

"I cannot help you, sir."

CHAPTER THREE

According to the project outline the one remaining Afarkil village was tucked within a grove of six stout Baobab trees a little over a mile south of the compound, on the extreme northern edge of some of the huge salt flats. Desmond, along with Ricky and Buddy in the Humvee's front seat and Mary, Donato and Schuyler with her camera in the back drove across the shimmering, lumpy landscape while Ricky read some printed information on the history of the clan over the frigid blast of the air conditioning.

"In the early-to-mid-1700s, most of the approximately 30,000 Afarkils lived as hunters and gatherers, organized into large bands of about twelve families. Each band had exclusive rights to an area of about fifty square miles and moved around their territory as one unit, changing home sites about once a year as they exhausted food or water."

"Thirty thousand into twelve families equals about 2,500 each," Buddy interrupted. "That's a lot of food and water."

Ricky glanced impatiently at Buddy then continued. "For hundreds of years the Afarkils were mistakenly called Bushmen by southern African and European Caucasians, but that all changed when uranium was discovered in the Danakil in the 1880s. Historians estimate over half of the Afarkils were subsequently wiped out by European uranium miners before they became even more nomadic. The 1973 famine was devastating to the clan, and it is estimated that half of the remaining Afarkils at that time either died or abandoned the traditional lifestyle, moving to Addis Ababa. Um ..."

Desmond looked over at him. "Bring us to 1984, Rick. We aren't going there to teach them a history lesson."

Ricky flipped ahead a page or two. "The Afarkils speak a unique linguistic derivation of Khoisan and Maban languages, distinguished by their distinctive clicking sounds."

"Anyhow," he concluded, as he finished reading from one brochure while folding the rest and placing them in the huge glove box. "They choose to live untouched by modern technology. The remaining enclave subsists a lot like their ancestors, in mud shelters, wearing long wraps or loin cloths and sandals made of skins. Women gather wild plants, which is their main food source. The men supplement their diets by killing small animals with bows and arrows. They also, for fun I guess, drink a fermented beverage made from the fruit of the Baobab tree. But between encroaching development, an unfriendly government, drought and the flight of the animals, they spend a lot of their time just surviving and ducking random bullets fired by drunk salt miners and hostile Marxists."

"The what tree?"

"Baobab," Ricky answered. "Giant, ancient trees. There's information on them and the Danakil in the glove box."

"Their fermented Baobab beverage," Buddy interrupted, trying to be a part of the conversation, "is much like what we call beer ..."

"Tell us about this mystery hospital, Rick," Desmond interjected, steering around a lava boulder. "Where the pregnant women are supposed to go."

"There is a long-held rumor that when Afarkil women are in their last week of pregnancy they go to this birthing hut, supposedly set somewhere away from the village so they can comfortably sweat out the remaining days and give birth in solitude," Ricky continued. "It is supposedly built away from the village and hidden to protect the women from the roving Oromos, and men are forbidden from going in there. It's kind of like an elephant's graveyard; rumored but never seen by white people. Once they give birth they can return with their baby to the village."

Mary was intrigued. "Why are the men forbidden from going there?"

"They believe that if a man sees them in the ninth month the baby could be born disabled, or even dead. Ancient Afarkil tradition considers pregnant women under a spell, and if men witnessed actual childbirth they will go blind. Also, if the baby dies, it is considered the woman's fault and she is forbidden from returning to the village."

"What happens to her?"

"Nobody knows. No other family will take her. But that's the old orthodox ways."

Mary shook her head. "You know, how did they ever think they would survive with such self-defeating traditions? They're like the Shakers of the desert."

"Agreed. It sounds to me like these Afarkils are killing themselves off," Donato muttered as the Humvee suddenly drove up to an enormous stack of old oil drums tucked behind a rock formation.

"Well, that's why they mostly abandoned the old traditions," Ricky concluded, finishing his thought.

"Now that's weird," Desmond muttered. All of them stared in awe as he tapped the brakes and drove very slowly around the stack. Hundreds of black drums were stacked at least thirty tall into a cubist black steel mountain that rose almost 100 feet off of the packed ground. "I heard about odd stuff like this in the desert."

"With zero environmental regulations the Danakil makes a convenient dumping ground," Ricky added. "We passed a pile of tires just outside the Eritrea border bigger than this, stacked perfectly, like by someone obsessive-compulsive."

A few minutes after circling slowly around what Ricky dubbed oil drum mountain, and after following a low ridge of red and yellow lava and sandstone formations, a ring of mud huts surrounded by six enormous old Baobab trees came into view in the distance.

As Desmond parked about 150 feet back, Ricky concluded his discourse on the lifestyle of the remaining band, his voice lowering almost to a whisper. "I read that their religion is a personification of the natural forces that produce sand and wind. They believe in the existence of the soul after death and in a deity named Sonto, who they believe will come out of the north on a huge, black Rhino with glowing eyes. They don't have temples or churches. And no doctors – they had sorcerers who were called in to heal the sick. There have been lots of times where they were almost wiped out by an easily treated minor illness, like the flu. Around 1920 they were almost obliterated by a measles epidemic."

"A sorcerer? Like in Fantasia?" Mary asked. "Did he have a long beard and a hat with stars on it?"

Ricky paused. "Um, no, I think he probably just looked like all the rest of them."

"I'm just yanking your chain, Rick! I'm actually quite impressed with your knowledge of them," Mary admitted, patting Ricky's shoulder from the back seat. Buddy watched the exchange, and laughed before reaching over and tousling Ricky's head, which really pissed him off.

Everyone got out of the Humvee. Mary parked her sunglasses on the top of her head and climbed out last.

"What are you staring at, you Brooklyn wop?" she asked Donato as she emerged tugging her skirt down. He was fiddling with a still camera.

"What the heck you think I'm starin' at?" Donato blurted, unfazed. "You wear a skirt like that you can bet I'm gonna look up, down and through it. And I'm not a wop. My ancestors had passports."

"So yer a Brooklyn greaser, then."

"One horny Brooklyn greaser."

"Will you two stop please?" Desmond asked, irritated at their childish flirting. "Mary, I do wish you'd lay off the racial slurs and reconsider your choice of clothing. We can't take a chance on offending the Afarkil men."

"I think these Afarkil men will be more impressed seeing a strong, fashionable western woman," she answered as she retrieved a clipboard and pen from the front seat. Ricky grabbed everyone a water bottle from the back as Donato began shooting pictures with a still camera.

Schuyler whispered something to Buddy and Ricky as she hoisted the video camera on her shoulder. Buddy laughed too loudly. Desmond sensed something weird about him – he was an insatiable ass kisser, but there was something else he could not put his finger on.

"One more thing," Ricky suddenly declared, almost as an afterthought. "It is possible these particular Afarkils have maybe never seen a white person. The last white people in this area murdered them and took their land, over 100 years ago."

Everyone stopped and stared at him.

"Wait a minute," Desmond whispered. "The last white people they saw were uranium miners? Who killed them? That's impossible! We're staying at a former UN camp so close they can spit on it! They had to have seen white people there sometime!"

Ricky grimaced sheepishly, almost sorry he mentioned it. "Yea, maybe. The white uranium miners are kind of cast as drooling, baby-killing monsters in their folklore. Besides, they're nomads, and our UN camp was long abandoned when they settled in this spot. They tend to live in remote places to avoid marauders, Dergs and white miners. I guess. I mean, last I heard."

Chastened by this latest news, Desmond and his team stared silently at the village from behind the dense wall of two close Baobab trees. Three very small young children wearing white wraps suddenly ran out of a hut. The six interlopers ducked simultaneously behind the massive trunks and root balls.

"But there have been others here, right?" Desmond asked. "Wasn't there another documentary team here not long ago? Surely some of them were white!"

"There have been only two attempts to document the Afarkils, and both failed," Ricky whispered. "A Danish team a month ago cancelled for no reason, and a British outfit about five years ago pulled out because of the weather. I understand the Afarkils at that time were much further south. I have no idea if they even met."

"Our challenge then is to convince them we are here to help them, not kill them!" Desmond acknowledged half out loud and half to himself as he peered around the tree trunk. The children ran into another hut without noticing the white people.

The village consisted of about a dozen plain mud and stick huts of varying sizes composed in a rough half-circle, with thatched roofs and strips of Baobab branches hanging in the doorways for privacy. A small campfire smoldered in the village center. Over to Desmond's left stood a six-foot tall tripod made of stripped tree limbs over top of an opening in the ground about a foot in diameter. A long woven rope tied to the top of the tripod disappeared down in the hole. Desmond concluded it may be a water supply. Behind the semi-circle of huts Desmond could see some old crates with UN stenciled on the side. Several pots, bowls and utensils were stacked nearby, some homemade, with many apparently UN-issued stainless steel ones. Unrecognizable small animal skins were stretched on homemade racks between two huts.

The six crouched silently in the inconsequential shade offered by the huge, old-growth Baobabs. Peeking at the village from between the thick, crusty trunks and jumbled roots, Desmond pondered how they should announce their presence. They didn't want to just stomp into the village and surprise them, since they may be considered drooling baby killers.

"Buddy," Desmond whispered, "I want you ..."

Buddy suddenly appeared at Desmond's side. "Yes sir, Mr. Desmond!"

Desmond put a firm hand on his shoulder. "Settle down and listen up! You know their language, so I want you to call out to them and announce our presence, okay? Now, this is very important. You have to word it just exactly right, because we may be the first white people they have ever seen, so please, please pick your words and clicks carefully. Very clear and very non-threatening."

Buddy looked at the village while the other five looked at him. "Got it, Mr. Desmond," he agreed. "I will announce in a loud and clear voice that we are from the modern world, and that we are here to save them."

"Don't say that!" Ricky interrupted, "they may not have a clue what 'the modern world' is, much less ..."

"Rick! Do you know the language?" Desmond snapped impatiently. "Do you have a better plan?"

Ricky stopped cold. "No sir."

Buddy stood, stepped between two trees and cleared his voice. He looked out the corner of his eye at his companions, who watched him intently. The air was smothering hot and dead still, as if everything – even time – temporarily stopped, waiting for Buddy to make his call. Not one Afarkil was in sight. Desmond watched; so far Buddy had seemed more like a sycophant than a linguist, and had given him little reason to trust his grasp of such a difficult language. Then again, he had given Desmond no reason to think otherwise, either.

Buddy looked hard back into the village and cleared his throat again.

"Mon <click> suh wah!" he called out. There was no response from the village. He looked intently around the village before he turned and smiled confidently at Desmond.

Well, Desmond thought, maybe he really is fluent. "Nobody heard you. Do it again." Desmond whispered, watching closely for any movement. "Louder this time."

Looking away from her viewfinder, Schuyler leaned over between Desmond and Mary. "What if they see us and panic?" she whispered, "What are they capable of?" Mary only shook her head, transfixed by the village and by what was about to happen.

"Mon suh wah!" Buddy called louder. "Mon suh wah <click> ungow-wa so meo."

Ricky looked at Buddy skeptically. "Are you sure you know what you're saying? Because that doesn't sound like ..."

"Ricky, Shut up!" Mary hissed, "Leave Buddy alone! He's doing a great job and this is too important for you to screw up!"

Turning purple with embarrassment, Ricky did as Mary ordered, electing to let nature take its course.

"I don't think they're home, Mr. Desmond," Buddy speculated, turning his back to the village, "I think they're out gathering food, roots or berries. Or something." Squinting through her camera's viewfinder, Schuyler zoomed and scanned all around the village and vicinity looking for any traces of movement.

Donato snorted as he stared through his camera viewfinder and squeezed off a few shots. "The only berries they'll gather in this hell hole are dingleberries."

Schuyler turned off the camera and looked at him with her most revolted face. "How childish! You are like middle school – plain disgusting! I cannot work with someone so childish and disgusting, Mr. Desmond."

Desmond looked up at Donato, whose eyes looked more bloodshot than normal. "Settle down, everybody."

"Aw, don't get yer panties in a knot, there, Miss Schuyler," Donato hissed. He seemed to love agitating Schuyler, who continued to glare at him, her fury building.

"I'll wrap them around your neck until you stop breathing," she mumbled as she refocused the camera.

"Sounds like a plan!" Donato whispered, laughing. "What do the perverts call that?"

"Donato! Cut it out!" Desmond scolded as he watched the huts, "People, please. We have a job to do here. I hardly think they would leave their children unattended." He looked over at Buddy. "Try again, Buddy. Louder this time. Schuyler, are you taping?"

"I will as long as this jerk beside me shuts up," Schuyler muttered as she peered through the viewfinder and framed a shot at the center of the settlement. "I'm going to kill you in your sleep, Donato."

"I'll go with a smile on my face!" Donato chuckled. "Hey does it got lace on it?" he nudged Schuyler, egging her further, "or uh, flowers or better yet little cherries on …"

"That's fucking it." Enraged, Schuyler hoisted the camera off her shoulder and set it on the ground.

"Schuyler! What are you doing!" Desmond exclaimed in shock. "For God's sake pick up your cam …"

The hot-tempered camerawoman ignored her director. "It's go-time, you obnoxious pervert." She grabbed the unsuspecting Donato by the left arm, spun around behind him, kicked his feet out and in no time at all dropped the art director on his stomach with a grunt and a cloud of dust, with her knee in the middle of his back and his arm pulled up behind him in an unnatural position. Donato never knew what hit him. The others watched in amazement at Schuyler's sudden burst of hair-trigger temper and incredible self-defense skills.

"Well, I'm impressed." Mary muttered. "Hey, don't hurt him, Schuyler!"

"Hey!" Donato growled through a mouthful of sand, surprise and an awful lot of pain, "What the hell! Okay ya bull dyke ya made your point now get the hell off me!"

"Everybody shut up!" Desmond ordered, standing and stomping in place to knock off some biting sand fleas, "Schuyler get off Donato and pick up your camera and don't anybody panic! "Donato leave her alo ..."

Then Desmond heard something right behind him that set him on edge. It was a voice. A stranger's voice.

"Son-toa, <click> so wa-too!"

Everyone froze. That wasn't Buddy. And it was right behind them.

"<click> Son-toa!"

"They snuck up behind us," a suddenly sobered Donato muttered. Schuyler got off of him and he struggled to his feet. "Think I'm gonna soil myself."

Frozen in fear, Desmond gradually turned to see seven, very lean and sinewy black men standing rock still. Their faces were dusted white, and they all had short-cropped hair, shaved on one side into an indistinct shape. One of them, who had an additional three stripes shaved into his head, held what appeared to be a spear of some kind made from a Baobab branch and a very sharpened rock. Each man had a single black horizontal strip painted across the bridge of their noses and wore only a loincloth decorated with simple abstract images.

Desmond finally turned all the way to face them, and then rose to his full height. He exhaled a bit. The men didn't move.

"Guys," he croaked nervously to his crew behind him, "stand up and turn around so these fine men can see you, please. Hands out where they can see them."

The others held out their hands and slowly pivoted to face the seven natives. Desmond suddenly imagined all of them being pinned like a cheap Caucasian shish-kabob against a Baobab tree by that very deadly-looking spear. Once they had all turned the two dissimilar groups surveyed each other: one a group of tall, terrified pale victims, the other a shorter group of black victors dusted in war paint wielding a weapon.

The man in the middle of the group with three stripes cut in his hair took one step forward and tapped the butt of his spear twice in the dirt. The six filmmakers held their breath. The heat was suddenly oven-like and unbearable – there was no air anywhere in the entire desert. The Afarkil man pointed at them.

"<click> Son-toa, mah–ya too!" Desmond heard him say.

Desmond smiled nervously. "What's he saying Buddy?" he murmured over his shoulder.

"He's telling us to get out," Buddy answered, his voice breaking. Mary actually held her breath, as did Donato, his black clothes covered in dusty sand.

"Get out?" Desmond asked, barely moving his mouth. "Are you sure?"

"I believe him!" Ricky hissed, "Let's get out! Get way out! Now!"

The leader more forcefully tapped his spear twice in the dirt and again pointed it at them. His voice was rapid and indistinct, and all Desmond heard was "<click> Sahn-yo toe mah heen-a san-toa <click> bal-o."

"Talk to him Buddy!" Desmond desperately whispered over his shoulder. "Tell him we're friends – tell him we're here to help! Tell him something for crying out loud!"

"Okay, Mr. Desmond." Buddy nervously cleared his throat. "Balla." The man looked at him warily. "Balla!" Buddy repeated, watching the leader watch him. He looked back at his director. "That's the word for friend."

A younger man stepped beside the lead one and muttered something while he pointed toward Mary. The leader looked at her, then he too pointed at her. "<click> sahn-ah mon-he mahnto," He stated, looking at Desmond.

"What'd he say, Buddy?" Desmond asked.

"He said look at the golden woman."

"Mr. Desmond?" Ricky interrupted, haltingly, "I don't know these people's language, but I do know ..."

"Ricky!" Mary exclaimed, curious about why she had been pointed out. "I want to hear what he's going to say about the 'golden woman'."

"<click> sahn-ah mann-he <click> mahn-to!"

"Um, I think he said he'll trade three of his women for Mary, Mr. Desmond."

Mary was shocked. "Three of his women? For me?"

The man stared at Mary with a disassociated, concerned look, unmoved by her attention.

"Mr. Desmond," Ricky pleaded, his arms stretched straight out, "I don't mean to disagree with our translator, but I can't believe that is what's being said! I mean these people may be simple, but they aren't primeval ..."

The leader shot an angry look at Ricky, shutting him up.

"What was the word for friend again?" Desmond inquired of Buddy, ignoring Ricky's pleas.

"Balla."

Desmond raised his right hand and took a step toward them. "Balla," he declared in his friendliest voice. "Balla."

The men held their ground, appearing angry. Desmond stopped, his hand in mid-wave. Apparently, he was pronouncing it incorrectly.

"May I make a suggestion?" Donato finally murmured, only his lips moving, "Can Buddy tell them good-bye, so we can get the hell outta here?"

"Maybe that's not such a bad idea – for now, anyway. We seem to have a cultural gap. We surprised them, so maybe this isn't the time to explain why we are here," Desmond acquiesced, slowly lowering his hand. "Buddy, tell them we will not trade with them, and that we will leave but come back tomorrow and discuss why we are here."

"Right." Buddy raised both hands out at the warriors. "Manna sanhe tua <click> moi santo balla. Moana see banna." The Afarkils remained emotionless.

"Good job Buddy. Okay, everybody," Desmond affirmed, turning slowly towards the Humvee, "let's go – don't get excited. Just keep your hands out where these gentlemen can see them." Schuyler groaned as she lifted the Betacam off the ground. The six of them walked as casually as possible back to the vehicle and climbed in. The men stood and watched them. Donato made sure he did not sit beside Schuyler after she loaded the camera in the back.

Once loaded Desmond started the vehicle, set the air conditioning on arctic blast, turned and drove back in total silence. In the rear-view mirrors he watched the Afarkil warriors get smaller and smaller, finally disappearing into the distance in a cloud of Humvee-induced dust.

There was silence in the truck almost all the way back. "That was too intense," Ricky finally muttered, his voice still shaking.

"No shit!" Mary remarked in an equally shaky voice as they arrived back to the compound, "He wanted to trade three of his women for me!" She turned back to Buddy. "Are you positive that's what he said?"

"That's what he said," Buddy confirmed in his own weak voice. "I'm sure I heard him correctly."

Desmond ignored their comments. He imagined those same three children running out a hut door and back into the first one, completing the narrative arc of their disappointing introduction.

CHAPTER FOUR

The next morning at 6:30 a.m., Desmond stepped out of his bunkhouse, greeted by blistering heat and the aroma of Bruny preparing breakfast at the catering building. He meant to grab a bottled water from his cooler on his way out but he forgot. He made a mental note to drink more.

Even though the night-time temperature in the Danakil sometimes dropped into the seventies, by daybreak it was too sweltering to sleep, so everyone was awake and milling about. Desmond was upset and worried about their meeting with the Afarkils yesterday; he had envisioned a bucolic, friendly greeting, much like the portrayals of the first meeting between the pilgrims and the Indians in the new world in the history books he studied in grade school. He imagined exchanging trinkets and eating a communal meal.

"Now they either think we're some sort of interloping white brutes or cowards worth killing," he mumbled as he walked past Donato finishing a very enthusiastic story to Buzzcut, Ricky and Buddy. He stopped to listen.

"... When all twenty of 'em are done, well Ricky here falls over in a heap. He's a mess, in terrible shape. I look at him as the chief says to me, 'And what'll it be for you? What will your punishment be?' And I look at Ricky, and I decide that I could never recover from Roo-roo. So I say to the chief, 'I pick death.' So the chief says 'Death it shall be. But first, Roo-roo!'"

All of the guys exploded in laughter at Donato's story before heading over to the chow line. Desmond managed a smile; it was a guy thing, and he presumed that maybe it was therapeutic for them to be able to laugh about yesterday's frightening encounter – although it did nothing to put a sheen on the crap that really happened.

He went to find Schuyler, anxious to view the footage she shot of their meeting. Despite the shock and surprise, it would be a compelling and candid look at the tribesmen in native warrior clothing in a genuinely confrontational setting.

Bruny was busy making someone a custom omelet, his lit cigarette burning on the cooktop edge when Desmond saw Schuyler already eating at one of the picnic tables under the awning. She looked lost in thought, just playing with her food. It was really too hot to eat. A few other crew members sat scattered under the awning. A large fan tried to move hot, dry air.

"Good morning, Miss Courtland!" Desmond announced in a chipper mood as he sat down beside her. "Don't pick at Bruny's food – it'll never heal."

"Hi Desmond. That's the second unfunny joke I've heard this morning already," she answered half-heartedly. "I'm sorry, I didn't mean ... when will the toilet be fixed?" she added, changing the subject.

Desmond saw she wasn't in a happy mood, and quickly got more businesslike. "I'll get that nonessential guy to fix it this morning, but first as director I have to address your dust-up with Donato yesterday."

Schuyler looked straight at him. Her eyes were cold and unblinking. "Donato's an alkie and a misogynistic ass, and I warned you I'll drop him on the ground as many times as it takes to get him to cut out the sexist and insulting comments. I know you're on the same page with me on this," she proclaimed, her irritation growing. "I damn near dropped him again this morning when he tried to tell me this repulsive roo-roo joke."

She looked back at her barely-touched breakfast. "I know no one, including you, wants it known that this is a hostile workplace for women."

Desmond had nothing to add to what she just said. "No, no they don't. Fair enough. But I question your timing with yesterday's encounter, and I wonder if it influenced the Afarkil's perception of us, seeing two of us fighting. It doesn't present the united front nor the image of peace and understanding I wish to project to them."

"Okay, I hear you. I apologize. Next time I kick Donato's ass in private."

"After breakfast I'd like to cue up the monitor and look at the raw footage you shot of our surprise party at the village yesterday."

"I already did," she replied, almost despondent. "And you aren't going to like it."

"Well, I'm sure we can pull some useable segments from it, at least for ..."

Ricky suddenly sat down across from Desmond and Schuyler. Desmond noticed his forehead was extremely sunburned – his fair complexion was going to take a beating in this broiler-like environment. He had about seven pancakes stacked on his plate.

"Mr. Desmond, I need to talk to you about our translator, Buddy," he chattered as he drowned his pancakes in syrup and poked in a mouthful. "I think he's a fraud, sir."

"Slow down Ricky, what do you mean?" Desmond wiped his forehead, thinking he felt hotter and queasier than usual. Was he even sweating? "And in case you didn't notice, Schuyler and I were having a conver..."

"Yesterday? At the village?" Ricky motioned toward Desmond with his plastic fork. "You know all that talk he did to those Afarkils who snuck up on us? Well his translations all sounded really familiar to me, and I'm thinking all last night and this morning, I'm thinking 'where have I heard that language before?' and a little while ago it dawns on me – the 1933 King Kong! Buddy's translations were lines from King Kong! He must have just watched it!"

"That's insane, Ricky," Desmond scoffed. "It's been years since I've seen the 1933 Kong, but I'm pretty sure those lines aren't in there."

"I'm positive! I don't know what he was saying to them in Khoisan, but his English translations of what they were saying were right outta King Kong!"

Schuyler rolled her eyes in impatience.

"Remember in the movie, the scene on Skull Island, when the chief talked to Robert Armstrong, and Captain Englehart translated? He said 'Look at the golden woman'! That's exactly what Buddy said about Mary! And in the movie the chief offers to trade six of his women for Fay Wray! Just like Buddy said! I'm telling you, it was almost line for line!"

"And I have proof, sort of," Ricky continued as he pulled an old paperback book from his back pocket, "I found this in the storage shed – it's a Khoisan and Tigrinya language guide, published by the United States War Department in 1941. It lists a ton of dialects, and I don't know if any matches theirs, but I flipped through and I could not find anything that sounded even remotely like what Buddy said. Remember he said 'balla' or something meant 'friend'? Not even close – it says here in the book that the closest word for 'friend' they have is 'nisi-hanu,' and that translates as 'one not family.' But, in King Kong the word for 'friend' was 'balla!'"

"Which leads me to something even worse," Ricky continued as he flipped a few pages. "They do have a word, 'bola' that translates roughly to 'cannibal!' It seems pretty close to 'balla' – instead of friends they may have thought you were calling them cannibals! That might explain why they reacted the way they did."

Desmond thought for a minute as a wave of dizziness washed over him. "I have to give Buddy the benefit of the doubt, Rick, and that cannibal thing seems to be a bit of a stretch. I will talk to him about his knowledge of their language, but he was hired specifically by Mary, on Mr. Carswell's recommendations, because of his language abilities. Christ it's hot."

"The thing is, the Khoisan and Tigrinya languages have over 25 dialects, and we aren't even sure which one the Afarkils speak," Ricky continued. "I just find it very hard to believe he is fluent in the one specific dialect we needed."

"Like I said I will talk to … Jesus Christ!" Desmond suddenly gagged when he looked down and saw his pancakes squirming with maggots. He jumped up suddenly, banging the picnic table with his knees as he extracted his legs.

Covering his mouth, he staggered over behind the kitchen out of everybody's sight and spit and retched for several seconds, trying to convince himself that he did not eat any of them and they would not kill him even if he did.

Maggots were his one really irrational fear. As a kid he sometimes dreamt he woke up, threw back the covers and found his body literally "alive" with thousands of the nasty, wriggling carnivorous little vermin.

Once somewhat composed, Desmond walked shakily back to his table, grabbing a water on the way and gulping it down. His plate was gone. "Sorry about that," he muttered to a rather surprised Schuyler and Ricky as he sat back down. The sudden introduction of cold water made his head swim and his stomach lurch.

"What the hell was that all about?" Schuyler asked incredulously. "And aren't you going to get breakfast?"

"What? Nothing. I choked on something. Ricky. I will take this under advisement, but I think you're overreacting. Now relax and check your pancakes for maggots. Schuyler?" Desmond asked, turning to his left, "let's take a look at that footage, if you're done. I've kind of lost my appetite."

Ricky looked in horror at his almost empty plate. "Check my pancakes for what ...?"

"Yea, thanks Desmond, I just lost my appetite too," Schuyler muttered as she got up.

As Desmond left the dining area, he veered over by Bruny. "Ready to eat, Mr. Desmond?"

"I made an ugly discovery on my plate," Desmond whispered to him in a low voice, "Please make sure it doesn't happen again. This shoot is far too important for that kind of distraction."

"What ugly discovery?" Bruny asked innocently as he scooped bacon off a grill and dropped it on a plate lined with paper towels. "What plate?"

"Let's just say I hope you do a better job of keeping disgusting crawling wildlife out of my food from now on."

Bruny set down his tongs and looked intensely at Desmond. "What food? What are you talking about? You never went through the chow line."

"It was maggots. There were maggots on my plate."

"That's a lie!" Bruny angrily raised his voice. "My plates are squeaky clean! You never went through the flippin' line so you must've got your breakfast somewhere else because you didn't get it from me! And I would appreciate you not spreading rumors like that about my cooking!"

Desmond stopped – Bruny was right, suddenly he had no recollection of going through the serving line. He could only remember stopping to listen to Donato, then sitting beside Schuyler to talk about the footage she shot yesterday. How weird, his timeline had a big gap in it and no matter how hard he concentrated he could not account for it. Did he have a blackout? He had not had one of those in over seven years, when he was going through his second codeine and vodka withdrawal phase.

He mumbled a half-hearted sorry to Bruny and walked over to meet Schuyler in the editing room, shaken by the moment.

As Schuyler reported earlier, her preferred monitor broke during unloading, and the backup needed some minor repairs to work, but she got it going as Desmond entered the tiny room, still mulling the maggot mystery. He grabbed another water and gulped it all down, then opened another one. He didn't realize how thirsty he was.

"Don't get your hopes up," Schuyler warned as she loaded the cassette and pushed "play." Desmond scooted a chair beside her, sat and anxiously watched.

The tape started with some jerky footage of the ground, a glimpse of the Humvee and some sky as she removed the lens cap and hoisted it on her shoulder. It then dissolved to static at about 1 minute, 15 seconds.

"See all this static?" she asked, watching the monitor as the noise danced in reflections off Desmond's face. "This is where the establishing shot of the village and the trees is supposed to be."

"So what happened?"

"I think it was because I loaded the tape outside of the Humvee, and sand may have gotten in the recording heads." After a minute of static Schuyler fast-forwarded past it all to 5:07. She stopped when the picture suddenly got clear again. "It cleared itself out at this point, I guess."

"That's strange." Desmond mumbled. He noticed that despite the heat Schuyler emitted a fragrance that his ex-wife wore that he couldn't remember the name. He had an assistant buy it for her several Christmas's in a row. He wondered if he suddenly leaned in and kissed her if she would drop him on the floor like she did Donato and threaten to kill him. Yea, probably.

"Now here comes the best part," she announced sarcastically, breaking Desmond's concentration. Donato's face suddenly appeared on the screen, crystal clear at 5 minutes, 31 seconds. "The only berries they'll find out here are dingleberries."

"Oh, that's perfect," Desmond moaned. "The best shot we have is of our art director saying 'dingleberry?' Christ almighty."

The screen went black briefly. It came back on and showed a one-second glimpse of a hut when the camera suddenly jerked sharply around, pointing at sky, then ground, then sky, then someone's shirt, then ground again before stopping on a cockeyed angle on mostly gray sand and a little corner of sky. Off-camera Desmond briefly heard Schuyler's voice threatening to kill Donato before it cut off. "Here – this is where I laid down the camera to take out Donato just before the Afarkil men surprised us."

"Enjoy the show," she suggested, leaning back in her chair, "because this is as good as it gets."

Desmond looked forlornly at the monitor. The scene had the excitement of a parking garage security camera. "What happened? Where's the sound? You got none of our conversation with the Afarkil men? Is this it?"

Schuyler erupted in anger and frustration. "It's not my damn fault! Donato pissed me off so much, then I was so terrified of being speared to death I didn't pick the camera back up, so I taped fifteen minutes of sand just after I must have accidentally muted the microphone!"

"But Schuyler, yes! This is indeed your fault!" Desmond responded, "You let Donato piss you off and you chose to beat him up rather than ..."

"I told you I was going to kill him if he didn't shut up!"

"I understand, but Schuyler, you let your emotions ...!"

Infuriated, Schuyler quickly got up and stomped out, leaving Desmond talking to himself and staring at a silent tape of desert sand. "... get the best of you." He watched the entire 19 minutes, 35 seconds almost without blinking, in a suffocating room with only his own disappointment to keep him company. His head was splitting, and he traveled back as he closed his eyes, swallowing down his frustration ...

"You were riding quite a wave, Mr. Desmond," Dick Cavett continued, trying to be light and chipper but seemingly aggravated by Desmond's silence, almost desperately trying to force him to speak as all three cameras slowly repositioned. Their motion made Desmond even more uncomfortable. "You directed two feature films that received remarkable receptions, especially for a new director, including two academy award nominations. Must have been a remarkable feeling! Some critics called you the next Godard, or better yet the new Hitchcock."

Desmond suddenly startled, almost like he had been dozing. "Hitchcock?" he blurted, ignoring the cameras' movement. "Why am I being compared to Hitchcock?"

Cavett almost jumped in his chair, delighted that the volatile director seemed to be coming to life, like someone slowly winding a giant key in his back, tightening his springs. "There are several who have made the comparison. But despite your two enormous successes, there are those who also referred to you, well, in a not very flattering way, to another director, the extravagant Eric von Stroheim, a personality ..."

"That's bullshit." Desmond hated being negatively compared to directors from the past, but Cavett persevered as camera 3 tried to nudge unnoticed several inches to Desmond's right. He watched – he knew the camera was moving.

"...from the silent era who was known for his pushy, excessive directorial ways," Cavett continued, ignoring Desmond's interruption that would have to be bleeped. "How do you respond to those accusations that you abandoned simplicity and basic tenets of storytelling, safety and common sense in favor of ..."

"That's a crock!" Desmond interjected, "Why am I being compared to von Stroheim? Who said that?" Camera 2 suddenly rolled an inch forward.

"I saw that!" Desmond shouted, pointing at the camera. It stopped just as suddenly.

As the tape dissolved to static then went black, Desmond shut off the playback, stepped outside in a disconcerted daze and saw Buddy eating breakfast with Buzzcut under the awning.

"Buzzcut you may leave," he announced as he sat down in front of Buddy. Like a good soldier, Buzz gathered his plate, water and utensils and scurried away.

"Good morning, Mr. D.!" Buddy declared with a huge smile on his face.

"Buddy, another crew member – oh, good morning – another crew member is concerned about your actual knowledge of the Afarkil language. It seems to be very complicated, and the question is how well you really know it," Desmond explained, being diplomatic as possible while staring unmoved at the pile of scrambled eggs on Buddy's plate. "See, we have to make absolutely sure that our communication is close to perfect to make this project work. Can you tell me a little bit about your experience in this?"

Buddy furrowed his brow and set down his fork. "Who's the crew member?"

"That's not important. Just tell me your experience."

Buddy shifted on the bench, picked up his fork and picked at his scrambled eggs. "My great-great uncle was Billy Bitzer, D.W. Griffith's cameraman."

Desmond waited for a follow-up, which never came. "Okay, okay, that's good, but your experience with the language, please."

"I'm getting to that. I studied African languages at UCLA and minored in film theory. A professor made us pick an obscure dialect to report for our final project. I picked one from an old NATO Central African language guide in our library archives called 'Nilo-Saharan Khoisan-Tigrayan dialect 5F' because it seemed simple. And it is, technically. The alphabet has only 13 letters, the entire vocabulary has less than 200 words, and frankly, it made a shorter report. I found out there were only two societies that spoke it – a small group of Afar farmers near Lake Afrera and the northern tribe Afarkils. I thought I could shortcut the project because with so few actual speakers it would be so hard to verify, but I found it was actually easy to learn once I got the hang of it."

Satisfied, Desmond stood to leave. "Very good. I hope you realize why I felt compelled to ask you this. I was not questioning your abilities at all." Desmond turned, then turned back to Buddy again. "One more thing – how exactly did Mary happen to find the one person in America who spoke this language?"

Buddy smiled. "That's where my great-great uncle Billy comes in. He had a vaudeville friend in Kansas City named Henry Hogan, who it turns out was also friends with Wallace Carswell. I met Henry and Carswell through a family member before Henry died in 1980 at age 108. Henry told Carswell that a young buck like me should work in the pictures, just like Uncle Billy. Carswell put me in his rolodex mostly just to placate Hogan, but he was obsessed also that I knew a bizarre African language. It was all serendipity, I think they call it. So here I am."

Satisfied of Buddy's abilities, Desmond found Donato and coaxed him into riding over to the village to get a look at the village in terms of color and composition for camera angles and what times of day were more conducive for filming, while the remainder of the crew tried to get their equipment repaired, cleaned and operable. Donato agreed to go but insisted on staying inside the locked vehicle with the windows rolled up so there would be no more surprises by angry natives.

"By the way, Donato, I spoke with Schuyler this morning about your incident with her yesterday," Desmond advised as he circled oil drum mountain. "Your confrontation resulted in us not getting any footage of our meeting with the Afarkils yesterday. I'm not very happy about it."

"What did she say? And that wasn't my fault. I was just kidding, but she has this fucked-up hair trigger temper."

"A temper that you intentionally aggravate. She told me she was going to file a grievance against me, and cut your penis off if you make any more sex jokes, including that insulting roo-roo story."

"You know, for some reason I believe her – damn, my back still hurts. I should file an assault charge."

"No, you're not, you're going to let it go and work with her." Desmond parked about 100 yards away from the ring of Baobabs. "I don't need someone filing a sexual harassment suit out here, Carswell would kill me."

Suddenly the Humvee air conditioning started blowing hot.

Desmond punched the controls several times. "What the hell ...?"

"The vehicle's eating sand, it gets everywhere," Donato maintained. "I got sand up my ass. I imagine the compressor needs blowing out."

There were no natives in sight inside the village as Desmond fiddled with the controls, making the air even hotter. "Tell me what you see, Mick."

"These damn trees are in the way of their huts, no matter where we place a camera," Donato observed, confident there were no natives within striking distance as sweat began pouring off his face. He rolled down his window to let in some air, but it was like being under a french fry light. "There's no good angles to frame the whole village. The only colors here a hundred shades of tan and a weak burnt orange. There ain't a blue or a green, or even a nice red in sight. Damn it's hot."

He continued, motioning to his left. "I noticed the sun set over this way, but even though it was clear the sky was a sort of milky white color, so we got no spectacular sunset or sunrise backdrop. Plus," he added as an afterthought, "Them Afarkils, from what I saw, are not very photogenic."

"Well, they are destitute," Desmond responded as he smacked the a/c control, thinking that would make it work. "What do you suggest?" He finally just turned it off.

Donato boldly produced a flask from his pocket and took a slug from it, right in front of his boss. Desmond watched him but said nothing. According to Mary, Donato's capacity for alcohol was almost legendary. "Mary and I discussed it last night, and I think she has some ideas on self-improvement. For the villagers, I mean, not the village. I'm not sure what to do about everything else – maybe burn it all down and start over."

A competent set designer in Hollywood for years before getting into art direction, Donato's politically incorrect but honest (and very blunt) opinions were crucial.

"How about some ideas other than burning everything down?" Desmond asked. "And what's in the flask?"

"Water. Want some?" Donato held the flask out. "It's warm but it's water."

Desmond knew better. "No, no thanks."

"Now if we want any decent pictures of their village, we need to take out at least one, maybe two or three of these trees," Donato continued, pointing at the grandest, oldest one directly in front of them. "They're damn huge and they block everything."

Desmond reached over and pulled Ricky's booklet out of the glove box and leafed through it. "I want to read you something ...

here ... it says here that the Baobab tree is native to this area," he began reading. "They provide not only shade, but their fruit, called monkey bread, is a major source of nourishment. Dissolved in water, the liquid from the fruit can be drunk straight or used as a sauce. Eating the fruit pulp treats a variety of fevers, including diarrhea and malaria, and its vitamin C levels are nearly six times higher than that of an orange.' Blah blah blah ..."

He flipped forward a few more pages. "...The leaves are eaten as a relish, especially during drought. The monkey bread seeds, which are eaten raw or roasted, yield edible oil ... Although the bark is unusable for building, it can be stripped and woven into a hemp-like substance to make rope, baskets and baby carriers. It can also be used to make nets or animal snares."

Desmond closed the booklet and tossed it back in the glove box. "So there you go. Their survival depends on the trees so we absolutely will not take any of them down. Period."

Donato shrugged. "Well I wasn't being totally serious about that, but there's still no color out here. Maybe we can get their permission to paint the huts. Those mud colors don't translate well up on a screen. Then again, it's so damn hot out here the paint might not take anyway. It's all a crap shoot."

"Well, their huts look like mud because they are made of mud," Desmond responded dryly. He realized Donato was thinking purely feature cinematic, not documentary. "Remember Donato we are not world-building for a feature blockbuster, we are documenting real life."

"Don't these people have any culture or anything? Any color in their lives? No art, no music ... I don't even see any of those, what do they call them? Bongos or something? It seems their whole civilization is centered around sand and mud."

"Apparently they choose to live this way," Desmond added. "The last members trying to cling to the old traditional ways. That's it, Donato – that's the lede of this story. Modern versus traditional."

Donato thought a moment before continuing. "Maybe we can

cover these huts in a veneer of painted plaster. That won't compromise the integrity of the original structures. We'll keep the stick roofs for authenticity. And I might whip up a painted sunset backdrop that would add a little flash."

Desmond thought Donato was finally coming back down to earth. "I'll get with Mary on her ideas, but don't go painting or plastering any huts just yet, I'm not completely on board with that." He started the Humvee and again jiggled the air conditioning buttons, to no effect. "It's all a moot point if we don't first make peace with these people. What the fuck is the deal with the a/c anyway? It's a blast furnace in here."

Desmond drove in a wide circle around the village to see if anyone was home. At his closest pass the Humvee – low on gas, as usual and sucking sand through the engine – stuttered and almost stalled. Desmond pumped the gas twice, and on the third time the engine roared back to life. And, the air conditioning miraculously kicked back on.

"Hey, we got air," Desmond proclaimed almost triumphantly. "Let's see just what this thing can do," he added in a sudden urge of bravado. He dropped it into low gear and stomped the gas, spinning the massive rear wheels in the loose dirt for a good second before they screamed off in a fury.

Just for fun Desmond deftly switched to 4X4 and raced the gigantic and vulgar Humvee out into the nearby salt flats. Powered by the massive 450 horsepower engine, the massive vehicle chewed through the gnarled bushes at over 50 miles-per-hour. Driving that oversize colossus made Desmond feel like a teenager again, although as a teen he never had a $75,000 mechanical monstrosity like this to show off his stuff.

Desmond noted with satisfaction that his brand-new military vehicle was crammed with every bell and whistle 1984 had to offer. This Haile-Selassie guy had great taste in vehicles. In addition to the upgraded V8 engine, the beast also was equipped with air-glide suspension, off-road roof rack lights, a CD player with upgraded Bose surround sound, aluminum trim package, four-zone a/c (when it was working) and oversize all-terrain wheels. The vehicle must have weighed almost 6,000 pounds, and its gas mileage was virtually nonexistent.

"Desmond," Donato moaned over the thunderous roar of the engine and the jarring landscape, as he held tight to the "Oh sweet Jesus" handle over the door, "I'm gonna lose my cookies if you don't slow it down." Every jolt was amplified by the vehicle's enormous bulk, voluminous weight and excessive speed, driven madly by a film director reliving his golden years as a teenage showoff during the Kennedy administration, nursing three reckless driving charges and two DUIs with a free-thinking, corn-fed, pony-tailed girlfriend in the passenger seat, all before his eighteenth birthday.

"I'll turn around at that tree up ahead!" Desmond called out, pointing to what he thought was one huge Baobab far off in the distance between two earth mounds. Aiming with great resolve, and laughing at the misery suffered by the hapless art director beside him, Desmond stomped the accelerator to the floorboard. The huge motor kicked into overdrive, with the massive transmission clanking into a lower gear and transferring maximum horsepower to all four of the huge knobby wheels. It was like riding the space shuttle.

Rocketing up to almost 70 miles-per-hour, still in four-wheel drive, the roaring acceleration pressed the two men back into their seats. Desmond glanced at the gas needle, believing it was actually dropping from a quarter-tank to almost empty in the brief distance to the turnaround.

Closing in, Desmond suddenly let off the gas and the vehicle unexpectedly slowed to half its speed, tossing an unbuckled Donato forward in his seat almost into the dash. The sudden rush of negative g-forces bucked Desmond chest-first into the leather-wrapped steering wheel, knocking the wind from him.

Slowing to a stop, Donato and Desmond caught their breath, and eventually laughed at the excessive, almost offensive speed and handling of the giant black tax write-off whose gas tank they almost emptied at the expense of some Ethiopian millionaire they never even met. "Damn, Mick," Desmond sputtered, out of breath at his own recklessness, "that was bomb! Damn! What a vehicle!"

Donato was so glad to be stopped all he could do was shake his head and take a long gulp out of his flask. Desmond, meanwhile noticed that what they thought was one big Baobab tree was in fact four trees packed closely together – and there appeared to be something pushed in between them. He looked curiously for a moment as the dust cleared.

"Desmond," Donato noted, apparently seeing the same thing, "what is that between those trees?"

Desmond peeked through the dissipating dust at a fairly large mud hut, about fifteen feet square, built solidly in between the four stout Baobabs and roughly disguised with branches. Desmond circled slowly to get the best view and shut off the engine as the two of them stared at it, so caught off-guard by another structure they really didn't know what to do. Finally, he spoke up. "Well, we'll never find out what it is if we don't take a look. Come on."

He and Donato climbed down from the vehicle and walked in the blazing sun all the way around the structure looking for an entry. It was very isolated; in addition to being tucked tightly between four trees and camouflaged with limbs and leaves, it was surrounded by two large mounds of rock up against a natural lava wall. It was just by chance that they even noticed it.

Finally, on the far side, nestled between two trees was an opening covered in Baobab thatch.

Donato stopped. "You don't think it's full of those hostile militia Ricky told us about, do you?"

Desmond stopped and looked at the doorway. "Valid question – but if it were full of militia they would have come out and filled us with a thousand rounds of soviet-made ammo by now. Remember we arrived here on a hundred-decibel 747. But I think I know what this is."

Desmond tentatively stepped through the thatch and was

surprised, almost shocked at what he discovered.

The inside was nearly pleasant. The floor was covered with fresh cut wild grass, sprinkled with wild herbs, kicking up a slightly jasmine fragrance with each step. It was not broiling hot inside; on the contrary, it was almost comfortable, dark and easily under a hundred degrees due to the shade of the generous trees overhead. The frequent molten blast of blistering Danakil wind was blocked by the mounds and lava wall surrounding it – part of the genius of its placement. The room was lit with several hand-dipped candles, with small holes cut in the walls just above them to draw out the black tallow smoke. The ceiling was Baobab branches, cut, bundled and stacked densely. It was the perfect place for someone to relax, someone like ...

... pregnant women. Sitting on straw tick mattresses were three beautiful young, but frightened, Afarkil women, staring warily at the white interlopers, all sporting the large, round shiny bellies of final month pregnancies. They wore long shawl-like wraps, with only their stomachs and faces exposed. Desmond noticed there was a tray of bread on the floor between the women, and beside it a woven basket brimming not only with the Baobab fruits but also with several other fruits and vegetables of unknown varieties. Several five-gallon cans with "U.N." stenciled on the sides nearby held several gallons of fresh water.

"I don't believe it," Desmond whispered coarsely. This discovery was the best news of the shoot so far. "Mick, we found the secret maternity hospital. It really exists! Dammit, we actually found it!"

Donato stepped inside and whistled long and low. "Son of a bitch, Desmond. Hell of a find."

All three women sat up and pointed accusingly at the two men. "<click> sahn-ah moan-she mahnoa-toa!" Desmond heard one of them say to them.

What's going on?" Donato asked, "She acts like she doesn't want us here."

"Oh, I don't think we're supposed to be here," Desmond

answered. "They've got some traditional notions about pregnancy and childbirth." The women motioned frantically toward the door, seeming to order the two white men to leave right away. One of the other women drew a linen sheet up over her belly to cover it from view. Her eyes were wide with concern, as were the eyes of the third woman. They obviously were quite angry and confused about the strange men in their presence.

"<click> sahn-ah moan-she manoa-to <click>! San-moan-she!" The woman gesticulated even more anxiously.

"It's all about their traditions. We need to leave – we'll get Schuyler here with the camera." Desmond motioned to the woman that they were leaving. "Yes ma'am, we are sorry, and are on our way out."

Desmond and Donato exited the hut almost giddy with their discovery. "What a great break this is, to instill hope in the viewer for the survival of the Afarkils!" Desmond exclaimed as he started the vehicle. "Maybe we can even film an actual birth, that would be so amazing!"

"This might go a long way to getting more of those other Hollywood types on board this project," Donato added as he took a self-congratulatory drag from his flask. "They love this touchy-feely shit."

"Damn right, and remind me to gas up the Humvee," Desmond observed as he drove slowly and sanely this time back toward camp, trying to conserve the precious few drops of gasoline left in the monster's belly.

Unfortunately, they sputtered to a stop a little over halfway back, and had to walk the remaining half-mile in the blistering sun.

Back at the compound, Eric met Desmond at the fuel storage reservoirs before Desmond even had a chance to ask him to take a gas can back to the Humvee.

"Bad news. A valve under the 50-gallon gas tank inexplicably started leaking," Eric informed him, pointing underneath the tank, "and well over half of our gasoline got out before I found it and got it shut off.

"What made it leak?" Desmond asked. "And the Humvee is out of gas."

"It's weird, the valve wasn't broken, it was just loose," Eric continued to his frustrated boss as he picked up and began filling a can to carry back to the Humvee, "and we lost it all down into a run-off ditch around back before I found it. It quickly evaporated, so there seems to be no fire danger."

Desmond's joy at finding the maternity hospital was suddenly tempered by the gasoline situation. "Is it because of the heat?"

"Most likely," Eric replied as he screwed the cap on the can and stood up. "But I definitely have to keep an eye on it. We don't want to run out of gas out here."

Desmond spent the rest of the day meeting with various members of his staff to plan the details of the documentary, reminding them all of their precarious gasoline situation until they could get it replenished. He had decided after consulting with Donato while walking back that out of respect for the pregnant Afarkil women, their maternity hut discovery would remain a secret for now.

Later that afternoon, Desmond and Mary met in front of the fan under the dining awning and discussed her ideas about the natives.

"Well, Donato and I were talking about how the environment, the village and especially these villagers, or at least the ones we saw, don't have strong screen presence," she explained. "They're small, they're ..."

"They're destitute," Desmond added, glancing unmoved at Mary's tightly crossed legs.

"Exactly," Mary concluded, not taking his sarcastic hint. "Monochromatic. If we want a project that will get the right attention we need to seriously dress them up, you know, jazz up those outfits they wear. They're minimalist and frankly boring. Now, black people in other African cultures have very colorful wardrobes. Remember that market we passed just outside Addis Ababa on the way here? Now those people had presence. I have some sketches here."

An excellent wardrobe designer, Mary's sketches depicted exaggeratedly tall, svelte classic ebony men and women in splashy fabrics, huge, dangling native jewelry and loud, elaborate headpieces.

"Viewers need color, movement and ceremony in an African milieu," she continued. "Nobody's going to really open their wallet to these people if we don't give them something good to look at, you know, a classic native look and classic native ritual that we cannot afford to lose. It's an expectation an American viewer has of a tribe, or a clan, based in Africa."

"We can't make these people out to be something they are not, Mary," Desmond cautioned. "We're not trying to prove they're worth saving only because they have pretty clothes."

"Oh no! Of course they deserve saving regardless of their clothing! We just should dress up their appearance for their screen debut."

"But ... I think you're missing the point of this documentary, Mary. We need to show how strong the Afarkils once were, contrasted with how destitute they are now. We'll lose the viewers' sympathy if we portray them not as impoverished but as dancing, colorful and happy-go-lucky."

Mary rolled her eyes. "Desmond! Be realistic! After our film runs its course how many of our viewers will actually see or even think about an Afarkil again? I'll bet almost none! They're the flavor of the month, you know that, that's the way things work. We need a film that people will watch, be mesmerized by and stroke huge checks to before they go back to their daily lives, feeling good about what they did and not thinking one more second about. When the day is over the only thing Mr. Carswell and our investor will want is asses in seats and checkbooks in hand and we only have one shot at that in a very limited window of opportunity."

"Besides," Mary continued, "destitute people can be colorful and happy-go-lucky – look at the dancing, singing slaves in Disney's Song of the South! And you see them in National Geographic all the time."

"And how do you think the Afarkils would respond to seeing themselves portrayed as colorless, boring and dying?" She added. "If it were me, I would be insulted."

Desmond was not fully onboard but he could see Mary's point. He remembered as an elementary school student in the 1950s studying slavery in pre-civil war America. The textbooks showed smiling black people in the south sitting barefoot on porches, singing, dancing, eating watermelon and playing the banjo, with the text explaining that slaves were happy had an "almost carefree life."

Mary made another good point: money notwithstanding, even if Hollywood celebrities lined up behind this project, dry, depressing documentaries traditionally didn't draw the right audience, get nominated for the right awards or enhance the career of the director. There was a fine line with this project, and his job was to walk it without crossing it. If the film was too depressing it could drive away the endorsements and future projects. Would just a tiny bit of color and ceremony really hurt?

"Mary, I trust you – but to a point," Desmond acquiesced, "I realize we have to walk a tightrope here, juggling harsh reality with screen appeal, but just don't get too carried away. I will maintain final say on any costume decisions."

"Now when do I ever get carried away?" Mary retorted as she closed her sketchbook, uncrossed her legs, stood and walked away. Nothing stirred in Desmond as he watched her backside. "By the way," she added, quickly turning around, "The damn toilet still isn't fixed."

Desmond jerked his eyes up to her face. Damn, he was going to get caught doing that. "I was not looking ... never mind, and all right, I'll get that guy right on it."

CHAPTER FIVE

Desmond snorted, but recovered from Dick Cavett's loaded question just as fast as he heated up. He sat back in his chair and took a long drink of the bottled water beside him. The cameras were finally still. "My last project ..." he started, pausing for great effect, staring at the bottle label, noticing he did not recognize the brand. "... was a noble effort for ..."

Suddenly camera 1 lurched forward another inch, like it was closing in. Desmond stopped talking and watched. He knew the guy moving the camera was toying with him. After a few tense seconds he completed his sentence.

"... for a noble cause."

"Noble ... some may dispute that term," Cavett interjected, trying to keep the conversation on track so viewers at home would not lose interest and turn the channel over to Johnny Carson. "In hindsight, Pyro was an expensive, audacious and vulgar concept, would you agree? Light years away from your first two films. Critics may have seen a lot of chutzpah and overkill but very little nobility."

Desmond felt his face suddenly heat up again. He did not appreciate his motives and descriptions questioned, especially by a host of a TV show. He closed his eyes and concentrated – he could see things moving, like wiggling little worms. This was not a good time to have a meltdown, not in front of this television crew. When were those cameras going to move again? Why were the men behind the cameras screwing with him in this manner?

Taking another long drink of what he guessed was cheap, house-brand water, he opened his eyes, regained his typical acerbic posture and launched into a rambling diatribe as he watched those damn cameras. "Pyro wasn't so far removed from my first two projects at all. It was the next in a planned sequence, a logical progression of idea, concept and story. I set out first to make the ultimate psychological thrillers, then to make the ultimate action movie, Mr. Cavett," he pontificated, emphasizing the word Mr. "I was singular of purpose and driven to fulfill my initiative, but there were exterior forces that thwarted my progress. I fell victim to meddling producers, incompetent scriptwriters and unskilled technical personnel. I was like a symphony conductor watching his musicians all play different compositions. I can only compare my experiences on that project to those of Orson Welles making Touch of Evil, or Kubrick attempting Napoleon. Like Kubrick and Welles, I was a visionary director pursuing alone a grand concept in the face of great adversity."

"But Mr. Desmond," Cavett implored, leaning forward. "Despite those directors' incredible commitment to their projects, no one died directly under Kubrick or Welles. But people died under you. You don't seem to grasp the reality that you just went too ..."

"Mr. Desmond, you better get out here quick!"

Desmond slowly opened his eyes to what he perceived in his hot stupor as a commotion somewhere outside. At first, he thought he heard someone yell "Get back!" and "Security!" He slowly rose and walked outside. Seeing what was going on, he broke into a run.

Bruny had arranged a sumptuous "welcome to the Danakil" American comfort food buffet. There was roast chicken and carved ham, the scent of which wafted all over the compound. There was a mouth-watering display of vegetables, including mashed potatoes, green bean casserole, and homemade macaroni and cheese. There were cold vegetables with dip, and an extensive array of desserts, including chocolate cake, strawberry cheesecake and even ice cream. Bruny was one of the only caterers anywhere who would successfully serve ice cream in the scorching Danakil.

Desmond was shocked to also see about fifty feet back from the far end of the table what looked like the entire Afarkil clan.

There were eight men and four women, including one holding an infant on her back in a carrier made of woven Baobab bark, and three young children, two boys and one girl. The little girl had a fresh patch made of mud and some sort of cloth over one eye.

The women wore full-length neutral robes that wrapped around their heads then down and around almost their entire bodies. They also wore two Baobab rings tightly around their necks. The men wore the same loincloths Desmond's group had seen yesterday, only their faces were not painted. They didn't say a word. They just stood there, staring quizzically at Buzzcut standing between them and the table seemingly holding them at bay. His AK-74 hung on his shoulder, his right hand brushing against it.

Mary looked over at her director. "Desmond! Finally! Do something!"

"Just move back from the food!" Buzzcut ordered the visitors. "No one will get hurt as long as you cooperate! Nothing to see here! Go back to your homes!"

"Our welcome wagon is going to kill our guests just for coming over to say hello," Donato stated to Desmond as his jaw dropped when he realized the horror of the situation. He couldn't even speak.

"Buzzcut!" he finally shouted, his voice breaking, "What are you doing!"

"Stay back from the camp!" Buzzcut again ordered, ignoring his director. "Back away! This is your final warning! Go back where you came from!"

"Idiot!" Ricky yelled, "They trying to be friends! For God's sake!"

The Afarkil people just stared quizzically at Buzzcut.

Desmond pushed through the crew past the table to reach his security detail. "Drop the damn gun!" he shouted.

Buzzcut turned, holding the gun out, pointed in the air. "Mr. Desmond, I was not going to shoot anyone, but my job is very specific to protect the camp and supplies from all outside interlopers ..." Buzzcut looked around at the entire crew, as if he were looking for validation. "the Oromo and other bad elements can easily disguise themselves and infiltrate us. History has shown that ..."

"Drop that gun NOW!" an enraged Desmond yelled. Gritting his teeth, he quickly reached and grabbed the gun barrel, an act he realized was unbelievably stupid. "These aren't outside interlopers or Oromo, they are the Afarkils we saw yesterday!"

"I was not on your scouting expedition yesterday, sir!" Buzzcut screamed as he wrestled for control of the weapon. "Without any identification I have no clue who they might be!" Both the crew and the Afarkils watched in breathless amazement. Desmond and Buzzcut both yelled for the other to let go when four shots abruptly fired off in quick succession.

"Hit the dirt!" Pandemonium broke out, and the staff scattered, screaming. A glass bean salad bowl on the table exploded. There was a clang in the background somewhere.

His ears ringing, Desmond finally pulled the gun from Buzzcut's hands. He stood back, shaking and out of breath as he did a worried head count of the Afarkils, who were backing further away from the camp. Thank God, none of them appeared to be hit.

He then turned his dazed attention to the deranged security guard with a mixture of amazement and genuine fury. "What the living fuck?" he sputtered through clenched teeth, shaking the weapon at him. "You were threatening with a firearm the very villagers we came all the way here to save! Christ, you violated like a thousand UN charters, not to mention ... that's it, I'm starting the paperwork to get you removed from this shoot!"

Buzzcut tried to sputter out his own response. "Sir ... like I said, without identification I cannot take any chances ..."

"Identification?" Desmond shouted, taking a step closer to him. "Were you going to ask to see their drivers' licenses? Birth certificates, or passports maybe? They have no identification you dumb fuck! And we'll have no project if you so much as harm a hair on their heads!"

Desmond turned and with the assault rifle pointed up in his hand addressed the entire crew, who were slowly returning to their feet after realizing they weren't dead. "There will not be a single death on any more of my film projects, period!"

He spun back to Buzzcut. "And I warned you! You are confined to the compound until I figure how to get you the hell out of here!" Enraged, he turned and carried the weapon back into his bunkhouse.

Once inside he dropped the gun on his desk, then rummaged through his junk drawer until he found what he was looking for – a large, old hammer presumably left over from construction. He took aim and swung it down as hard as he could on the end of the gun barrel. The hammer glanced off the side, knocking the gun off the desk across the floor, then clubbed his right knee in a jolt of fierce pain. Swimming in misery, anger and frustration, Desmond fell down on his hands and knees and beat furiously on the gun barrel with both hands, madly chasing it around the floor with each errant strike and seemingly not worried that it could accidentally go off ...

"I should have known better than hire Paramount flunkies to be in charge of my pyrotechnics! How long does it take to wire a squib?" Desmond remembered shouting in a rage at his pyrotechnic technicians as they tediously connected a thousand explosive squibs to walls, ceilings and the backs of dozens of stunt people on the set of Pyro. "If your ineptitude re-schedules my exploding 727 Jumbo jet scene, you assholes will all be out of jobs!"

Drowning in sweat and finally satisfied Buzzcut's gun was rendered useless, he picked it up, hoisted himself with a grimace and walked with a pronounced limp back outside. The Afarkils were gone, and most of the film staff was gathered around his bunkhouse sporting concerned looks that indicated that he was in there doing something stupid.

"Told you he wasn't beating himself," he heard Eric say to Donato. "Where's my ten dollars?"

Desmond felt everyone watching him as he walked uneasily toward Buzzcut and stopped in front of him, holding out the mangled weapon in a shaking hand.

"You were warned."

Buzzcut looked at it and frowned. "It's no good to me now," he muttered. "That was a $300 weapon."

"Fine." Desmond walked back toward the dining area, still clutching the ruined weapon. He knew the shooting probably drove the Afarkils away as he dropped the gun into one of the black bag-lined trash barrels with a muffled thump.

"Where are the Afarkils?" He asked no one.

Mary pointed into the bleak horizon. "Gone that way. Buddy tried to get them to stay but they wouldn't. They seemed pissed, and I can't blame them."

Dinner was eventually served to everyone but Desmond, who was too angry to eat or even talk about the incident. He spent the dinner hour sitting at his desk, staring at the wall. He had just gone through the trouble of introducing his team to the Afarkils now his oblivious security guard was threatening to kill them. But was he correct maybe? Could there have been murderous infiltrators hidden among them? Was he naïve for enforcing an open-border policy, where the Afarkils were welcome to come into the camp at any time?

He wondered why they had walked all the way to the camp – was it to apologize for the encounter with the men? Maybe they came to warn him to stay away from the maternity hut. Or was it an effort to make friends, and to maybe have that communal meal he envisioned? It made sense since the women and children came also. Christ, who knows?

Well that opportunity was blown to hell. Drooling white killers, indeed. Shit. He had dug out a form from his briefcase to make the case to ship Buzzcut off the project but it was seven pages and he was too sick and angry to fill it all out.

That night around midnight, Desmond lay in his bunk and stared at the ceiling as he continued to obsess over the incident with Buzzcut and the Afarkils. It was unusually hot for this time of night, and his sheets were damp with sweat. He heard Bruny give several large bags of dinner garbage a heave-ho into the dumpster around back. A pinpoint of light shone through a small hole up by the ceiling. It was probably a bullet hole made when he was wrestling Buzzcut over the gun.

Things were going badly. He feared this shoot was another Pyro, only in slow motion. He closed his eyes and recalled to his regret a familiar story …

Dick Cavett rubbed his chin, more confused than enlightened by Desmond's seeming inability to grasp the scope of the disaster on his last film. "I guess I'm having trouble understanding your vision," he began hesitantly, as camera number 2 slowly tracked a few inches from Desmond's left. "It was an action film." Then off the top of his head he added, "Directors make action films all the time. So, had you simply scaled back and focused on what worked for you before – well, would that have been an option?"

"Excuse me?" Previously only annoyed but suddenly infuriated, Desmond lurched to his feet and faced the startled host. The cameras followed him up out of his chair. "Only an action movie? Scale it back? Let me tell you something about this particular action film, smart guy – I endured weeks of slack-jawed incompetents for a crew, and special effects technology that was obstinate and lackluster to say the least!" Desmond jabbed his finger toward Cavett, spit flying. "This film was to be a groundbreaker! My conception was absolutely epic, light years beyond any other, but apparently only I could grasp the scope of my own vision."

"Talking head punks like you should get on your knees and thank directors like me who have the balls to stick their necks out and create a larger-than-life product that is worth your time and money to go experience!" He continued in Cavett's direction, only sometimes his eyes seemed to wander off of him over his shoulder, or down to the floor, like his brain was operating independently from his mouth, which never slowed down. The little cameras inside his head could not stay focused where they were supposed to be, they kept moving around.

"Damn theaters would be empty if it weren't for fresh, visionary directors like me enticing people into them with high-quality products, not scaled-back, mainstream bullshit!" Desmond went on, his voice rising and working to stay focused. "You can say a lot of things about that movie, call it whatever you want, a lazy production in an easy-sell market catering to the lowest common denominator or whatever, but one thing you cannot say is that Tom Desmond does not make money for the studio and Tom Desmond does not pack them in the theaters! And yes, we had an accident and people died ..."

Desmond suddenly stopped and stared at the floor. The director and cameramen held their breath, but Desmond actually could not breathe. The enormity of his own words suddenly suffocated him. He shut his eyes tightly.

Suddenly Desmond scrambled out of bed, shot out the bunkhouse door and dropped to his knees. The camp was black and still as his back went into a long graceful arch before he violently threw up, then raised and repeated the procedure. People died. People died. A strand of spit hung like a rein from his parched lips. All this time, and the words still cut like a knife ...

His mind racing and unable to sleep. Desmond finally got up, his knee screaming. He staggered back inside and sat down at his desk. It was still suffocating hot – his fan did nothing but move heavy, oven-like air. He absently reached for the short-wave radio he kept on the floor beside his nightstand, turned it on and started tuning.

This for years had been his favorite nocturnal activity when he could not sleep, and it was one that always relaxed him. It made him feel as if he and the radio were the only two alive in this entire world; that all the other idiots he dealt with didn't exist. It was the only remnant he kept from his childhood and what he hoped was the perfect outlet from all the pressures of saving exotic races of peoples from extinction.

Clutching his radio like a newborn, he lay back down in bed. He turned the volume down low as the phosphorescent green from the dial eerily illuminated his little world. This is how he did it as a little boy in the early 1950s as he waited for his Dad to come home from shift work. He remembered how he heard the front door open around 12:30 at night – his cue to put down the radio and pretend to be asleep. His dad then came in his room, pulled up his covers and kissed him lightly on the cheek, the Old Spice cologne that his "li'l feller" gave him for his birthday still lingering on his stubbly face. Desmond was only nine – just before his parents divorced. After that his dad never did that again. He never understood why his dad just cut him off the way he did.

Craving companionship, he hunted for a distant voice from the outside world. As he tuned, he recalled the very last time his dad kissed him goodnight – Christmas Eve, 1954. His mom let him stay up until 11:30 p.m. to watch Arthur Godfrey, as long as he promised to be in bed asleep by the time his dad got home.

Desmond turned his head slightly, and placed his ear very close to the speaker as he deftly turned the dial with the acuity of a safecracker. The radio only hissed. Reception was nonexistent below sea level and a seeming million miles from anything. He thought he briefly heard a scratchy woman's voice, but was unable to find her when he backtracked.

"Where is everybody tonight?" he whispered, lying there in the green glow of the tuning band, starting to feel more and more isolated, alone and sorry for himself as he finally drifted into a restless sleep.

Come in, London.

He startled awake from an impenetrable, partially erotic dream only an hour later, drenched in a nervous sweat. His radio was face down on the floor, the back broken off and the dial face cracked and darkened. Dammit. But he suddenly knew what he had to do. He had to go apologize and make things right with the Afarkils.

CHAPTER SIX

Even though it was still the middle of the night, Desmond got up, wiped off his face and hair with a moist towelette and shaved – something he had not done since arriving. He still felt dazed and weakened from the evening's incidents and from eating no dinner and drinking too little water. He walked outside his bunkhouse and while sidestepping his barf noticed that with the exception of one of the constantly running propane generators that kept the freezer and pantry cold, the compound was quiet. Even Bruny was asleep.

Passing the porta-john with the "out of order" sign taped to the door, Desmond stopped, knocked gently, then jiggled the catch. It seemed to be locked from the inside. How does a portable toilet get out of order, anyway? Wasn't the nonessential Eric supposed to fix it?

Looking up as he got in the Humvee, Desmond noticed the night sky was so hazy no stars were visible. He started the giant vehicle and drove slowly out of the compound. "I'm going to make peace with these people if it kills me," he noted out loud. He didn't need or want his translator tonight – he needed to be alone for this, and felt, somewhat idealistically, that he could clearly communicate to the Afarkils how sorry he was for what happened at the compound, and that he wanted to be friends. Surely the Afarkils would understand the international signs of friendship.

With the air conditioning going in and out, Desmond circled around the giant silent black oil castle. The headlights illuminated only the bottom few rows, adorned in unpronounceable Middle Eastern refinery names and logos.

Soon the sleepy Baobab-surrounded village was in his sight. He slowed to a stop just outside the ring of trees and got out, leaving the engine running and the headlights shining on high beam directly onto the mud huts. This was no time to be shy or scared, and he hated to wake them up but he had to clear the air between them.

"Hello!" he shouted. Nothing. He reached inside the vehicle and blew the Humvee's obnoxiously loud horn several times, shattering the night's stillness before he stepped around directly in front of the lights and stood there with his hands on his hips. The desert was dead still, hushed and ominous, as if it was holding its breath, waiting for the next person to make a move.

Suddenly, he saw movement. He squinted, and saw the awakened Afarkil villagers warily emerging through their thatched doorways.

"Hello! Hello!" he shouted again. After a minute it looked as if all of the adults were standing out in their central yard to see what the commotion was about. They squinted and stared, apparently unable to make out anything in the blinding high-beam Humvee headlights.

"Hello, Afarkils!" Desmond happily shouted again.

Suddenly, one of the older Afarkil men put his hand up to shield his eyes. He suddenly turned and addressed his fellow villagers. Some of them nodded, then he turned to face Desmond.

"Sonto?" he shouted, pointing at Desmond, "Sonto?" He looked at the man beside him, who also squinted into the high beam of the headlights.

Desmond watched curiously as all the Afarkils looked in his direction in curious surprise. "What?" he thought to himself, "What the hell are they looking at?"

Suddenly another one called out something that sounded like "Ma-bua Sonto!" Two older men took a few steps closer, still squinting to see.

"Well, I seem to have their resp ... wait a second," Desmond thought. What was that story Ricky said about their religion? What was their God's name? The one that would come on the black Rhino?

"Sonto?" he heard again.

"Oh my God!" Desmond declared as the reality dawned on him, "They believe I'm their God, Sonto." He realized he was bizarrely illuminated only in silhouette by the Humvee's headlights, which he guessed the Afarkils thought were the glowing eyes of the black rhino.

He was thrilled but torn by the revelation. He certainly would gain their respect and cooperation for the filming if they thought he was their God. Then again, was he being deceitful to pretend that? If and when they found out he wasn't really their God, what would they do?

Knowing he needed to repair the damage done to their relationship at the compound earlier, he raised himself to his full height and marched as he imagined to be god-like a few more steps toward them, being careful to stay masked as a shadow in the lights. He was an academy award-nominated movie director, after all, and knew how to use dramatic lighting to its best effect.

"OK, now what?" he thought. He decided to let them see what he thought they wanted to see. He raised both arms out high and shouted in perfect pronunciation, "Listen to me, Afarkil people!"

The Afarkils looked tentatively at each other, then the two closest men broke into a smile. "Good," Desmond muttered, rubbing his hands. "I'm communicating with them."

"I am from across the ocean, far away," he annunciated, making rudimentary motions with his hands in the belief that would make his English more comprehensible to them. "I," he added, making a cranking motion with his right hand, "use camera, to film YOU." He pointed at them with both hands. They didn't move. "I come to save your civilization."

Desmond was in the center of a bizarre dream, only not terrifying like the ones he usually had or the semi-erotic one he had before coming here. This was the dream he always imagined, where he was regarded as a Deity. Oh sure, he used to be worshipped in the film industry by sycophants, suck-ups and hangers-on, and of course there was that lady at New York's Studio 54 who knelt before him and promised to worship him, only not in the way he really desired and who turned out to be a man anyway. In this dream, he was in a

Godforsaken desert in the middle of the night, lit by monster headlights and communicating with a vanishing desert clan that he was saving from extinction; a clan whom he believed considered him their Lord and Savior, who had finally arrived on a massive rhino with a 500-horsepower engine and a Bose sound system.

"I am sorry for the man with the gun," he continued, trying to apologize for Buzzcut's actions earlier. "Hope your people are okay." The Afarkils stared back, seemingly in astonishment – the men in front appeared to be holding back laughter, which Desmond attributed to nerves. They undoubtedly were excited to come face-to-face with Sonto, and showed their respect differently than Americans.

"I will come back tomorrow," he forewarned, knowing they understood because he spoke loud, slow and waved his hands. "Bring friendly white people. Bring camera to tell your story and save your tribe … clan." He made the cranking motion again. "Goodbye good Afarkil people!"

Desmond backed up until he disappeared behind the Humvee headlights. One of the closest men turned to his fellow villagers and announced something that made all of them smile. Suddenly they all almost simultaneously raised their hands and made bowing motions. Desmond may have assumed in any other culture they appeared to be mocking him, but not understanding their unique cultural eccentricities, he instead slipped into the vehicle, gunned the engine in a mighty roar, threw it into reverse and backed away from the village so the Afarkils would think he was on a black Rhino and not an obscenely expensive SUV that he hoped had enough gas to get him back to the compound. He was absolutely elated – finally he was getting the esteem he deserved, the ultimate respect.

Tomorrow was going to be a great day!

***

"I have an announcement to make!" Desmond called out the next morning under the dining awning after all the staff got coffee and seated themselves.

"We're packing up and blowing this stinking hellhole?" Donato answered. He had on opaque sunglasses and was ghostly pale.

"Not even close! Last night I went to the village and made peace with the Afarkil people!" That certainly seemed to wake everyone up. "So this morning we start filming. Finish up breakfast and let's get a move on."

"Desmond?" Mary asked as she threw her Styrofoam plate in the trash can and watched her boss load up a plate with scrambled eggs. "I was on that crap two-way radio for over an hour last night to Mr. Haile-Selassie's office making plans to make some ... you know, adjustments, to the villagers and to their village before we started actual taping. So what's your rush? And why in the world did you visit them last night? Did you take Buddy with you?"

"I did not, because I had to communicate one-on-one with them, which I did, magnificently, after the situation with the Buzzcut. And what you say is true, Mary, but time is getting away from us, and the first scene is a simple establishing shot of the children scampering through the village," Desmond explained as he took a couple bites of eggs then scraped the rest into the trash. He knew the scene by heart. "Once we get set up, we'll be able to film just the first and maybe the second scene, which is also a simple shot of an Afarkil man stepping out of his hut, stopping and looking to his right."

"I think you're jumping the gun, but you're the boss," Mary conceded as she turned away. Desmond watched her as she walked off before noticing Eric walking in the opposite direction carrying the porta john door and a toolbox.

Desmond was pleased with himself. It was good to hear Mary sort of acknowledge him as the director – it put him in control. He had also earned the respect of the Afarkil people, and Eric was finally fixing the toilet. Things were improving considerably.

With breakfast over, Desmond, Donato, Mary, Schuyler, Ricky, Buddy and Eric loaded the Betacam, tripod, sound equipment, the

Scriptboy clapboard that flashed 12:00 and some other assorted paraphernalia into one of the trucks. Ricky and Buddy took one of the jeeps. Desmond was in the Humvee's driver's seat and Eric was in the back when Mary, carrying a final cup of coffee, got in and promptly spilled it on her white shorts.

"Dammit!" she muttered, dabbing the stain with a napkin.

Eric looked down at her shorts as they drove. "My partner spilled some cappuccino on white pants at a Starbucks, and found that soaking them in cold water with baking soda got it out."

Mary suddenly looked at Eric suspiciously as they traveled to the village. He was a rugged young man, about twenty-seven, with short, gelled jet-black hair that even though it was lying naturally, looked as if he had just left the stylist. He had a shaped five o'clock shadow, and thick, defined upper arms that stretched the sleeves of his T-shirt. The dude was in serious shape.

"Your partner?" Mary asked tentatively. "Would I know her? And Christ it's hot in here! What's with the air conditioning, Desmond?"

"Not a her," Eric smiled. "Charles and I have been together three years. He's a model for the Ford Agency. He does Abercrombie print ads."

"Sorry Mary," Desmond answered, "the a/c stopped working."

At the village, everyone climbed out of the vehicles and unloaded equipment. Eric hoisted a huge cooler filled with bottled water and set it on the ground.

As Desmond surveyed the village, he overheard Donato approach Mary. "I could have told you about Eric if you just asked," he explained, his alcohol-saturated voice throaty and rasping, "We've worked enough jobs together. But I can assure ya, Donato doesn't swing that way. Donato loves to yodel in the valley."

Mary shoved him backwards a step. "Get away from me. Brooklyn greaseballs aren't my type."

"I don't believe that for a minute!" Donato staggered as Mary walked off, as if a wave of nausea washed over him. "Ooh, dammit."

"Mary and Donato?" Desmond asked, waving his hand-written

shooting schedule, "Do you think you could get with the program over here?"

A few Afarkils observed as the filmmakers prepped. A couple of men squatted on the ground, smoking a very long pipe made from a Baobab shoot, watching them carefully. A curl of smoke wafted from a small campfire. It was all quite picturesque.

Desmond stood and watched the scene for a minute with his arms folded. "What are they doing?"

"Well ..." Mary shrugged, "Whatever it is they do, I guess. Why?"

"Never mind. Hey Buddy?"

"I could have told you they needed improved optics," Mary muttered. "Correction, I did tell you that."

Buddy trotted over to Desmond's side. "Now, just tell them we are here to do a simple establishing shot, and we want to film their children running through the village from that hut ..." he pointed to his far left, "... to that one." Desmond pointed to his right. "That's it. Just three kids running playfully, having a good time. Children and their laughter are crucial to this project."

"Okay, Mr. Desmond, but are you sure everything's on the up and up?" Buddy asked. "They're not mad about what happened at the camp?"

"They're fine," Desmond answered, putting his hand on Buddy's shoulder. "I spoke to them last night. They know who I am and what I want." He looked at the village scene unfolded in front of them. "I'm more than a friend to them, actually."

He nudged Buddy and turned around to face his crew. "Drink lots of water out here everybody."

Desmond watched as Buddy approached a group of men and two women standing in front of their huts. They appeared unmoved. Buddy looked back at Desmond and waved.

With Buddy busy communicating, Desmond ordered his crew ready. Schuyler set the camera on a tripod at Desmond's direction and verified that it was operational. Ricky had the mini boom mike and sound recorder cued. The others watched. It was all up to Buddy.

Buddy stood several seconds among the Afarkil villagers. Desmond couldn't hear him but could see him getting more and more animated. Finally, Buddy coaxed one of the children, a little boy, over to the hut. Then he ran with him over to the second hut. He let him go and yelled "See?" He glanced at Desmond to make sure he was watching.

"They don't get it," Desmond mumbled, watching in frustration. Unable to stand by any more, Desmond grabbed a reluctant Ricky by the arm and marched with him into the village.

"Come here Buddy," he ordered, pulling him and Ricky into a doorway with him.

Ricky made a face. "What is that smell?"

"Now watch!" Desmond requested. "OK, guys, run!" Buddy and Ricky trotted from one hut to the second, a distance of about thirty feet. They stopped and turned. "Children, do the same!" Desmond yelled to them. The Afarkils shook their heads and smiled, as if maybe they understood, but made no attempt to cooperate.

The entire village population gathered and sat on the ground watching as Desmond, Buddy and Ricky demonstrated to them several times what they wanted. Buddy and Ricky looked as if they were about to pass out in the heat from all the jogging back and forth.

"Now the children," Desmond finally pronounced, sizzling in drying sweat as he gestured at the two boys and girl seated giggling on the ground. A woman coaxed them to stand, and they obediently walked with him to the doorway of the first hut. Ricky was right – it smelled very bad behind the fabric-covered doorway. "Schuyler are you ready?"

Schuyler picked up the camera and tripod and tiptoed around the seated villagers, warily watching them out the corner of her eye as Donato positioned her for the best view. "All set, Desmond," she reported, squinting through the viewfinder. Suddenly the lens popped off the camera. "Wait! Wait!"

Desmond paused impatiently as she picked up the errant lens, wiped it off and snapped it back. "The keeper's cracked on one side, it won't stay in place."

Desmond pointed to Ricky. "Okay with sound, Ricky? I'm hoping to get some children's laughter here."

"Good to go." Ricky groaned, picking up the boom mike and putting on his best face. All that running in the smothering heat and that unknown odor so close to breakfast seemed to make him sick to his stomach.

"Great ... you're looking whiter than white there, Rick ... Mary, you're up."

Mary walked out into the center of the village in front of Schuyler in her white shorts with the coffee stain on the front. She held up the Scriptboy clapper flashing 12:00. "Afarkil documentary, scene 1, take 1." <clap>

"And ... action!" The kids stood still. "Run!" Desmond yelled. They still stood there.

"Cut!" Desmond once again demonstrated how he wanted them to run from the one hut to the next. It felt 300 degrees inside that village.

Ricky lowered his boom and looked quizzically at Desmond. "Mr. Desmond, this is a documentary – why are you doing multiple takes? Shouldn't you just point the camera at them and film them?"

"As I have explained, it's called creative nonfiction documentary, Rick," Desmond answered. "It's the way I do things. I like my features traditions. Mary, continue."

"Afarkil documentary, scene 1, take 2." <clap>

Ricky shrugged and picked up the boom.

"Action."

One of the boys walked a few feet, stopped and stared at the camera, then started laughing. In fact, most of the villagers were snickering as well.

"Afarkil documentary, scene 1, take 3." <clap>

One boy ran two steps, then fell down.

And on and on it went.

Tucking his flask inside his pocket, Donato wandered over beside

Mary, who was watching under the shade of the Baobabs. "Hey, Desmond and Mary?"

"What Donato?" Desmond noticed his art director's voice was inebriated and too-loud.

"... I thought the Afarkils was one of those tribes where the women went topless." The girl disappeared inside a hut. The two boys just stood there. The Afarkil adults seemed highly amused, and seemed to laugh louder at each botched take, to Desmond's growing annoyance.

Mary was unmoved by Donato's observation. "What ... is this a joke?"

"Again, Mary," Desmond impatiently instructed.

All three children took off running a few steps, but in the wrong direction.

Desmond rubbed his eyes. "Donato lose the topless talk and leave Mary alone. Let's try again."

"Afarkil documentary, scene 1, take 7." <clap>

Donato shrugged. "I think a documentary with the women topless would be a good draw."

Desmond repositioned the children. "Again, please. Donato, your suggestion is juvenile and will never fly, so stop."

The three children finally ran over near where they were supposed to, stopping just short of their goal, where they got distracted.

"That was a pretty good one, Desmond!" Schuyler yelled from behind her viewfinder, "You better go with it!"

"No, let's keep going – we can do better!"

"Afarkil documentary, scene 1, take 10." <clap>

The three ran around to the back of the hut. The adults laughed even harder. They seemed to be having a great time.

"This side of the hut, please!" Desmond pleaded at them, "This side!"

"Wait!" It was Schuyler – her lens popped off again.

Donato turned his drunken attention to Schuyler after she got the lens back in place, "Hey Schuyler," he slurred in the form of a shout,

"I got a question."

Desmond rubbed his eyes in frustration. He saw Donato was drinking and now heard him pestering Schuyler. He wondered if she was going to go worldwide wrestling on him. He would have to clamp down on him.

Schuyler glanced a quick, hateful look toward the apparently drunk art director. "You know I'll break both your legs if you get sexist with me again. And Mr. Desmond knows it."

"Aw come on," Donato whined, placing his little flask back in his pocket.

Desmond called out to him. "Donato?"

"Where's your sense of humor?" Donato continued to Schuyler. "I'm thinking of a number between one and 100 ..."

"Hey Donato," Desmond called again.

"I'm not interested in your stupid pubescent games Donato." Schuyler sharply replied without looking away from the viewfinder.

"Let's break," Desmond announced as he stretched and touched his sunbaked lower lip. "Lots of water, people. Donato, get the hell away from Schuyler before she hurts you." Failing also to get a rise out of Schuyler, Donato laughed and walked unsteadily around back of the other huts.

During the five-minute break Buddy approached Desmond. "How did I do, Mr. Desmond? I like to get feedback on my work."

"You did just fine Buddy. Okay can we ..."

Schuyler walked up and interrupted. "If you don't put a stop to Donato I will. He has no business here being drunk, sexist and abusive. He needs to go back to camp and dry out."

"I agree, Schuyler, and I have already noted to have a long talk with him." Desmond looked back at the village. "Let's just try to get these shots in the can. Mary, can we move on?"

Mary went back to work. "Afarkil documentary, scene 1, take ... take 9,876? Take 11." <clap>

The kids ran perfectly in the right direction but Donato wandered from around the huts pulling up his zipper, right through the middle of the scene. "Cut! Dammit Donato, move it! You're in the shot!"

Donato only stopped, raised his hands and bowed grandly. Desmond would have cussed the stupid art director if he weren't so flipping hot and frustrated with the Afarkil children. "Just get out of the shot and go sit in the Humvee. Mary, continue please."

This time the kids took off running. They looked great. Desmond watched breathlessly – perhaps this was going to be the one. Suddenly, one of the boys just stopped short. Collective moans rose from the staff.

"Can we use that one, Desmond?" Schuyler asked, "I got my doubts about the camera. It doesn't sound right. I can edit that."

"No. Let's try again. The next one will be the one."

"I'm not getting this!" Schuyler called out. The camera rattled horribly then abruptly cut off. The kids ran perfectly on cue to their marks. It was spectacular. "Desmond!"

"Perfect!" Desmond exclaimed. "Didn't I tell you that the next one would ..."

"Desmond!" Schuyler screamed, "Listen to me, I didn't get it! The tape jammed! The camera's full of fucking sand again!"

The crew groaned again. It was as if their last-second touchdown had been called back on a penalty. Desmond rubbed his forehead as he stared at the ground. "I tried to warn you!" Schuyler scolded as she opened the side of the camera to retrieve the mangled tape and blow out the insides. Nearby, Ricky sat unmoved, appearing to keep from puking. It was boiling hot.

"Tell you what," Desmond suggested, "let's give the kids a break and shoot scene two."

He looked around. "What is that damn smell?"

Mary vehemently opposed the plan. "We don't have the huts or the clothes the way we want them yet, Desmond," she interjected. "It'd be pointless to ..."

"It's an extreme close-up," Desmond cut her off. "Nothing but a head shot with dark background. Let's get set up, people." Schuyler went inside the Humvee to load a new tape into the camera.

Everyone went to work setting up scene two, much to Mary's resistance. "This scene should be a no-brainer, people," Desmond claimed. "Schuyler, get positioned about ..."

Everyone suddenly recoiled at the sound of someone violently throwing up. Ricky, on his hands and knees in the stifling desert heat, finally lost his cool under the Baobabs.

Donato glanced over toward him. "Looks like it was the nerd's turn to park the Buick."

"Get it together Rick," Desmond asserted in a somewhat cross tone, trying to get everyone back on track. "I'd like to get on with this scene quickly. I'm getting a headache."

Ricky struggled to his feet, more sallow than normal. "Hey," he moaned to anyone who may be listening, "Somebody tell Bruny that from now on he needs to cut me off at three boiled eggs."

Desmond decided to involve Donato in the process to stem his drinking until he had a chance to talk to him, so he asked him to pick out one of the men with an interesting face for the close-up shot – a face that displayed the best example of a long life of difficult living in a harsh and unforgiving environment but that also would exude empathy in the audience.

After a minute Donato brought to the hut one of the older men he nicknamed "Harvey" – who was actually the leader of the group who surprised them the other day.

"He's your man, Desmond," Donato announced, "He's ready for his close-up now."

"Very good," Desmond muttered, barely noticing the three stripes shaved into the side of his head. "Buddy, tell Mr. Harvey what we would like him to do."

"Can do, Mr. Desmond." Buddy looked briefly at the schedule and approached the man as Donato placed him on his mark just inside the hut.

"Mah son-to wanna," Desmond heard Buddy explain to the man as he pointed to Schuyler and her camera. "Mo wanna san te." Harvey nodded that he seemed to understand. Buddy turned and smiled at Desmond. "All set. Did I do okay?"

"Here we go," Desmond stated as he knelt behind Schuyler and framed the shot.

Mary walked in between the hut and the camera and held up the clapper. "Afarkil documentary, scene 2, take 1." <clap>

"Action."

Deadly serious, the Afarkil man pulled the thatch to the side and walked out of the doorway. He stopped. Then, perfectly on cue, he turned his head to his right. Then he burst out laughing, as did several of his fellow villagers watching.

"Cut! Perfect!" Desmond was relieved he got one, and even smiled in response to the man's laughter. "Schuyler, let's do one more."

"Afarkil documentary, scene 2, take 2." <clap>

"Action."

The Afarkil man again pulled the thatch to the side and walked out of the doorway. He stopped. Then, on cue, he turned his head to his right and held it there. The other villagers watching laughed again, seemingly at the man's steely seriousness.

"Cut! Great! We're on a roll people – let's go back to scene 1 and try that one again. Quickly please!" The Afarkil man broke into a broad smile as Donato shook his hand.

It took several more takes to capture the children running. Donato kept disappearing behind the huts and Schuyler's lens came off twice and the camera jammed again, but finally Desmond had what he thought was a (somewhat) decent shot of what turned out to be only two of the children (the girl and one of the boys) walking (instead of running) from one hut to the other.

Once they were finished, and loading up the Humvee to return to the compound, Donato scrambled out from the village, his face white.

"Shit! Shit!" he sputtered, suddenly quite sobered, "I think there's a dead body in that biggest hut! Shit!"

"A body? What kind of body?" Mary asked, her face dropping.

"A dead body? Uh oh ..." Desmond ran back into the village passing Donato in the opposite direction. As he approached the largest hut "Harvey" raised a hand to stop him but he pushed aside the fabric over the door and ducked in anyway. Inside he found a body laid out on the floor, wrapped completely in some sort of white linen. Like the maternity hut, the floor was covered with dry thatch, sprinkled liberally with what appeared to be some local herbs. Two homemade tapers burned beside it. The decay smell was overpowering.

Holding his nose, Desmond knelt and gently pulled back a small area of linen from the head. It was an African man, but not an Afarkil, as he feared. This man had a moustache, his cold, green eyes were open, and he oddly had on a plaid shirt.

Buddy walked into the hut also past the objecting "Harvey" as Desmond looked down at the man's face. "Is it really a dead body, Mr. D?" he asked, looking down. "He doesn't look like an Afarkil."

"Nothing to see here," a visibly shaken Desmond declared as he folded the linen back over his face and walked out of the hut, with Buddy coming out a moment later. The Afarkils stared angrily at them both. All of the crew but Donato stood somberly off to the other side beside the truck.

"Is there really a corpse in there, Mr. Desmond?" Ricky asked in a shaky voice as Desmond approached. He looked as if he were about to lose it again.

Desmond thought for a minute. "Ricky?" he asked, "What do they do with their dead? Why is he laid out wrapped like that?"

Ricky struggled to explain. "Well, according to the book it's very elaborate ..." he replied nervously, looking at the villagers, who had obviously lost their sense of humor and appeared quite perturbed with the crew. "And first I don't recommend any of us go back in there. They got a thing about living people seeing their dead."

"Good grief, they got a 'thing' about everything!" Desmond suddenly blurted, shocked and frustrated by this discovery. "They don't want people looking at their pregnant women, they don't want people looking at their dead, they don't like people ..." He paused, suddenly remembering he was not a normal white male in their eyes.

"If they believe I'm Sonto," he thought, "this may not be a problem after all."

"In any case," Ricky continued, "they let their dead lie in state for something like twelve days, and no one is supposed to see the body while their God Sonto comes and takes the soul," he explained, trying desperately not to be sick again. "On the second day they, um, they eviscerate the body, and, um ... excuse me ..." Desmond and Buddy watched Ricky trot off behind one of the Baobabs and bend way over.

Schuyler approached Desmond. "Is the kid going to be OK?" she asked, pointing over to Ricky.

"He'll be fine," Desmond absently replied, sensing his staff was stunned by this recent discovery. "He said they let their dead lie in state for twelve days – so is it possible this man was dead before we even arrived here?"

Schuyler shrugged. "Sure, it's possible I guess."

"Harvey" walked over to Desmond, then put up his hand in front of him and Schuyler. "<click> soa mon-a mo he." It was obvious to Desmond what he was saying.

"Let's go back to camp, people."

CHAPTER SEVEN

"It was a man," Desmond announced as he and Schuyler joined the others at the vehicles. Schuyler got behind the wheel of the jeep by herself, presumably so she wouldn't have to ride with Donato.

"What do you mean?" Ricky asked just as he wiped his mouth and popped in three Lifesaver mints.

"The body was a man," Desmond repeated sadly, "I pulled back the covering and saw his face. He had a moustache and a plaid shirt."

"Oh ... I wish you hadn't done that. You've dishonored their dead by looking at him," Ricky explained as Desmond started driving back to the compound. "That's a grievous offense in their burial ritual ... wait, he had a moustache and a plaid shirt? Are you sure he was an Afarkil?"

"That's what I wondered," Buddy interjected. "And he had curly hair."

"Grievous offense? What kind of a culture strangles itself with so many bizarre rules it practically guarantees its own extinction?" Mary blurted, "My God, can anybody ..."

"Wait, wait, Ricky and Buddy have a point," Desmond interrupted. "It's possible that was not an Afarkil – Afarkils don't have moustaches, and he sure was hell was not dressed like one."

"Maybe he was a captured or killed Oromo," Buddy cut in. "I didn't notice they were short one man, Mr. D."

"Then maybe they killed him?" Ricky exclaimed, agitating the others. "This is a concerning development ...!"

"Everyone settle down and listen up!" Desmond announced loudly. "I actually may have done them a favor by going in there, so ease up on them. It's a long story. Rick, regardless of who it is, what exactly is their burial ritual?"

Ricky heaved a big sigh. "All I know is after they remove the organs and bury them Sonto will then take the soul as the body lies in the hut. Then they can bury the body. That's the old tradition anyway."

"Pardon me, Mr. Desmond," Donato asked, "but exactly how did you do them a favor by going in there?"

"Like I said it's a long story ..." Desmond muttered before he got lost in thought. The death of an Afarkil could be devastating, and possibly linked to him if it occurred after his arrival and especially after the altercation at the camp between them and Buzzcut. His only hope was that it was indeed an Oromo or other outside intruder.

"In any case, we can't let this development sidetrack us. I want to see the best of today's rushes. I'll ask Schuyler for a rough edit. We'll have a viewing before lights out tonight."

Back at the compound Desmond first had a word with Donato about his behavior at the shoot, and told him he could no longer drink during working hours and to stop the sexist flirting and joking. He then went looking for Buzzcut to question him about the shooting earlier, to see if he knew if any of the bullets could somehow have hit someone outside the compound, but he was nowhere to be found.

Giving up, he went back to his oven-like shed and laid down for a rest while the rest of the staff unpacked equipment and Bruny prepared dinner. He had only been down about fifteen minutes and just started to drift off when there was a knock at the door. "What is it," he answered crossly.

"Mr. Desmond? It's Eric. Mary thought you should come see this."

"See what?" Desmond muttered as he crawled down out of bed, sore and dehydrated from the day's activity. "Are they ready for me to see the rough edit already?" he asked Eric as he came out of his bunkhouse. Then he noticed Mary standing by the kitchen, looking to the south. She turned and motioned him over before pointing to a plume of black smoke rising from the distance.

"Could that smoke be coming from the village?" she asked. "It's in that direction, right? It looks like they're burning something pretty big."

"Yes, it is," Desmond agreed, watching the smoke as a sickening worry welled up inside. "And I don't know."

"Mr. Desmond?" Ricky asked as he approached Desmond's side, "I can't say for sure if this has anything to do with the smoke, but Buddy did tell me a little while ago that he tipped over a candle inside the hut where the body was."

Desmond's stomach dropped. Not another goddamn fire. "Who tipped over a candle? When?"

"Buddy." Ricky pointed toward Buddy as he walked away from the dining area. Desmond shouted him over. Buddy turned, stared at them for a second, then started toward them.

"Buddy, Rick tells me you tipped over a candle inside the hut – is this true?"

"Yes, but I picked it back up." Buddy clarified as he casually ambled over. He was holding an apple with a bite taken. "When I left the hut. It was an accident, but they shouldn't have put candles on dry grass."

"Clumsy oaf!" Mary exclaimed to Buddy. "Why didn't you say something?"

"I didn't think it was a big deal!" Buddy suddenly squealed, backing up a step, seemingly worried Mary was going to take him down like Schuyler did Donato. "I made sure there was no fire! I stomped the grass where it fell!"

"Um, Mr. Desmond?" Ricky mentioned, hesitantly.

Desmond ignored him. "Buddy I swear if you started a fire in their village I will ..."

"That's impossible," Buddy insisted, "it was completely out when I left. They must be burning something else."

"Mr. Desmond!" Ricky countered, even louder.

"Dammit, what?"

"How will they put the fire out?"

Desmond froze. There didn't seem to be enough water in the area to keep a houseplant alive, much less extinguish a fire. "Grab some cases of bottled water and put them in the Humvee! Let's go people!"

"We've really stepped in it," Ricky continued to Desmond as he, Eric and Buzzcut hurriedly loaded six cases of water into the back of the vehicle. "First you went into the hut and saw their dead, if it was their dead, which was bad enough. But if Buddy set the hut on fire … the Afarkils believe that desecrating the dead before their soul is taken is a sign of contempt to their God. According to their more orthodox tradition, the clan elder must commit ritualistic suicide to appease Sonto if a dead body is corrupted, even if accidentally, to replace the missing soul. I don't know if this particular clan still subscribes to that belief, but …"

Desmond turned to him. "Suicide?"

"That's the old custom. It's a very serious matter to them, and I think this time you should take some responsibility for what has happ …"

Desmond angrily looked at Ricky. "Responsibility? What are you saying? What do you mean 'this time'?"

Flustered, Ricky realized he slipped and attempted an answer. "Well, um, no, I'm saying only that … we really need to get to the village Mr. Desmond!"

"You're saying that I'm somehow responsible for the consequences of this fire because of my previous experience with fires? Is that it?" Desmond shouted, enraged at Buddy while attacking Ricky's suggestion that he was somehow liable for the Afarkil's responses to his crews' actions, however clumsy. This was becoming the Pyro explosion, fire and litigation all over again, and he was again getting blamed for it. He slipped into five-alarm damage control; he could be removed from the shoot over this and his career would be dead. The threat of fire to the Afarkils was superseded by the threat to his career.

"I am only responsible for the actions of my crew, so I take full responsibility for what Buddy did inside that hut, if that's what really happened," Desmond loudly exclaimed to Ricky, his fury peaking.

"But I'm not here to change the Afarkil culture, Richard. I am only here to document their culture. If the clan elder commits suicide, it is a tragedy, but that is their belief system, and I have to respect it and am powerless to stop it! We are here trying to save their way of life, which includes their customs and beliefs, however self-defeating they may be, and which none of us have any right to interfere with or question! The fire may be Buddy's responsibility, yes, and I will fix that if it is, but if their clan elder takes his life because of something this fire did, then that is their tradition and on their conscience, not mine!" Ricky backed up a step in the face of his boss's meltdown. "I will not be responsible for another fire! Am I clear? Am I clear?"

"If you really care, and I think you do, perhaps you should go there, like right now," Ricky continued, stern yet browbeaten by Desmond's sudden fiery temperament and twisted attempts to cover his own ass. "Go to them, put out the fire. If that's what it is, and try to stop any rash actions. You might save a life, or even the village."

In his blind rage Desmond realized Ricky was correct – he believed that the Afarkils probably thought that he, as their God, was angry for burning their dead, and that if he intervened, he could stop the clan elder from killing himself.

"Buddy, you are confined to the compound until further notice," Desmond heatedly told the contrite interpreter before turning to Ricky. "Rick, you are disrespectful but you made a good point. And since you found that old language guide, you are now our translator. Now, where's Schuyler?"

Ricky tensed then relaxed, like he was expecting a punch or something. "Probably in the editing room. Why?"

"Schuyler! Schuyler! Come quick!" Desmond walked quickly to the editing room. "Rick! Grab your book and come with me."

Schuyler came out of the stuffy, dark room, soaked in sweat. "Where's the fire?" she asked, unaware of the irony of her question.

"Get the camera and come on! We gotta go back to the village, quick!"

Schuyler hustled back into the editing room and grabbed the Betacam and another lens before she, Ricky and Desmond hopped into the Humvee. As they raced around oil drum mountain, she snapped the new lens into place, loaded a fresh tape and hoisted it onto her shoulder at Desmond's request. In the back-seat Ricky flipped nervously through the book, confounded by all the bizarre symbols, sounds and pronunciations that made up the myriad vernaculars of the Khoisan language, if that was even the language they spoke. The book said it had over twenty dialects, each radically different from the other.

"I hope we're in time," Desmond fretted as he skidded to a stop at the edge of the village. "Ricky be ready, and don't cock this up."

Ricky shot him a worried look in the mirror from the back. His expression reminded Desmond of a dog being taken to the vet.

"In time for what?" Schuyler asked as they all clamored out of the vehicle and jogged into the village.

Sure enough, there had been a fire, confined to the one hut, but it was extinguished. The roof was gone and there were scorch marks around the window. Desmond's head swam in the sickly-sweet miasma of burnt flesh and grass, bringing back uninvited memories of the Pyro accident.

All of the villagers were gathered in the center of the settlement, near the campfire. They quickly gathered in a circle as the three approached, looking down at what appeared to be a person on the ground.

Schuyler glanced at the burnt hut as they hustled past. "What happened here?"

"Never mind, just start rolling," Desmond reminded her as they walked quickly into the village center, followed by an apprehensive Ricky. "Keep the camera on the villagers. Do not film the burned hut."

They crept up behind the ring of villagers and stood silently.

Desmond nudged Schuyler and pointed for her to film a prone figure on the ground among the feet. After a minute the people raised their heads, turned and slowly stepped back, leaving the man on the ground exposed. Desmond and Schuyler walked uneasily closer, the camera humming.

"What am I filming, Desmond?" she whispered, clueless as to why they were there. "Why is this man on the ground? Is he sick?"

"Shhh ..." he answered, looking down. It was Harvey – the one who was in the close-up shot. His eyes were closed but he was still breathing. Desmond thought he looked asleep.

One of the men angrily approached Desmond as the others stood watching. The man stopped right in front of Desmond and pointed at the destroyed hut. "<click> sahn-me banna?"

Desmond blinked. "Rick, what is he saying?"

Ricky was silently mouthing the words as he thought he understood them as he flipped through the book. "Um ... hold on ..."

"<click> sahn-me banna?"

"I, I ... I don't know," Desmond stumbled, "I'm sorry ... no understand. Any day now Rick."

"<click> sahn-me banna?" The man pointed at the prone man on the ground. The other villagers also appeared angry. Schuyler kept filming, panning between the prone man and Desmond's confrontation with the tribesman.

"Uh, I think he is saying ..." Rick spoke into his book, "he might be asking if we know ... about a body, maybe?"

The man turned and picked up a sprig of some sort of plant that lay on the ground. He held it out to Desmond. "<click> sahn-me!"

"'Son me' means either sleep or cholera, I think," Ricky mumbled. "Or hungry maybe."

Frustrated by Ricky's inability to communicate, Desmond assumed cautiously the elder on the ground was attempting suicide by eating some kind of poisonous plant. He knelt down, placed his hand on the man's wrist and held it. There was still a strong pulse. He stood up as the other man watched him. If this was the case, there was nothing he or anyone else could do.

"Is he dead Desmond?" Schuyler asked from behind the camera.

"There's still a pulse, but it will be any time now I'm sure. I'm fairly certain he poisoned himself. We were too late."

"<click> Sahn-me Banna?" The man pointed to the burned hut.

"Goddammit Rick, a little help here!"

"Uh, it appears he is asking us if the hut is asleep ... I'm not sure."

"The hut? For God's sake ... even I can see ..." Desmond finally acquiesced, annoyed and distressed. "Shut it down Schuyler. There's no more we can do here."

Desmond faced the Afarkil villagers and pointed to the burned hut. "I am sorry about your hut, it was an accident," he said loud and slowly. "We will fix it, like brand new!"

The man grimaced and turned to his fellow villagers. He raised his right hand.

"<click> sahn-me! Boa me sanna! <click> me sanna!" was all Desmond heard. All the villagers moaned and shook their heads, as if they were disgusted about something.

Desmond, Schuyler and Ricky left the village, got back in the Humvee and sat silently for a minute as the Afarkils angrily watched them. "Did that man really poison himself, Desmond?" Schuyler finally asked. "Why would he do that?"

Desmond shook his head, seemingly in a daze. "Ricky, you were right. You said that the clan elder would commit suicide to appease their God if one of their dead was desecrated. Evidently this is what happened. He ate a poison plant, and they were asking for my approval of their sacrifice."

"One of their dead was desecrated?" Schuyler asked. "The one in the hut? What happened?"

"It seems Buddy kicked over a candle and set the hut on fire," Ricky answered.

"Oh, for the love of ... that dumb shit," Schuyler muttered.

The reality of his crisis sinking in, Desmond's head dropped to the steering wheel, unexpectedly causing the horn to blow a short burst, startling the three of them. He jerked back up with a yelp.

"Why do they need your approval?" Ricky continued. "They

need to appease their God, not you."

Desmond sighed – he was annoyed with Ricky and his never-ending questions, but was not going to give away his secret. "That's what I meant. It's a ..."

He turned to face his rookie translator. "And by the way I suggest you not only learn to keep your mouth shut, but seriously crash-course this language if you want to stay employed with this project. You embarrassed me and yourself in front of them."

Ricky shut up and slid down in the seat, buried behind the book he was probably sorry he even found.

"Regardless, it was very noble of you to try to stop that from happening," Schuyler affirmed, leaning over and placing her hand gently on Desmond's knee. He held his breath. "I'm sorry we didn't get here soon enough – it would have been very compelling footage, you talking that man out of killing himself. It would have shown your heart, understanding and commitment to saving the people."

Desmond looked at Schuyler. Her compassion suddenly made her the most beautiful woman he had ever seen. He would have leaned over to kiss her if not for the suicide and the presence of the currently worthless passenger in the back.

"The thing is, Schuyler, you may be right – originally I wanted to get here in time to stop his death. But then again, at the same time, I think I just as much wanted to get here to catch his death on tape. It sounds sick – that was the old Tom Desmond. And I can't say with certainty which one of those reasons I came here with just now. I thought I was more of a changed man than ..."

"Wait a minute, Mr. Desmond?" Ricky interrupted as he read from the back of the book. "Excuse me, but it says here that the Afarkils adopted many new customs in the late 1930s, and one of them was they replaced ritualistic suicide with the clan elder lying on the ground pretending to be dead as a symbol, while the others chanted, spread herbs and prayed over him. And they don't just do it for their own dead, but for anyone, as a sign of respect."

Ricky looked up and made eye contact with his director in the rear-view mirror. "Didn't you say the man had a pulse? Maybe he was just acting dead. And maybe that dead man in the hut was not an Afarkil after all, he could have been a lost traveler or something."

Desmond reflected on this new information. It would have been like their own second Vatican Council – out with the old, in with the new. "Well, I can't be sure ... but don't say anything to the others," he implored to both of them, "I don't want this to get out yet." Schuyler and Ricky promised as they turned to drive back to the compound.

Looking in the mirror, Desmond hit the brakes and suddenly expressed an overwhelming sense of relief.

Schuyler looked at him. "What? Why did you stop?"

"We're off the hook," Desmond exhaled as he gunned the engine and continued driving. "I just saw the dude on the ground get up and walk away."

CHAPTER EIGHT

Later that evening, after a dinner that Desmond skipped of smoked turkey breast sandwiches, mashed potatoes, corn on the cob, peach cobbler and unlimited sangria, Schuyler informed him that the day's rushes were done and the best of them were ready for him to view. As he entered the editing room she, Donato, Buddy, Mary and Eric were seated in folding chairs and seemed in good spirits, listening to Mary tell a story about her childhood.

"... Think that's bad?" She responded to someone's story, "my last name, Semper, had been a constant source of bathroom humor while I was at All Saints Catholic High School near D.C. They called me 'Mary Semper Virgin,' a joke taken from the confession in the old Latin Mass ..."

"Beatæ Mariæ semper Virgini," Donato murmured. "To Blessed Mary, ever Virgin.' I remember my Latin still."

"Hey Desmond, some of us were just talking about our favorite Christmas growing up," Mary announced as he came in and opened a folding chair. "What was your most unforgettable Christmas?"

Desmond thought for a few seconds. "I'm really not much in the mood ..."

"Come on, just for fun. We could use some fun here."

Desmond heaved a sigh. "Unforgettable? That would be Christmas, 1954," he answered emotionlessly as he sat in his chair. He was still reeling from the fire and the almost-suicide in the village. "I was ten. I got all these cool presents, but just after I opened them my dad confronted my mom about having an affair with the Dr. Pepper Silver Dollar Man."

Everyone stopped.

"It was true – I even liked the guy at first because he stood when I came in the room and extended his hand. He would go 'Hi-ya, hi-ya young man, I'm the Dr. Pepper Silver Dollar man,' and shake my hand. He was the first adult who ever initiated a handshake with me, and it made me feel like such a grown-up."

"Who or what exactly was the Dr. Pepper Silver Dollar man?" Mary asked.

"His name was Jerry something, and he was part of a promotion – a man who went around to people's homes on Saturday mornings and asked to see if they had bottles of Dr. Pepper in their refrigerators. If they did, he gave them a silver dollar for each one." Desmond paused. "After the first visit, he came back several more times over the next few weeks to check our Dr. Peppers, and always while dad was at work. I looked forward to the Dr. Pepper man's visits because whenever he showed up mom always gave me fifty cents to walk to a filling station down the block to buy an ice cream or these purple smoke bombs and browse the magazines. I loved those trashy true detective ones. I assumed at the time that mom had Dr. Peppers squirreled away all over the house, and the man needed several follow-up visits to count them all. I was ten, what did I know?"

"Then one day I got to the filling station and a sign on the door said that Mr. Hicks' wife was ill and the station was closed, so I went back home, and I heard the Dr. Pepper Silver Dollar Man and mom in the basement rumpus room I assumed looking for Dr. Peppers. I went down a few stairs, thinking I was going to hear him counting out silver dollars and stuff but instead I saw mom bent over our ping-pong table, and the Dr. Pepper man was forcing her head face down onto the table with both hands. There was a sock or something in her mouth. His shirt was unbuttoned and his pants were around his ankles and he was furiously screwing my mom from behind, going 'hi-ya hi-ya hi-ya' the whole time. I was mortified – it looked like he was killing her. Then he raised his hand, made a fist and punched her in the back of the head really hard, bouncing her head off the table."

Everyone in the room was frozen.

"I cried out 'Stop! You're hurting my mom!' and ran back up the stairs in terror. They heard me, and he came bounding up the stairs behind me."

"'Why are you home so goddamn early?' he shouted, catching me by the arm in the hallway. There was raging fury in his voice. He was out of control and I was afraid he was going to kill me. He squeezed and twisted my skinny arm, saying 'your mom told you it took about thirty minutes to count your Dr. Peppers you little bastard!'"

The crew watched curiously while Desmond rubbed his right arm, grimacing and recalling the dreadful moment.

"I was shrieking like hell when mom ran upstairs and yelled at him to let go of me, then she sputtered that what I saw was not what it looked like, or some bullshit, trying to cover herself. Her face was swollen on one side and her makeup was smeared. Then that asshole silver dollar man cornered my mom and started yelling at her about what a nosy little shit I was and why couldn't she control her kid. He punched her hard twice, with her shouting 'Jerry! No! Stop!' before he shoved her into the washer and dryer then left and never came back. Turned out he broke my arm and I had to wear a cast for six weeks."

The crew sat spellbound, their eyes wide and their mouths hanging open in horror. Mary had her hand over her mouth in silent, horrified alarm. Desmond continued to rub his arm.

"Apparently mom admitted the whole thing to my dad, but he didn't understand how victimized she had been by the guy, like Svengali, like he had her in a spell. He was furious over my arm getting broken, though. He blamed her for that and for letting Jerry back in the house and he moved out right after that Christmas.

"Shortly after that the silver dollar asshole was found shot and almost dead behind the bus station. He claimed he knew who shot him, but he never said who it was while he spent over a month in the hospital. Turns out he was an imposter, anyway – he never worked for the Dr. Pepper company."

"My dad moved out west after that, near Albuquerque, I think, and I lost all contact with him. No letters, no nothing. It was the 1950s, and he was old school and apparently wanted total separation from the marriage, and I got caught in the middle. It really hurt, because I was crazy about my dad."

By that point the entire crew was expressionless, staring dully at Desmond's story, which hung in the air like greasy burned popcorn. Donato took a hit out of his flask. And Desmond could not stop talking.

"It's funny – the last thing I wanted was to go to the hospital to see that son of a bitch, but mom's traditional Irish Catholic forgiveness came out and said she needed to see him and pray over him because he almost died, and that he had been through a lot worse than he had put her through. She obviously had some sort of Stockholm Syndrome – sympathy for her attacker. I had no sympathy, and sat in the waiting room. She came out of his room crying – he told her something really upsetting. I remember seeing two other women there in the waiting room with black eyes, and there I sat with my right arm in a cast."

"Apparently Jerry got himself into houses to supposedly count Dr. Peppers. He flirted and earned the women's trust, seduced them then got violent. He hurt a lot of people and broke up a lot of families, I'm sure. He sure as shit broke up mine. Hate still pours out of me toward that lowlife."

Ricky entered into the soup of unbearable gloom just after Desmond's story. Desmond only rubbed his arm and stared at the floor, as did most of the crew. "I thought we were watching rushes?" he asked tentatively. "What the hell happened? Did someone die?"

Desmond suddenly stopped rubbing, realizing what he had done. "Look, I'm sorry, don't let my depressing life story ruin our mood right now," he explained, snapping back to life. "Pump it up, Schuyler – show me some flash."

Donato looked at Mary. "Never ask Desmond to tell another story."

Schuyler leaned ahead, mumbled "seriously" and pushed PLAY and they watched about a ten-second scene of a young boy and young girl, staring straight at the camera, jogging from the door of one hut to another, where they just stopped.

The screen went black. Everyone in the room sat stunned.

"Christ have mercy," Donato muttered, "Desmond's Dr. Pepper story was more lighthearted than that."

Desmond looked around at the others. "That's it? That's what we spent 10 hours and 27 takes in the roasting sun doing? For, what ... maybe ten seconds of screen time?"

He suddenly stood. "People! The outline said the kids are running playfully! These kids are mostly walking!"

"Desmond, it's the best we got," Schuyler broke in. "The other takes the kids are all over the place. We stopped where you said to stop – that's the take you said was perfect."

"Yea Desmond," Mary chimed in, "it does suck but you said ..."

Ignoring Mary, Desmond sat back down and crossed his arms. "That's completely unusable, what we have there. It's zero. May I see scene 2 please?"

Schuyler rolled her eyes, mouthed an expletive, cued the tape and pushed PLAY again.

Scene 2 was a medium shot of "Harvey" walking out of the door of a hut. He turned to the right. The screen went black. Take 2 played immediately after. He walked out, then cut close up to his face as he turned. Then black.

Desmond stared at the monitor with his mouth open in stunned dismay. "Schuyler," he finally exclaimed in a too-quiet voice that seemed to alarm the others, "Would you play that again, please?" Schuyler rewound and nervously pushed PLAY.

After the scenes Desmond had his head in both hands. He sat like that for several moments as the others exchanged concerned glances. Finally, Mary spoke up. "Okay, okay Desmond, so we got a couple bad shots, but at least ..."

Desmond dropped his hands and stood. "Please, Mary. What we have here is not just a couple of bad shots. What we have here is something that is physically sucking the very life from me right now. It's ... it's a video black hole."

Desmond's admonishment infuriated Mary. "Don't you hush me! And you can't be blaming us!" She seethed, "Because we followed your lame direction to the letter, Mr. Desmond!" She put an unnatural emphasis on "Mr." "We told you to wait until we made some adjustments to the village and to the people, but no, you had to rush in right now and ..."

"Let's be objective here, Ms. Semper," Desmond interrupted, his voice rising in anger. "Okay, disregarding the amateur home movie that is scene 1, let's look only at scene 2, shall we? First the video quality is, okay. A little monotone, but all right. Second, Schuyler, for reasons known only to her, used what looks like a 24-millimeter wide-angle lens shot from neck level looking up, making the man's head look more like a fucking alien than a destitute Afarkil!" Desmond grabbed the back of his chair and banged it out of pure frustration while everyone winced.

"We are supposed to care about these people while watching this film!" He shouted in frustration to his crew. "I am supposed to feel some compassion! Some empathy! We should watch this and feel compelled to jump into action to save this culture! But honestly I could care less about the bizarre man I see on that monitor!"

Disgusted with Desmond and not wishing to be subjected to a tantrum, Mary stormed out, followed by Eric, Ricky and Donato, who slammed the door. Even Buddy tiptoed out. After they all left Schuyler also stood up to leave.

Desmond plopped down in his chair and stared at the monitor as she opened the door. "Schuyler?"

She stopped but wouldn't turn around to face him. "What."

"Why did you use a wide-angle lens for a close-up?"

"Because the portrait lens I had there turned out to be broken and kept falling off. I thought I could fake it."

"Do you have another fixed portrait lens?"

"Yep. But so you know, it's 55-millimeter."

"Have you viewed the deceased man or the clan elder footage yet?"

"Nope."

"Let me know when you do? And no more faking."

"Yep." She stomped out. Desmond could sense the anger pouring from her pores.

Left alone, Desmond continued to stare at the black monitor. This was probably his own fault – he never should have told the Dr. Pepper story. It ruined the mood.

The door suddenly opened – he at first thought it was Schuyler coming back in to break him in half but it was Bruny. "Hey, they told me you were in here. I got a couple turkey sandwiches and some mashed potatoes left over from dinner. I'm going to shitcan it unless you want some. How about it?"

Desmond cued tape 1 to the beginning. "No thank you Bruny," he answered absently without looking at him, "I'm not hungry." Bruny shrugged and closed the door. Desmond sat and watched all 27 lousy takes of the children, interrupted only once by the crash of Bruny heaving dinner trash into the dumpster out back.

All the takes were identically awful, and as he watched, his mind drifted back ...

While he stared at the studio floor, seemingly stunned by his own admission, the two outside cameras slowly wandered around his right and left, and he knew what was going on: Camera 2 in the center was distracting him while 1 and 3 tried to surround him.

Desmond slowly looked back up at Cavett, who was almost ready to put a stop to the interview. "People died," he whispered to his host, accidentally knocking his off-brand water bottle onto the carpeted floor. He noticed the show director, cameramen, and crew looking at each other with concern as he stopped and looked down at the bottle, which had spilled numerous maggots out on the floor. He stopped breathing. The two cameras stopped with him.

Losing his concentration, Desmond bent over, gently picked up the errant bottle from the floor and shook it out to make sure there were no more vermin inside. Rising back up, he squinted while he read the label. Cavett and the crew held their breath in total silence. A little guy wearing headphones inside Desmond's head focused his two cameras on the bottle label, centering on the tiniest details. Outside the big guys in the big headphones also stopped and focused their cameras on Desmond, concentrating on the big picture. They were not going to miss a second of the famous director's impending collapse, even though they were at one time, huge fans.

Finally sick of watching the children scramble and the big-head tribesman step out of the hut and look to the right, Desmond shut off the monitor and trudged back to his bunkhouse and laid down in his suffocating bed, staring at the ceiling, which seemed to nauseatingly spin.

"My crew and I are out of alignment," he decided after much thought of what could be wrong, including the dreadful realization that maybe he had lost his filmmaking skills altogether. "My vision is opposing with theirs because we have no concrete plan of action. Our disorganization may have led to a fire and to a man carrying out a custom of mock suicide. I don't believe my staff grasps the intricacies of the culture or the scope of their responsibilities. Saving an entire race of people is a grave obligation and I have to put my foot down on what I want this project to be, and what it is to accomplish. It's time to take charge, and I need a real script. It's how I work best."

Desmond decided to clean up and change clothes. "A fresh start," he announced with optimism, "because tomorrow is a new beginning." He hadn't even changed his socks since arriving – it was just so easy to flop into bed and pass out every night without screwing with the formalities of folding, washing and putting away clothes.

He sat down in his desk chair, reached down to untie his boots and noticed that they were cinched into dirty, impossible knots. With great difficulty he untied them, then separated and loosened the flaps. He crossed his right leg over the left knee and started tugging, and after a few seconds of finagling the shoe finally groaned and fell off his foot, followed by an accumulation of sand and grit.

"Should do this more often," he muttered.

The other boot came off just as difficult as the first. He looked down at his socks. They were the same mud color as the Afarkil huts.

He raised his pants leg an inch and picked at the top of the sock until he had enough to grab with his fingers. He attempted to draw the sock down, but it wouldn't go. It was as if the sock were attached to his ankle with Velcro. He grimaced in pain as he slowly tried to literally strip the sock from his ankle. "Taking off socks isn't supposed to hurt," he complained as he stripped it another half-inch. It was like peeling an unripe avocado. The sock was so hard to get off he actually had to stop to rest, wondering if he was going to have to cut them off.

He attempted to jerk the sock off in one quick tug but the pain cut through like a jile, a razor-sharp Oromo hunting knife. He bent down to examine his foot, and was astonished to see that his socks seemed to have fused with his skin, and was actually peeling off, revealing muscle underneath.

Suddenly swimming in fear, and terrified he was going to bleed to death, Desmond quickly pulled the sock back up and squeezed it into place, hoping that he could fuse the ripped skin back to his leg faster. He abandoned the idea of changing clothes; if his socks were so hard to remove what would his pants be like?

His head reeling, he looked at his pants and shirt. The buttons, zipper and belt looked permanent, like iron, and they would never come off. His belt buckle was a padlock, for God's sake. He was trapped, like a prisoner, in his own clothes.

He laid back and took several cleansing breaths. This was crazy. No one gets trapped in clothes. It was a ridiculous notion, and he actually managed a smile about it. Things would be different tomorrow. He was hot and exhausted. He just needed some sleep.

And water. Good Lord he was suddenly thirsty. He got up and dragged a shrink-wrapped case of bottled water from under his bunk, cracked one open and chugged it all down without pausing. When had he last drank? He couldn't remember. When did he last pee? He couldn't recall. Jesus, why did his arm hurt so bad? He opened and drank another one, then a third before he laid down to rest.

After a fitful night filled with rapid-fire, repetitive nightmares of slithering maggots and angry Dr. Pepper men, Desmond got up, went outside and called a before-breakfast emergency meeting of all essential staff, most of who were already in the breakfast line, except for Buzzcut, who had apparently filled a plate and disappeared.

With much groaning and complaining the staff left the line, walked over and gathered around Desmond's podium. Buddy snuck over and stood behind Eric, neither of whom technically were supposed to be there.

Many of the crew still looked angry and frustrated at their director. The air was dead, and the sun was rising as a beastly hot, murky orange wad in a milky white haze. Most of them held ever-present water bottles.

"First off, I want to apologize to the folks who were with me in the editing room and endured both my wrist-slitting Christmas story and my tantrum yesterday," Desmond announced a little sheepishly as morning sweat fueled by the sudden influx of water into his system dripped off his nose and chin onto the podium. Apologizing was not his forte, but at least his ankle felt better. "It was a most unprofessional display. Christ it's hot this morning."

Buzzcut then walked over, holding a coffee cup.

Seeing Buzzcut reminded Desmond he was supposed to fire him. "See me after the meeting, Buzzcut. As I was saying, I carried on in a most unprofessional manner," he explained patiently. "There were some developments yesterday that were upsetting to me. But, I am ready to begin anew, as I hope you are also. I am announcing some changes in our project. We are going to get organized and on a strict schedule. I want this to be the best project anyone has ever seen. I want the viewing public to look at our documentary and be moved by the plight of the Afarkil people, to regret and shed a tear for what has happened in the past, to be offended by the present, but hopeful for the future. I don't want a dry eye watching this documentary. The oppression of the Afarkils stops now, with our work. And, I am cognizant enough to realize a good director does not hold back his most talented people."

The crowd perked up, with some nodding of this seemingly positive direction. "Mary?" Desmond asked, singling her out, "What was that idea you had about the people and costumes?"

Mary suddenly came to life. "Well ... I can still make it happen, I have a small logistical detail to work out still, but ..."

Desmond held up his hand, as if to say "quiet." It suddenly occurred to him how nauseous and dizzy he was, and he struggled to stay upright. "I trust you. Go do it. You have my full approval."

Rarely given full directorial approval to do anything, her stunned surprise soon gave way to sheer joy. "Hell yes! Whatever you say!"

"Donato?" Desmond asked, spotting a black t-shirt and bushy eyebrows hidden behind black Ray-Bans, "We talked about their huts? And a painted backdrop?"

Donato appeared equally woozy and skeptical. "Yea ...?"

"If you can get permission from the Afarkils, go for it. As long as it does not compromise the structures in any way. But you must, must, must get full approval of the villagers to do anything at all. Work with Ricky on that. Oh, and I need you and maybe Eric to rebuild a hut at the village that accidentally got damaged. By the way everybody," Desmond announced as an afterthought, "Buddy is confined to camp for misbehavior. Ricky is our new translator. He found a book."

"Will do, Mr. Desmond," Donato half-heartedly mumbled.

Desmond sensed the crew was onboard with him. He instructed Ricky to jazz up the audio any way he could, and to add music to the soundtrack, maybe even some rock and roll. "Try to work in some Madonna, Cher and Bono. They're driving forces behind this project."

Ricky seemed stuck between skepticism and delight. "Well it's a little premature, and there might be copyright issues to ... but I'll do what I can."

"Keep me updated. Okay, everybody," Desmond continued, speaking again to the crowd, "I'll give you all of today to prepare. Tomorrow at this time I expect to see some real progress!"

The crew scattered, seemingly excited at their new prospects and opportunities, leaving Desmond standing, dry, dizzy and alone at his podium. He had just successfully re-set the clock, turning back time to day one of this project. He nodded in appreciation of himself as he watched his people disappear to their respective duties.

Suddenly, a bearded, rumpled older man suddenly stepped from behind him. The stranger had on baggy khaki pants, a long-sleeve dark yellow shirt, and his wire-framed glasses sat crooked on his face. He held an unlit, bent cigarette in his mouth, which poked through the bushy white beard that surrounded it. His hands were jammed in his pockets.

Desmond squinted at the strange man. "Yes? Who are you? Have we met?"

"Um, no, no we haven't," the old guy mumbled. "I just got here last night. My name is Gerald Camber. I'm a scriptwriter, and they sent me here to write you a script. I understand you don't have one."

Desmond noticed Camber's brilliant blue eyes as he produced a box of wooden matches from his pants pocket and busied himself trying to strike one.

"Gerald, is it?" he asked. "I know it's been a real nuthouse around here, but where did you come from? And who told you to write me a script? This is all news to me, and I'm not sure I like it."

"Carswell first called me weeks ago. He gave me a run-through and asked me to have a treatment done before you arrived. I believe that's the fax you been carrying around. I never heard of a documentary needing a script before but a job is a job, right? Then he told me to come here to see it first-hand. Set me up with this General in Addis Ababa who got me a driver here late last night."

Gerald spilled most of the matches on the ground. "Ah shit." He reached down with a groan and picked up a couple of them.

"Everybody was asleep and I stumbled around in the dark for a while but I finally found a shed to stow my gear and get some shut-eye."

Desmond was suspicious of this new arrival and wished he had some notification, but communication was poor in this part of the world. Mary had the only radio within miles in her bunkhouse. "Camber – that's an odd name. I've never seen it before, and I'm sure I would have remembered it. Have you done much documentary work?"

"I started in motion pictures in Germany in 1925 as a prop boy for Fritz Lang. Came to America and went to work for Bob Flaherty. Froze my schnootz off in Canada loading film canisters on Nanook of the North." His match finally lit but went out before he could light his cigarette with it.

Desmond's eyebrows rose. "You worked for Fritz Lang? And for Bob Flaherty on Nanook of the North?"

"Yea," Gerald nodded, indifferently, the unlit cigarette bobbing up and down as he spoke. "Stayed with Flaherty up till 'round 1940. Got out of the movies for a few years in the fifties, then went back writing scripts for John Grierson, up into the sixties or so when documentaries went to shit. I've been around the horn, in case you're wonderin'. Done it all, so to speak."

Desmond thought an on-site screenwriter was an unnecessary example of Mr. Carswell's interference in the project when he was perfectly capable of drafting his own script, but decided to put him to work. "Nice to have you aboard, Gerald. Now, this project outline is impossible to read now and it was mostly for some reason in Japanese and badly-translated English. I need a scene-by-scene re-write in English, based on my notes. I know a documentary typically doesn't use a prepared script but I come from a features background and I am more comfortable working this way. I of course will have final approval and credit."

Gerald nodded, seemingly receptive to Desmond's ideas as he continued. "We need to reflect the immediacy of this crisis. Our job is to bring the plight of the Afarkil people to the big screen, and provoke cries of outrage at the raping of this culture. I'm not looking for a lot of dialogue, just three acts of scenes and activities that tie together and tell the story of this tribe and gives the viewer enough hope for the future that they will write big checks."

Gerald started to ask a question, but Desmond cut him off.

"This is indeed a documentary," he reiterated, "but I am experimenting with a new concept I am calling creative nonfiction, and I don't want anything left to chance."

Gerald again unsuccessfully struggled with a match and shrugged. "Ya know, a lot of people don't know but during Nanook, Flaherty accidentally dropped a cigarette in his film can, destroying all the original footage, so he had to re-create it all."

As Gerald finally lit his cigarette while talking it dropped from his mouth onto the ground. He looked down at it then back at Desmond. "Fuck. Maybe I'm the one who burned up all of Flaherty's footage."

"You say you found quarters, Gerald?" Desmond stepped on the dropped cigarette, remembering the gasoline situation. "And maybe you shouldn't smoke within 50 yards of our gas and diesel tanks. We had a leak."

"I'm set up in the storage shed over yonder. Got my Old Royal typewriter, a bottle of Wild Turkey and a ream of onionskin. I can get you 90 pages in 24 hours - guaranteed."

Desmond stood with his hands on his hips, watching Gerald as he shuffled away. "Damn scriptwriters ..." He suddenly remembered he needed to talk to Buzzcut, but he was gone. It would just have to wait.

Everyone spent the morning hard at work on their fresh start. Donato spread out a 20'x25' stretched canvas and went to work creating a gorgeous sunset in latex. He also prepped about fifty gallons of plaster of Paris; gathered trowels, floats, blocks of foam, 2x4s, plywood and other building paraphernalia, and mixed several diluted gallons of water-based paint. He directed Eric to get the dozer and backhoe down off the flatbed, gas them up and make sure they were ready to go – a task Desmond watched him accomplish wearing only a pair of Speedo swim trunks, flip-flops and wraparound sunglasses.

He certainly seemed to know his way around heavy equipment.

As Desmond walked to lunch at noon he was approached by Eric and Donato. "Hold up Desmond," Donato requested, still not looking well. "Eric has bad news."

Eric shot an aggravated look at Donato, then turned to Desmond. "Appreciate it Mick. I found the gate valve on the diesel storage tank damaged," he explained. "It looks like we lost almost all of our diesel down in that ditch out back. Luckily the dozer and backhoe are already full, but there is almost no more after that. We have to plan carefully – the stick indicates less than five or six gallons left inside."

"Damaged how?" Desmond asked. "Like someone deliberately damaged it? Sabotaged it?"

"I can't say, Mr. Desmond," Eric explained, his eyes looking to Donato for help. "The rubber seals in the valve coupling could have dried out in this heat and ruptured. Either that or sabotage. We dodged a major bullet, though – that could have made a hell of a fire in this heat."

"No shit," Desmond moaned. Why did everything have to be so damn complicated? "This is a harsh and unforgiving environment. What do we have that uses diesel?"

"Only the backhoe and dozer," Eric explained. "The other vehicles and the generators use gas. And we have exactly 18 gallons of that left. Funny how we've had a leak of both our fuel sources."

"I'll talk to Mary about getting our investor to deliver more fuel," Desmond sighed in frustration. "Meanwhile no unnecessary travel."

Ricky demonstrated to his boss some theme music samples and sound effects. He suggested the song "Africa" by the group Toto would serve as a killer opening theme, if he could secure the copyright. He also accumulated several minutes of tribal drums, dance and pan flute music for background. None of it was authentic Afarkil music – in fact, most of it was electronic South American world groove lounge music, but he told Desmond that according to his guide the Afarkils did not even seem to have a word for "music."

Schuyler got out her filters, and although two of them had been broken in the trip, she still demonstrated to Desmond that she had an impressive assortment, along with some specialty lenses and a few undamaged gobos that could help her map out some video effects. But no more faking it, she promised.

Even Bruny got into the act, suggesting theme dinners based on African folklore he pieced together from 1966 World Book Encyclopedias Ricky found in the storage shed. Mr. Haile-Selassie had provided a shrink-wrapped suckling pig in the cooler, so he and Eric brought it out, dressed it with sauce, herbs and dressing then roasted it all afternoon on an authentic Baobab-style spit to celebrate their "new beginning."

With the night temperature in the balmy low 80s, it became a party. After a hard day of preparation, the crew chowed down on Bruny's perfectly roasted pork, drank large amounts of red wine and sangria and danced the night away to Ricky's eclectic CD collection, wired to two enormous floor speakers. Flame torchiers and smudge pots usually used to signal rescue helicopters illuminated the night air in red, dancing plumes of flames and smoke.

A few even made it a costume party. Eric wore a "warrior loin cloth" cleverly made from what looked like a Laura Ashley bed sheet. Donato, wearing only a homemade "grass skirt" (really strips of burlap tied at the waist over a pair of shorts) and a lei partially covering his hirsute belly, got completely hammered on sangria and whatever beverage he carried in his flask. Drunk and impotent, he spent most of the evening sitting and swaying to the booming, trance-like music.

Mary wore a bikini top and a wrap skirt fashioned somewhat after the wraps worn by the Afarkil women but slit very high on her hip. Desmond overheard Donato speculate to Ricky that there was no room left for anything underneath, which certainly seemed to pique Ricky's interest.

But it was Schuyler who most impressed Desmond by showing up in a baseball cap, cowboy boots and a sleeveless tank top with a small rip at the neck, but especially in a pair of daisy duke cut-offs that highlighted her smooth, muscular tanned legs that he saw for the first time. She kicked back in a lawn chair and contented herself with eating a whole lot of pork and sipping red wine.

Wearing his trademark black jeans and a t-shirt, Desmond stood off to the side, nursing a large cup of sangria. He enjoyed watching the others dance, but he specifically was entranced by Schuyler and her remarkable legs. To him, sexy was not what he saw, but who he saw it on. Of course, Mary looked sexy dressed in a skintight slit skirt because she worked to look that way. On the other hand, Schuyler, in a sleeveless T-shirt and tight jean cut-offs was smoking sexy, without even trying.

Schuyler may have been an enigma, but with each sip of sangria Desmond became more and more aware of what a strong and beautiful enigma she was, noticing with great pleasure the broad, straight shoulders and V-shaped back of a woman who played tennis or swam competitively. Her upper arms were toned and well-defined, and in the tank top he could see her stomach was board-flat – very impressive for an American in her mid-thirties who seemed to shun plastic surgery.

Desmond smiled, remembering when she placed her hand on his knee in the Humvee. Was it an invitation? Should he go up to her, admit she looked amazing, and invite her back to his cabin? What would those amazing legs feel like wrapped around his waist?

Then he remembered – he could not seem to get his clothes off. How embarrassing would that be? And of course, Donato had already raised the specter of sexual harassment, so he needed to tread lightly.

Taking a deep breath, Desmond walked up behind Schuyler until he was close enough to smell her hair. She turned and flashed him a quick smile, then turned her attention back to her dancing crew members. He got up his nerve and put his hand on her shoulder. "Hey Schuyler?"

She never looked up at him. "You're drunk Desmond. Not going to happen."

He jerked back his hand, taking a huge and embarrassed gulp of sangria. "But I was going to ask you about the shoot tomorrow!" he sputtered, backing up a step.

"No you weren't," she snapped, not even looking his way. "Do it Donato! Do the twist!" she suddenly shouted into the crowd as Donato attempted his best Chubby Checker impression before she lowered her voice so only Desmond could hear it "so maybe you'll break your damn neck."

Desmond suddenly was the befuddled kid at the high school prom whose date left with another guy.

Confined by Desmond to their quarters during the party, Buddy and Buzzcut were eventually forced out because the fumes from the smudge pots drifted into the bunkhouse they shared, filling it with noxious red smoke. The only one missing was Gerald, who apparently insisted on finishing his script, even at 11:45 p.m.

The party truly came to life at almost midnight when everyone did the limbo. "Don't worry about falling!" Eric shouted when Bruny attempted the tricky five-foot level, "The backhoe is gassed up and ready to pick ya back up!"

As the bar lowered and everyone became either too drunk or too inflexible to clear it, Schuyler suddenly stopped eating pork and stood. Desmond watched her closely.

"Rank amateurs," she announced, "here's how it's done." With the bar set at about three feet, Schuyler approached, studying it. Everyone watched as she threw her cap to the side, spilling her black hair around her shoulders. She faced the bar, threw back her head, then in one smooth, uninterrupted motion slowly lowered backward to the ground. With her back arched and greatly accentuating her breasts, and those amazing thighs flexing, she easily slithered under the bar as smooth as honey, to the silent amazement of everyone.

Desmond was floored. It was just about the sexiest sight he – and all the guys, judging by their expressions – had ever seen.

She stood, took a bow as everyone cheered, and sat back down. "Show's over."

Around 2:00 a.m. the party sputtered to a stop when everyone – drunk and stuffed on fatty meats and rich, red alcohol – finally had enough. Unbelievably, almost all of the pig had been eaten, and gallons of wine and sangria consumed. The guys had gotten far too drunk to care anymore about Mary's slit skirt, but Desmond guessed all of them still held enduring memories of Schuyler's flexing thighs and her tossed-back hair as she limboed far lower than anyone thought possible.

He stayed up much later than he wanted until he got to watch Schuyler walk back to her bunkhouse, then close and lock her door. He tossed back one last cup of sangria, crumpled his Styrofoam cup and tossed it without success toward the trash can. He stared at the devoured roasted pig skeleton as Bruny glowered and squatted to pick up the discarded cup.

"This is what Mr. Carswell will do to me if I screw this thing up," Desmond announced to the head of the picked-over Sus Scrofa. "Who's a dead pig? Who's a big, dead pig?" he asked the skull in a slurring child's voice, cradling it in both hands.

Staggering drunk back to his quarters, he considered stopping by Schuyler's bunkhouse under some bogus pretense just to see what she was wearing. Knowing she would see right through him, he decided instead to go by Gerald's shed to see how the script was coming. Seeing a dim light under the door, he stopped and listened to the "clack, clack-clack, ding zip clack clack-clack" of his Old Royal typewriter as he banged it out.

"That old fart's a hard worker, I'll give him that," Desmond muttered as he grabbed the doorknob and jerked open the door.

Startled, Gerald looked up from his typewriter under the glow of a single desk lamp. A fifth of Wild turkey sat at his side and his ubiquitous unlit cigarette was propped in an ashtray. Desmond saw no bunk, and the shed was wall-to-wall junk. "Hi-ya! You startled me, Mr. Desmond. I was just finishing up act 2 of this script you been fussin' about ..."

"Gerald, old boy, I've been thinking," Desmond stammered

drunkenly, still standing outside but swaying and holding onto the door for balance. "If you're as good a scriptwriter as you say you are, and with my direction, we should have no problem pulling together a banger ... bang ... bang-up production that will save these people and make us all rich."

"Mr. Desmond?" Gerald asked, curiously taking a pull on his unlit cigarette, tapping it and returning it to the edge of the ashtray, "Can I be frank? I'd love to save these people too, but sometimes despite our best efforts, things just don't work the way we intend. You know about the Aswan Dam? In Egypt?"

"Yea, it's a dam."

"Yes it is, and it was built in 1970 to stop flooding and to fertilize and irrigate fields. But, it caused the Nile River to deposit the fertilizing sediment at the bottom of Lake Nasser, where it couldn't be recovered. Today the dam exists only to provide electricity to fertilizer factories needed to nourish the fields made barren by the construction of the Aswan Dam. It was a response to the flooding and farming problems, but not the solution to it. And despite the best efforts, it backfired and failed its original purpose."

Desmond blinked. "And your point is?"

Gerald took another drag on his unlit cigarette and returned it to the ashtray. "Okay. In the 1960s NASA was worried that bad weather would delay the construction of the gigantic Saturn 5 rockets that would carry the Apollo astronauts to the moon ..."

Desmond stomped in impatience. "Gerald, I really don't have time for ..."

"Let me finish! So they built an enormous building to construct the rockets inside. Turns out the building was so massive that it generated its own weather. The Saturn 5 rockets, while under construction, were pelted with lightning, rain and hail inside the goddamn building."

"So where are you going with this?"

"I'm just telling you, Mr. Desmond, that sometimes despite our best efforts to fix something, we just can't. And, we make things far worse by even trying. We can't change the natural course of things that are pre-ordained by God and nature. Everything we attempt has unintended consequences, and we can't control them. If this Afarkil tribe is doomed, then it's doomed, period, and nothing we do will change that. Due to the course of nature, it either survives or it doesn't, and we cannot 'make' it survive. The harder we try, the greater the probability of failure. You are a response to the disintegration and eventual death of the Afarkil culture, but you are not the solution to it. Nothing is. Nature is going to do its damage and there is not one single thing you or I can do to change that."

Desmond hung to the door frame, trying understand what the fuck Gerald was talking about. "The Afarkil society is mine to save, and your theories are gibberish," he finally retorted, his voice slurring but his perseverance fully intact. "So either you are on board with me on that, or you're on the next truck back to Addis Ababa. So chew on that, old man."

Gerald took another drag on his unlit cigarette and snickered. "I hear you, Mr. Desmond. A job is a job, right? But you need to leave me alone now, and let me finish this here script if you uh, want it by tomorrow."

"Whatever. You're a dying breed. You know what, I just realized I was talking to a pig over by the kitchen, now I'm talking to an old goat!" Desmond chuckled and slapped shut Gerald's door. "A really stupid old goat."

He stumbled back to his bunkhouse and passed out in his bed, sealed up in his clothes.

CHAPTER NINE

At 8:15 the next morning Desmond could barely stand just outside the Afarkil village, leaning against a Baobab, hung over, dehydrated, shaky and virtually helpless, as Ricky – also hung over and almost as helpless – attempted to tell a reluctant "Harvey," the unofficial Afarkil spokesman, the plan for filming that day. Last night Desmond had a gallon of sweet red sangria, a plateful of pork, and not one drop of water. His mouth was as parched and gritty as the salty sand under his feet. He watched briefly as Harvey angrily stood with his arms folded, frequently shaking his head no, as Ricky squinted into his book, trying to piece together a coherent plan and make it somewhat understandable to the villagers.

He looked down at the undulating ground and concentrated. Despite brushing off Gerald's warning that he was chasing a hopeless dream, he nonetheless was haunted by his words today. What if this were a desperate pursuit? What if there was no way the clan could be saved, that the natural order already ordained that it would collapse and there was no way his efforts could rescue it?

God, it was hellishly hot. He closed his eyes to stop the world from spinning.

People died, Mr. Desmond.

As that realization grew after Desmond dropped his water bottle, he mortified everyone, especially Dick Cavett, when he pulled a handgun out of the back of his pants. His original plan was to start shooting, something, anything, with the expectation a studio guard would shoot him dead. Suicide by proxy, they called it. He didn't have the guts to shoot himself, so he would entice someone else to do it for him. Only he realized he couldn't bring himself to pull the trigger at all.

"How did that asshole get a gun in here?" the producer shouted into everyone's headphones from a remote studio down the hall ...

"... Bad news Mr. Desmond," Ricky declared as he walked back out to his boss, who opened his eyes, shuddering from the horrifying memory. "The Afarkils won't let us in their village."

Desmond sort of heard him, but he was distracted by a very sick Donato slowly pulling up to the village in the flatbed truck, loaded down with his paint and supplies, followed by the remainder of the crew in the Humvee and one of the Jeeps. Eric was on the bulldozer, and backed it up to the largest beautiful, thousand-year-old Baobab. He looked as if he were ready to shackle a chain around it and with no reservations yank it out of the ground to make a better shot.

The entire filmmaking convoy, most if not all of them pallid, woozy and lightheaded from the party, pulled up beside the flatbed, each loaded with everything they could find to not only "dress up" the Afarkil village but rebuild the burnt hut. Buddy crept up on the backhoe, holding the mistuned engine throttle wide open while belching a tornado of black diesel. He stopped beside the bulldozer, in front of Desmond and Ricky, grinning ear to ear, obviously proud of his abilities to drive heavy equipment.

Desmond paused – why did they need heavy equipment, anyway?

"Eric just showed me how to drive this Mr. D," Buddy shouted from the seat as he tried to power down. Desmond could only stare in confused disbelief, as he could swear Buddy was supposed to be confined to the compound. Was no one listening to him? Mary arrived in a Jeep and got out, wearing black sunglasses, a hat and a thundering headache.

"Wait!" Desmond suddenly shouted over the din of the equipment and his own bewilderment. Everyone stopped. Eric powered off the bulldozer. Buddy searched for whatever shut off the backhoe. Even the Afarkils stopped and looked.

"Desmond," Mary groaned through dark sunglasses, "please stop screaming."

Desmond turned to Ricky. Something deeply terrifying passed from his lips through one ear and out the other, and it was so terrible he suddenly thought he was going to self-destruct if he did not hear it. "Ricky, please finish what you were about to tell me."

"I can't hear you over the backhoe, Mr. Desmond," he shouted back

"Buddy!" Desmond shouted, "Shut that goddamn thing off!"

"I was saying, the Afarkils are refusing to let us film them," Ricky repeated loudly, holding up his book over the roar of the backhoe as Buddy nervously jiggled and pulled every switch and lever until finally it powered down to a dull sputter.

"Didn't you see? The man there grabbed my book out of my hand, pushed me away, then threw the book at me. You were standing right here, Mr. Desmond, didn't you see any of this?"

"We're dead meat," Donato announced as he walked up.

Suddenly someone yelled "duck!" as the backhoe bucket roared back to life then unexpectedly swung around and smashed into the rear of the bulldozer with a deafening, explosive crunch, demolishing the rear protective grate and nearly tossing Eric to the ground. Desmond raised his head, and could only watch as Buddy, in a panic, reversed the bucket but hung a tooth on the dozer's fuel line and it sheared like a gunshot. Gallons of oily, precious diesel began pouring onto the ground.

Eric yelled "You dumb fuck! Shut it off!" before he jumped from the dozer over onto the backhoe, shoved Buddy out of the way and powered it off. Everyone else seemed to hold their breath as Desmond bent over and placed his hands on his knees. It was quiet now. And Christ, it was hot this morning – brutally hot. Lights started shooting off in his head as the gushing diesel fuel formed a black, oily pool on the ground.

A young television director in a plaid suit and a bulbous 1971 knit tie screamed to cut the damn cameras at the sight of Desmond's pistol but the cameramen was by then cowering on the floor. Despite having no operators, cameras 1 and 3 continued their slow semi-circular tracking around a 1950s-era woman nude from the waist down, bent over a ping pong table while a young man in a crisp white shirt with his suit pants down around his ankles pumped her from behind, his eyes shut and saying hi-ya, hi-ya hi-ya with each thrust, just before he punched her in the back of the head. Then again, and again, the poor woman's head bouncing off the ping-pong table with each strike. Desmond thought he saw one of two security guards unsnap his holster, get down on one knee and place his hand on his service revolver while his partner snuck around the perimeter of the set, just like the cameras, to try to get behind him as he tried to scream at the couple in the center of the floor to stop, their sex growing more violent and the pumping and the hi-ya's increasing in intensity. Many crew members were down on the floor, crouching or hiding from the crazed director when there was an explosion off to Desmond's left and he stopped trying to scream at the couple to see several cordite canisters exploding prematurely in sequence people splattered with jellied low-grade burning napalm with two of them completely engulfed in flames ran in random jerky angles across the set before one of them fell face first to the floor right in front of him in a panic Desmond turned to his right to see the security guard kneeling in front of him, his hand on his weapon thank goodness I'm here he thought the guard shouted at him we've got a code orange cheap bottled water the guard stood whaddya say you lay down the gun Mr. Desmond so we can clean this place upthenwe'llgogetyousomebetterwaterthanthischeapshit ...

Everything grinded to a stop. Then it started up again, but at a different speed, like someone switched the record player from 78 to 16 rpms.

It's not the water that's cheap. Desmond put the barrel of the gun in his mouth and pointed it up. He may have brought the gun to "clean the set," so the tabloids would have something to talk about tomorrow, but he got his nerve, and this idea was better – this will show them. The barrel was cold between his lips. And just before he squeezed the trigger, the man screwing and beating the blazing stuntwoman on the ping pong table looked up at him.

Didn't I tell you I needed about thirty minutes to count your Dr. Peppers?

A jolt then silence. Everything floated in clear, viscous liquid.

***

Desmond opened his eyes to find himself lying on a cot. A doctor and a nurse with blurred faces hovered over him, which reminded him of that time his arm got broken by the Dr. Pepper Silver Dollar Man and it was put in a cast. In fact, for a few seconds he thought he really was in a hospital, as the room was cool, he was covered in a blanket and he had an IV in his left arm. But then as he became more alert, the doctor and nurse's faces cleared, and he realized they were not a doctor and nurse at all, but Donato and Mary, and he wasn't in a hospital room but a food storage pantry in the Danakil Depression – the only comfortable building in the entire compound, in the entire desert, on the entire African continent.

A thought occurred to him: why hadn't he come here to escape the heat before now?

"Desmond?" Mary asked, her voice dense and moldy as she squeezed his hand. "Can you hear me?"

Desmond raised his head off his pillow. He knew where he was and what he was doing in the desert, but he had no memory at all of how he got on a cot in the pantry. He laid back down.

"I hear you Mary," he whispered. "What happened?"

Mary and Donato both looked at each other relieved. Mary squeezed his hand even harder, then raised and kissed it. There was a tear in her eye. "We really thought we lost you back there," she confessed, her voice breaking. "You started ranting nonsense then your eyes rolled back and you fell. Your heart rate went to like 200 beats a minute, and you were completely unresponsive. We brought you here. Schuyler said you were having a severe heat stroke, so she found some medical supplies and started an IV. The bag went out of date about six months ago but she said that was okay. You've been out for several hours."

"I remember talking to Ricky about the Afarkils," Desmond whispered after a few sips of water to cool his gritty throat. "It wasn't good."

"No, it's not good, it seems they refuse to let us film them," Donato affirmed. "Ricky said the Afarkils made it very clear that we are not welcome anywhere near them."

Desmond closed his eyes in frustration. This was a disaster, and it was going to end his career. He suddenly recalled living in a truck stop motel back in the mid-seventies when he was at rock bottom. He was heading back to that point in his life right now, he thought.

No. No he would not.

"This is unacceptable," he finally professed, his voice growing stronger. "We have to make this documentary, whether the Afarkils want us to or not. Don't they want to be saved? Christ, the whole world is lining up behind this project – I can't fail! People will say Tom Desmond had a chance to bring the plight of the Afarkil people to the world and he failed! Then the extinction of the Afarkils will be on me!"

"Desmond, calm down," Mary warned.

He let go of her hand and pushed it away as he fought a wave of dizziness and nausea. "Don't you see? I will go down in history not as a director of two successful movies, but as the guy who killed people on a film set, then tried and failed to do something really stupid with a gun on national television! Then when given a second chance years later, failed to save a dying tribe! I'll be an industry joke!"

"Desmond, stop and listen for a minute, you're making yourself sick," Mary insisted, placing her hand on Desmond's chest and gently easing him back down on the cot. "Donato and I have been talking about this situation, and we might have a solution, but you have to be open-minded, okay? Are you willing to listen to us for a minute?"

Desmond exhaled and lay back down. Tears welled in his eyes, as they always did when he found himself vulnerable and someone tried to help him. It used to happen with his mom. He should be happy that two of his crew were looking for a solution to the problem rather than wallowing in self-pity and formulating an exit strategy. For once, he needed to shut up and listen.

"All right, Mary. I'll listen."

Mary took a deep breath, glanced at Donato and looked back down at her boss. "Do you remember yesterday morning, at the meeting, you said that a good director does not hold back his most talented people?"

"... yes."

"And do you remember, you told me I had full authority to do whatever I felt was necessary to make this project come together? And you also told Donato that he could do the same thing?"

"Yes."

Mary looked up at Donato and he finished Mary's explanation. "Well ... Desmond, Mary and I have been talking while you were passed out, and we came up with what we think, is a pretty good solution to this whole problem. You see, we have a ton of building supplies here, left over from construction, I guess. And since the Afarkils locked us out ... anyway, we think that, well ..." Donato hesitated, as if he didn't know how to pick the right words. "We think we can build a fake village. And make it look like the real deal."

Desmond almost laughed in Donato's face. "Am I still having a heat stroke? You are kidding, right?"

"Desmond, listen to us," Mary insisted. "You need this documentary, don't you? Like Donato said, the Afarkils have shut us down. We can't make a film about a culture that won't let us film them, or even come anywhere near them anymore. We have no options left."

"So we build a fake village, then what?" Desmond inquired. "If the Afarkils won't let us film them in their real village, they sure as shit won't let us film them in a fake one!"

Mary exhaled deeply and looked at Donato again before continuing. "Well, we thought of that too," she divulged hesitantly. "A day or so ago I spoke on the radio to our investor's office in Addis Ababa, and ..."

"Christ, Mary! You didn't tell the investor about our problems here did you? He'll pull his money out!"

"No! Shut up and listen!" Mary insisted. "I told them things are going great, but that we needed a little assistance with something, and Mr. Haile-Selassie has made an incredible thing happen."

Desmond paused. "What incredible thing?"

"Well, he is going to send us some local actors. We can use them to play the Afarkil villagers ..."

"Mary that was insanity! Now our investor knows we have no villagers! What is he going to think ...?"

"Desmond!" Mary stood in anger. "For God's sake! I lied to him, okay? I fucking lied my ass off! I told him we needed a few actors to play peripheral roles and be stand-ins and since he apparently knows nothing about filmmaking he bought it! But realize right now we have nothing here! You promised you would not hold me back, and Donato and I have tied ourselves into a knot trying to come up with a solution to this stupid situation we are now in while you laid in here in the cool air having your little stroke! You know you aren't the only goddamn martyr here, I have just as much at stake in this as you! We all do! I stuck my fucking neck out to Wallace and to Mr. Haile-Selassie! I lied to him about why we needed actors, and right now the world is waiting for a documentary you can't deliver! What will you tell the press when you get back? What will you tell Mr. Carswell if he wakes up? What will you tell Mr. Haile-Selassie – who I hear is like head of the Ethiopian mafia or something – when he demands a return on his investment? What will you tell Cher, Madonna, Michael J. Fox and every school kid in America? Sorry folks, I failed?"

Donato stood and looked down at his prone boss. "Think about it Desmond," he warned. "All of our reputations are on the line, especially yours, and the way we see it, this is our only way out of this mess. Come on, Mary. Mr. Desmond has some thinking to do." He and Mary turned to leave.

Desmond took a long drink of water from the bottle beside his cot. This idea was absurd, but it was true he had no fallback strategy. He would be fooling the entire world, tricking them into believing he made a documentary when in fact he made just another bullshit feature film pretending to be a documentary. He would be another Robert Flaherty, trying to re-create Nanook of the North.

This was becoming his burning cigarette in the film can.

But Donato and Mary had a point – without the cooperation of the Afarkils, he had no project. Mary was keeping the investor satisfied, because if he found out Desmond lost the Afarkil people and had no film, he would pull the money and he would be ruined. Plus, if he really was head of the Ethiopian mafia, who knows how he would retaliate when he found out the truth?

"Wait a minute," he whispered as Mary and Donato opened the door. They paused and looked back. "I have a special personal relationship with the Afarkils, and I am confident I can reach an agreement with them, and they will allow us back in. But I will agree to one thing: Donato, I want to see a drawn-up plan of what you propose for a replacement village, but do not build anything yet. Mary, I cannot imagine any scenario where I could go along with using actors, period. That is just dishonest. I'll come up with a different idea."

As the two left Desmond lay back and covered his face with both hands. What the hell was he going to do?

Desmond startled awake some time later in a haze to an angel changing his IV bag. "Did they tell you the saline is out of date?" he thought the angel asked. Yes, they did, he thought as he looked up at her. She looked familiar. After checking and re-taping the needle in his arm the angel sat back and looked down at him.

"Do you remember earlier that Buddy accidentally swung the backhoe bucket into the bulldozer?" the angel whispered in Schuyler's voice. Desmond started coming back down to earth. He shook his head. Yes, he did remember. "Eric wanted me to tell you that when Buddy ruptured the fuel line almost all the diesel ran out on the ground and down a sinkhole. They were able to drive it a short distance back before it conked out."

"Who's filing the EPA report?" Desmond asked in a rasping voice, surprising himself with a coherent question. Schuyler looked amazing to him at that moment, and he was touched by her humanity although not overjoyed by her news.

"Mary told Buddy and Eric they had to do it," she answered as she reached up and adjusted the drip. "Are you drinking lots of water?"

"Yes." Oh God, yes, he would do anything the angel over him asked. But there was something he had to tell her. "Schuyler," he whispered, grabbing her wrist as she got up to leave. "I'm sealed up inside my clothes and I can't get out."

Schuyler patted his hand then removed it. "What clothes? What are you talking about?" she asked as she turned to go out. Surprised, Desmond lifted the blanket and looked underneath. He had on only a pair of boxer shorts.

"Thank God!" he mumbled before he happily closed his eyes. Even his glued-on socks were gone.

Desmond ignored the security guard's offer of better bottled water, then he squeezed the trigger into his own mouth right in front of Dick Cavett. The bullet left the barrel and passed through his upper palate, bouncing off his upper jaw and shattering several teeth before veering slightly up through his sinus cavities, glancing off the cheekbone. Flattened, the lead ball just missed his optic nerve before it slammed the bottom edge of his left orbital socket, blasting through that side of his head under his eye. Blood, bone fragments and tissue exploded in a white flash from the side of his face as several people screamed and flailed on the floor in desperate attempts to save themselves.

The concussion flipped Desmond backwards, and he landed flat on his back.

Lying there on the floor of the NBC Network studio, he dreamily felt the jagged tunnel he just blasted through his own head. There was no real pain, just a vague, unsettled feeling that part of his face was missing. His fall backwards seemed to last ten years to him, and when he finally landed it was like falling onto a feather bed. His mouth and sinuses reeked of bleeding hot sulphur, and he was briefly aware of burns inside his mouth. He also realized that even though his head lay in a puddle of sticky liquid he suddenly could see everything clearer, and as he drifted slowly into unconsciousness, he replayed the terrible chain of events of 1971 that took him to that despairing point.

Little did he know at the time, however, that he would have to continue that descent until he bottomed-out as a broke junkie who would have to claw his way back.

***

Sometime later, Desmond awoke to Donato entering with a large roll of paper. "You up for looking at a plan?" he asked, sitting down and unrolling it. Desmond shook out the cobwebs and propped on his elbows. He was feeling much better.

"I have some ideas for the village, like you wanted. My idea is to have the huts sit more in a semicircle, rather than the random formation the real ones are in," he explained, pointing to an elaborate pen drawing. "I made peace with Schuyler long enough to agree on exactly which structural shapes and layouts would be most conducive for better camera angles and shots. Eric right now is at a visually appealing site just around oil drum mountain, in front of some salt formations, laying out each hut with a chalk line and specifying whether it is a complete hut or just a façade – that will save us some time." His sketch showed a gathering/dining area in the village square, with a huge cooking contraption centerpiece, complete with elaborate spits and stew pots and pulleys and levers to operate the whole thing. It was right out of Swiss Family Robinson.

"To create the replacement huts, I'll nail together 4x8 sheets of OSB plywood, with 2x2 x-bracing on the back," Donato explained, "I then can sketch a hut front with a piece of charcoal, then Eric and Ricky can cut it out with scroll saws. I can cut up and piece together some oil drums, rope and pulleys laying around here to build the centerpiece."

"Donato, what the hell are we doing?" Desmond asked, trying to comprehend the elaborate ruse they were concocting. Although Donato seemed to be on top of his game, he could still smell alcohol oozing through his pores.

"Saving a culture but saving our own asses, too," he answered without missing a beat. "You should go ahead and approve construction of this, Desmond. Even if the Afarkils let us back in we can use the backup village for scene, location and even green-screen shots. Trust me on this."

Donato then leaned in real close. "Please, I need this. I need it bad. I got to get back into the inner circle – fucking digital and 20-year-old computer punks are stealing my livelihood. I need to prove I can design and build and pull my weight. I'm too young and too fucking broke to become an industry has-been."

Desmond sighed. He was too weak to argue. "Okay, Donato, but put some distance between this and the real village so I'm not reminded constantly of why we had to do it."

Donato winked as he rolled up the drawing. "Get some rest Desmond."

Desmond closed his eyes and remembered.

About three years after the Dick Cavett incident, the resulting surgeries, rehabilitation and litigation, Tom Desmond lost everything and was reduced to living in a truck stop motel. Of all the places in his memory to go, he had to go there. Maybe his mind was reminding him he has been in worse places in life than on a cot in a pantry recovering from almost lethal heat stroke.

The self-inflicted gunshot wound had healed badly, and it took three major surgeries to make his face right again. While he no longer resembled the elephant man on that side of his head, the pain at the time was so excruciating it got him hooked on a variety of narcotics, even angel dust, to dull the pain. How ironic, the role of angels both in the motel and in the pantry. But no angel ever came in the truck stop to change an IV.

He remembered all the unnecessary and ugly overnight outside noises while recovering at the truck stop: gunning diesel engines, drivers swearing and cat-calling the hookers that propositioned them; loud, anonymous footsteps walking and sometimes running past his door down the breezeway. Sometimes as he lay in that wretched place, numb and strung out on whatever drugs he could find, he heard drunken voices outside his door, then his doorknob suddenly jiggled, as if someone were testing to see if it was really locked. He heard police and ambulance sirens out in the darkness often. Would the next ones be coming after him? Is that a cop beating on his door, jiggling his doorknob, ordering him to put down the angel-dusted joint and open up?

He remembered being almost jealous of long-haul truckers who did not have to deal with belligerent producers, fumbling production assistants and egotistical talent, or have their livelihood threatened with the outrageous claims of prosecutors with dollar signs in their heads who ironically painted him as a monster only out for the almighty dollar. Driving a truckload of string beans from Pennsylvania to Georgia couldn't possibly have the appalling stress and financial ups and downs of filmmaking. He remembered in the time following the accident he went from eating a porterhouse steak on Sunday to thawing a frozen hot dog under a hand dryer in a gas station bathroom on Friday. He thought if he was permanently forced out of the film business, he could pursue a career as a truck driver, and be free of the impossible obligations he lived with.

But dammit, he was a filmmaker. Nothing else clicked. He had to get out of that damn motel.

Desmond awoke to Bruny rummaging through the pantry rounding up some dinner items. "Excuse me Mr. Desmond, I didn't mean to wake you up," he apologized with an armload of gallon cans. "Mary said they would be back here by 9:00 and for me to have dinner ready then."

Desmond sat up and stretched. He looked at his arm. His angel had removed his IV and there was a small bandage where it had been. He felt normal – in fact he felt better than he had in the last few days. "What time is it Bruny?"

"Just after seven. At night. You've been snoring like a bastard."

"And how many days have we been here?"

Bruny paused, initially confused by Desmond's question. "Well, today ends my fourth day here. But you and Mary were here a day before me. So you've been here five days. Why?"

Desmond smiled. That's what he thought, but he wanted to make sure he hadn't slept through an entire day or something. He laid back the blanket, swung his feet to the floor and stood – then promptly sat back down, his head swimming.

"Whoa, easy there," Bruny warned, setting down the cans and steadying Desmond with both hands. "You've been through a lot – why don't you lie back down? If you feel like eating, I'll call you when dinner's ready."

"No, I'm going back to my bunkhouse and make some notes, it's time I got back to work. I'm a filmmaker, dammit, people are counting on me."

Bruny helped Desmond to the door, and he was jolted by how blistering hot and bright it still was at 7:00 p.m. As he stepped outside, he also noticed the ground was broiling the bottom of his bare feet, making him trot as fast as his tortured knees allowed in only his boxer shorts back to his bunkhouse. There he found his black pants and shirt, even his formerly glued-on socks, washed and folded on his desk chair.

Queasy and aching from his walk in the heat, he climbed into his bunk and lay down. Suddenly he missed the coolness of the pantry.

Once in his sweltering bed he closed his eyes and finally remembered the worst night of that worst time of his life in that terrible truck stop, when his wife and career were gone, he was out of money and out of drugs. It around 3:00 in the morning and the motel room TV was on a pay-per-view porn series called "Loni Andersin's Adult Pleasures." Sick, shaking and wearing only a dirty V-neck T-shirt, he sat in bed as he watched Ms. Andersin introduce the next feature.

She started to speak but her script took a strange turn.

"Mr. Desmond," she suddenly remarked, in the middle of introducing a film titled Rear Admiral. He stared into her bizarre face, his mouth hanging in surprise. Was she really talking to him? He noticed she bore only a remote resemblance to the straight actress Loni Anderson. "You've really screwed things up. You've just about lost it all."

He blinked as she seductively licked her red lips in the darkness of his room. His penis lay flaccid, slumbering on his lower abdomen and not at all interested in the television while someone shouted a cluster of profanities outside in the parking lot.

"So tell me," she again whispered, leaning forward into the camera, "how do you plan to get your life together? How will you make your spouse support payments? What will you say to the lawyers when they arrive and serve you with a civil suit over the accident? What will you say to your ex-wife's lawyer? What will you tell anybody?"

"I don't know," Desmond answered softly, engulfed in the otherworldly bluish light of the television. "What can I do?" He could hear an argument starting through the wall in the next room. A prostitute and her john were arguing over a payment. It happened all the time in this place.

"You need to stand up and face the music," Loni Andersin insisted as she half-heartedly brushed her hand over her artificially enhanced breasts. His penis yawned, stretched and briefly looked up before lying back down. "But first you gotta get off the junk. You're going to die a very bad death in this shitty truck stop."

"Get yer *mmff* clothes and get the hell out!" a muffled, raspy man's voice shouted through the wall, "You *mmff* the hell *mmff*!"

The camera pulled back and Desmond saw her right arm was in a cast, bent at the elbow, just like the one he wore as a child. It was scrawled not with names of friends but multi-color magic marker obscenities.

"People are dead because of me," Desmond replied to the television, louder this time, ignoring the fracas next door as he stared at Loni Andersin and her cast. "What am I going to do? I have nowhere to go and no money left. Maybe it's fitting that I die in this shitty place."

"No, that would be the coward's way out. And we know you suck at shooting yourself."

"Or," Loni Andersin continued through her pursed red lips, "make an even bolder decision to remain alive and turn your life around. Maybe you'll have to probably go to prison first, and that might be rough, but it would part of your rehabilitation."

Desmond imagined himself in an orange jump suit. Then his mind was flooded with an image of him bent over a bed frame, that jumpsuit around his ankles, his face pushed down into the filthy mattress, with a fold-out picture of Loni Andersin from Hustler magazine duct-taped to his back while several fellow inmates took turns sodomizing him. He closed his eyes tight – the image of them beating him in the head and chanting "hi-ya, hi-ya" made him want to throw up. His right arm throbbed.

"No worries, though, you're a white man," Loni Andersin continued, breaking the image. "A good lawyer will get you out quickly, I'm sure."

"It was 23 dollars *mmff*!" A shrill woman's voice cut through the walls like a sharp knife. "*Mmff* the son of a *mmff* you and *mmff* gonna pay out the *mmff*!"

It sounded like somebody threw and broke something. Desmond glanced at the cheap owl lamp on his bedside table and imagined if it would make the same noise he just heard if he threw it against the wall. God knows he wanted to.

He closed his eyes tight and rubbed them with the palms of his hands. He was taking life advice from a pay-per-view television porn star, for crying out loud. The door to the room beside him opened and slammed, shaking the walls in his room. "*Mmff* you!" the irate woman shrieked through the wall. Desmond heard her stiletto heels clack by angrily. The booming and thumping suddenly ceased. After a minute of silence, as Desmond closed his eyes, he heard the TV through the wall click on to a commercial for Frosted Mini-Wheats cereal.

He opened his eyes and looked up at the ceiling of his bunkhouse. That was a period of his life long over. The porn star was wrong, he did not go to jail, thanks to testimony by a pyrotechnics expert that verified mistakes were made. He had indeed clawed his way back. This heat stroke was a stubbed toe.

Praise God, he was okay now.

CHAPTER TEN

Desmond startled awake to someone beating on his bunkhouse door. "What time is it?" he whispered to no one as he groggily sat up. Sunlight poured in through his window. He sat for a second, then looked at his watch and was stunned to see it was after 9:00 a.m.

"Desmond! You okay in there?" It was Mary. "There's something here you need to see – are you able to come out?"

"Coming," he croaked. His throat was desert gravel. He painfully rolled out of bed. He had slept either in the pantry or his bunkhouse for most of the last 24 hours, yet he sure did not feel refreshed, only confused, grumpy and sweltering hot.

After putting on his clean clothes and grabbing a water, he went out to see what Mary wanted. The morning sun was blinding. "Okay, Desmond," she announced excitedly as she grabbed him by the hand. "I hope you're feeling better and I want you to keep an open mind, okay?"

She led him to an older model Greyhound bus that was enveloped in a heavy burn smell, parked near the other vehicles. The rear hatch was open and a strange man in shorts, a long-sleeve plaid shirt and dirty dress shoes, whom Desmond presumed was the driver, was peering into the engine and muttering to himself.

As they approached the door, Eric stepped out carrying a large cardboard box that had "costumes, desert project" written sloppily in a black marker on the side.

"Nobody's taking this bus anywhere," he remarked to Desmond as he walked by, nodding toward the man in the rear of the bus. "No oil. Genius back there burned the engine up."

"You got costumes?" Desmond asked Mary, coming slowly back to life and recoiling from the burned oil stench drifting from the bus engine.

"Yes, costumes, but something else," Mary admitted, almost holding her breath. "I know you said no actors but ..."

Out of the bus behind Eric stepped a very tall, muscular, handsome black man, wearing a sleeveless dark muscle shirt and khaki pants. He had very dark, perfectly smooth skin, and was completely bald, with a chiseled jawline and a small sterling hoop in his left ear.

"... but they have arrived anyway," Mary announced, looking the man up and down with much interest. "They're our talent. This is Isaiah. He's originally from Cameroon."

Desmond could only stare in wonder as he shook the man's hand. He was 6'-6", and built like an Olympic swimmer.

"... no, no the pleasure is all mine," The man stated sarcastically in a French-accented baritone after waiting for Desmond to say something. "I have to get out of this sun," he added, looking around with a grimace as he flipped open a pair of Vuarnet wraparounds and placed them on his face.

"Mary ..." Desmond's voice trailed off as Isaiah just walked away. He felt as if he was having another heat stroke. "... What the hell is going on?"

Following Eric and Isaiah was the first of several women. Mary ignored Desmond's question and introduced herself to her. "Welcome to the shoot. My name is Mary Semper, assistant to the director."

The woman shook Mary's hand. "You may call me Mazaa."

Despite his growing anger, Desmond noted that Mazaa looked to be in her mid- to late-twenties. She was quite attractive, with pure ebony skin and her coal black hair hung to the middle of her back in thousands of ringlets. She immediately winced in the heat.

Not knowing how to react, Desmond could only offer his hand. "My name is Tom Desmond, the director of this project." Mazaa looked suspiciously at Desmond's hand before she shook it lightly.

"I've never heard of you," she confessed casually in a strange accent before just walking away from him.

"Can't say I've ever heard of you either!" Desmond harshly snapped to the woman's back as she kept walking. Now he was truly infuriated.

"Hey, hey, Desmond!" Mary interjected, "Don't talk to the talent that way! They've had a long hot trip and they're not in the mood for small talk!"

"They don't know anything about long hot trips," Desmond griped. "Mary, can we speak? Now?"

As he pulled Mary off to the side five more Ethiopian men and women got off. Desmond just got angrier as he watched them stream by, all squinting and complaining about the brutal heat and the long ride. Many of them reeked of marijuana. "Mary, I am really shocked that you deliberately went behind my back and got actors after I told you specifically not to! And how dare you call yourself assistant to the director! You are the ..."

"Get off your fucking high horse Desmond!" Mary hissed. "It was too late for me to stop them! They were already on the road when I was changing your diaper inside the pantry! And, seriously, is this the thanks I get for saving your ass back at the village? They are here, and you just have to deal with it."

"They're going back."

"They're on contract, so they get paid whether they go or stay. Besides you heard Eric – their bus is broken down." Mary took Desmond by the arm and turned him. "Look, I swear I'm not trying to screw you over, Desmond, I'm trying to help you. You haven't even attempted to talk to the Afarkils again. But I'll make you a deal – if you get the Afarkils to agree to be in this film, I will send the actors back. And if the Afarkils don't agree – well, then we have a backup plan, don't we? The one Donato and I told you about."

Desmond looked at the talent as they congregated under the dining area awning, taking water bottles offered by Bruny. Mary had a point, and while he slept off a heat stroke she had planned ahead – something he had failed to do. He hated to admit he had been out-strategized.

"Who are these people, anyway?" he finally asked.

"Mr. Haile-Selassie got them. His office told me they were all local actors, fashion show models and Ethiopian music video dancers. He said two of them won the African equivalent of a daytime Emmy award, and one was a Dinner theater guild winner, whatever that is," Mary bragged, encouraged by Desmond's evolving attitude. "Desmond, this documentary of ours will be one for the record books if you just let me handle things." She glimpsed and smiled at Isaiah's muscular, shiny and perfectly triangular back out the corner of her eye as he peeled out of his shirt.

Desmond stopped cold. "Wait a minute ... Mary!"

"Lower your voice to me!" Mary answered him, almost as loud.

"If these people are award winners we absolutely cannot use them! I can't have people on the screen that viewers will recognize from African daytime television and music videos! For God's sake, Mary, did you not think of anything?"

Mary's face dropped in stunned realization – apparently, she never considered this predicament. "But ... Desmond, Mr. Haile-Selassie went out of his way to get these people here on short notice. It would be completely disrespectful to him ... look, with convincing acting, and, maybe a lot of makeup, no one will ..."

Desmond raised his hands and turned his head. "No way, no fucking how. I will pay the Afarkils out of my own salary before I'll use recognizable actors in a documentary. Get on the radio to your millionaire friend and tell him to send a cab, a plane, a blimp, or something to get them the hell out of here. They will never appear in my film. Period." He turned and was startled to be face to face with the man who had been staring at the bus engine.

"Mr. Sir," he gestured in broken English, "my name is Carl Haile-Selassie and I need pieces for my bus! You must help me call in to order the pieces to repair my bus!"

"Haile-Selassie? My God ... how many of you are there?" Desmond asked. "Are you any relation to our investor? His name is also ..."

The man's eyes widened and he got frantic. "Yes, yes, Gabriel Haile-Selassie. He contracted me to drive these people here and return. I am no relation – he controls all salt mining in Ethiopia, I only drive a bus. He is very powerful, I am a simple man and I have another job that I must get to right away, otherwise Mr. Haile-Selassie will ... I need to have correct pieces sent here right away to repair my bus!"

Very powerful? Controls all salt mining? Desmond suddenly was even more wary of their only investor – what was Mary getting them all into? She wanted to be in charge, so by God he was going to put her in charge of this problem as well. "I am sure my production manager can help you with getting your bus fixed."

"The woman? The woman will help me?"

"Yes, the ..." Desmond repeated as the man suddenly hustled away from him to hunt down Mary.

Desmond stood very worried of the bus driver's fear of the mention of their investor. That man could notice the lack of progress and acrimony between his crew and the Afarkils. He could report back and get the production shut down or worse, just piss the man off, prompting a surprise visit. That prospect was simply unacceptable.

Things were getting away from him. He needed to make peace with the Afarkils as soon as possible and stop drawing so much unwanted attention.

Since he and the crew were stuck with the newly arrived talent until Mary could arrange transportation back, temporary bunk rearrangements had to be made. According to Mary's instructions from Addis Ababa, no more than two actors could share a bunkhouse; therefore everyone else had to triple and quadruple up. Buddy, Buzzcut and Ricky had to sleep on the bus with the loudly complaining bus driver. Bruny slept in the food pantry on the cot, which suited him just fine. Donato had a windowless 7' x 7' shed with a six-foot ceiling. Schuyler had to sleep in the tiny, unventilated editing room. Gerald still had the combination storage/junk shed. Against Desmond's wishes, Eric had to move in with him.

At the request of Mr. Haile-Selassie, most of the fans in the compound had to be confiscated by Mary and placed in the talent's bunkhouses to keep them as comfortable as possible in the almost intolerable weather.

Sensing the tension among his crew, and terrified the bus driver would also sense it and report back to their boss in Addis Ababa, Desmond called an emergency staff meeting that evening to hopefully stave off an insurrection.

"Where's Donato, Eric and Ricky?" he asked as Buddy, Mary, Schuyler, Buzz and Bruny gathered around his podium. The bus driver also was not there, and Desmond worried he may have been told about the replacement village or worse, their relationship with the Afarkils.

"They're at the replacement village," Mary answered. "Donato said you ordered them to build it in thirty hours so they've been there all day."

"I said no such thing ... ah, fuck. Folks, I know the arrival of this talent caught us by surprise," he announced in as reassuring a voice as he could muster. "Believe me, it has inconvenienced all of us – Even I have to share a bunkhouse with nonessential staff. But this is just temporary until arrangements can be made to send them back. Mary, did that bus driver get with you about the parts he needs to repair his bus? It's apparently high priority."

"What? No," Mary answered, looking bewildered. "I haven't seen him since he got here. What do I know about bus parts?"

"Well, you need to find him. I don't want him wandering around here and reporting something negative back to the real Mr. Haile-Selassie."

Mary shrugged as the others started grumbling at the mere mention of the newly-arrived actors before she suddenly stood and faced them. "Look, I hear your bitching but you don't know how lucky we are to have talent of this caliber here!" she scolded. "You're just going to have to put up with some more rearrangements while we figure this out!"

Desmond was very suspicious of Mary's words. He had no personal experience with the sometimes impossible on-location requirements of foreign actors, having only heard unpleasant anecdotes from other directors.

"What rearrangements, Mary?" he inquired. "Regardless of their credentials they're on the first wagon train out of here – and we've already switched all the bunks around. There aren't more arrangements we have to make for them, are there?"

"I asked Mr. Haile-Selassie – the investor, not the bus driver – to put them under contract for this project before you shut the idea down," Mary stated crossly to Desmond as she unfolded a sheaf of papers. "I had to make a shit-load of concessions, and it's too late to back things up, so working or not, there are still accommodations we as the crew have to make for them as long as they are here. If they are not used or leave the location we are released from these obligations."

Mary then ran down a laundry list of rules and procedures. The talent had first priority on everything, from cold drinking water, fans and clean bed linens to laundry and premium, individualized food service. "And at meals the talent goes through the serving line first," she announced. "I informed Bruny on their arrival that many of them have special dietary requirements and to meal plan accordingly ..."

"What dietary requirements?" Desmond asked, growing even more frustrated with this situation. Bruny only grimaced, seated at a picnic table with his arms folded.

"Well, Isaiah, for example, is on an ultra-high protein, ultra-low-fat diet, and Mazaa cannot have more than 10% total polyunsaturated fats, with no bleached rice or grains," she explained, adding that several others were either meat-only, vegetarians, vegans or on juice fasts, ultra-low carb or liquid meal replacements. Desmond frowned, knowing that for Bruny, meals were going to become excruciating day-long ordeals, with him laboring over the nit-picking requirements of the talent so much that he and the production crew were going to have to settle for bland, quickly prepared basics.

"Bruny are you okay with this?"

Mary answered for him. "He has no choice."

Bruny shrugged. "You heard the lady."

"Look, people, these are small prices to pay for this level of talent in this environment," Mary continued after clicking off all the accommodations. "Whether we actually use them or not, just please bear with me – things will work out perfectly."

"This is on you, Mary," Desmond warned, suddenly feeling dizzy. "I hope you know what you're doing."

Exhausted after the meeting, Desmond spent the rest of the day resting and recuperating while Donato, Eric, Ricky and even Schuyler worked on the replacement village. That evening at dinner, after all the talent had gone through the serving line and as Desmond stood and flicked a spoonful of unsalted instant mashed potatoes off the spoon and picked through a pile of fried sliced bologna, Buddy approached him.

"Mr. Desmond? And Mr. Bruny?" he inquired nervously, "Mr. Isaiah would like a word with the two of you."

Bruny muttered obscenities as he scooped the last two bologna slices off the griddle and walked crossly with Desmond over to the talent's table. Isaiah sat with his arms folded, his almost picture-perfect dinner before him untouched.

"Are you the chef?" Isaiah asked, looking at Bruny.

Bruny looked around. "No, I'm the owner of this waterfront paradise."

"Settle down, Bruny," Desmond warned, noticing Isaiah's fancy china plate as he held a sagging foam one. "What do you need, Isaiah?"

"When Mr. Haile-Selassie approached me and my fellow actors about this job we were very hesitant to come here," Isaiah explained in halting English. "I knew how brutal the working conditions here would be. In fact, I initially refused to come at all, and discouraged my fellow actors from coming too."

"Could you make your point please?" Desmond asked, not

wanting to hear a drawn-out soliloquy. "My fried bologna is getting cold."

"Mr. Haile-Selassie is a fair man, but also very persuasive. So he and your production manager, a Miss Semper, the woman, I believe, guaranteed certain accommodations to make up for these horrific working conditions. Housing, fans, clean water, and especially the food, were all promised and more importantly, contracted, to be exactly as agreed."

"So what is the problem?"

"The problem is this fish has been grilled, not baked," Isaiah announced as he motioned toward his meal. "It is a common Terkana Perch, not the Nile Catfish. It is frozen, not fresh, and it has been seasoned with cumin. I left strict instructions per our contract, which were to bake my fresh Nile Catfish filet, and season it only with fresh cracked pepper and serve it with a single lemon twist – which, by the way, I do not even see at all."

He handed his dinner to Buddy, who carried it over and scraped it into the trash can. "I expect my dinner prepared correctly this time," Isaiah continued as Buddy set the empty plate back down before him. "And in the future, I prefer my food to not be seasoned with the sarcasm."

"Isaiah, as I'm sure you can understand, certain food items are impossible to serve in this desert, including catfish from the Nile, which is like hundreds of miles from here," Desmond explained, staring at Buddy and trying to keep Bruny from exploding and doing something stupid. "We are hampered also by storage and preparation limitations and ..."

"My requests are in line with what was contracted and promised to me by Mr. Haile-Selassie and your production manager, Miss Semper," Isaiah articulated in his rising baritone, as the others under the awning sat and listened. "Along with a personal assistant. Buddy here is filling in until a legitimate one can be arranged. If you have a problem with these terms ask them to show you our contract. Meanwhile, I see no food in front of me."

Suddenly not hungry, Desmond threw his plate away and walked over to Bruny, who had stomped into the freezer after his encounter with Isaiah and was then laboring to disguise a frozen Perch filet as fresh Nile Catfish. "Bruny I know this is an inconvenience, but I promise I will ..."

"An inconvenience? That's the understatement of the fucking year! What's the deal with fucking Mary guaranteeing these people certain food items without even consulting me, or asking what we have in stock?" Bruny angrily exclaimed, interrupting his boss. "The frozen and refrigerated foods were pre-stocked by that actor's boss, so they should know what we have. And those other two guys," he groused, pointing to two short, muscular men who sipped fruit and protein frappès and made disgusted faces. "They wanted organic wheat germ powder in their meal replacement shakes. I ain't got organic wheat germ powder! I got normal granulated wheat germ, but that ain't good enough!"

Bruny picked up a carving knife and held it out menacingly. "One of those women actually ordered a free-range skinless young chicken breast tenderloin, unsalted, brushed with extra virgin Italian olive oil and broiled with only rosemary and chives. What the hell? I'm tellin' ya, Desmond, these people are ..." He suddenly stopped himself and used the knife to trim the filet in front of him.

"Just put a lid on it Bruny," Desmond warned, sensing a potential uprising. "As I said before, we just have to all pull together during these trying times until these people go back. This is all temporary. I will not compromise our project over petty bickering. Is that clear?"

Bruny laid down his knife and took a deep breath. "Sure," he huffed, "whatever you say." Desmond knew he was going to have to have a long, heart-felt meeting with Mary about what else she and Mr. Haile-Selassie promised the talent.

With the completion of the replacement village according to Donato less than a day away, Desmond was eager to talk to the Afarkils and start filming. After dinner he found Mary by her bunkhouse poring over the costume boxes and picking out several outfits "Mary," he asked, "Have you got your copy of our new script yet? And you and I need to meet about what all you promised the talent."

"What script? This is a documentary."

"THE script. I left instructions for Gerald to have it ready yesterday morning! Good grief we start filming tomorrow morning!" Desmond unconsciously stared at Mary's breasts while he fussed at her.

"Desmond, I have not seen any script. And who the heck is Gerald?" Annoyed, she stood, looked at Desmond and tugged at her tank top. "And you won't find a script down there."

"Oh, sorry." Desmond quickly looked back up. He had heard Gerald's typewriter clack-clacking away for what seemed like 24 hours a day for the two days prior to his heat stroke, and assumed the man had to be done by now.

"Hold on, don't go anywhere, you and I need to talk when I get back," he added before hustling over to Gerald's storage building.

"I hope he used carbon," he muttered, remembering that he had not seen the mysterious man since the night of the party.

Desmond walked up to Gerald's door and knocked. There was silence, no clacking. Maybe he was done. "Gerald? Are you in there?" Buzzcut approached and watched as Desmond waited.

"Who ya lookin' for?" he asked as he spit half on the ground and half on his right shoe. "Ah, dammit."

"Gerald, the scriptwriter. I want to get his script – and he better be finished."

"I didn't know we had a scriptwriter named Gerald here," Buzzcut replied, pulling a folded sheet of paper from his back pocket. "What's the last name?"

Desmond turned to Buzzcut. Wasn't there something he wanted to speak to him about? There was so much piling up on him he couldn't keep any of it straight anymore. "Well, we do, he came late, in the middle of the night a couple days ago, and he has been typing my script, only now he won't open his door. His last name is Camper or something."

"I don't know, Mr. Desmond." Buzzcut studied his paper then scraped the side of his shoe on the ground, trying to clean off the tobacco spit. "Honestly there is no Camper on my crew register, and I haven't seen nobody here working on a script, and my job is to know the whereabouts of every crew member at all times. It's all part of my security de ..."

Desmond tried the doorknob and, finding it open, stepped inside. Buzzcut stopped talking, shrugged, and lit a cigarette.

Gerald's workspace was nothing more than a sweltering hot, 8' x 8' junk-filled storage shed. According to Ricky it was one of the buildings left by a team of United Nations surveyors trying to resolve a boundary dispute in the late 1970s. It had been occupied by various squatters, aid workers, militia men and UN peacekeepers since then, who left it a wreck. Trash bags, old clothes, filthy, ratty blankets, food cans and wrappers and assorted junk were stacked everywhere. It reeked of a dry, dusty forgotten smell.

On the right was Gerald's table, but the Old Royal typewriter was gone, and in its space on top of a pile of waterlogged paperback books was a loose stack of about 100 sheets of the translucent typing paper he had seen in front of Gerald the night of the party. Thankful, he picked it up.

"This must be it." The top cover page was titled:

<u>Parasitic Inf ection in Indigenous Afar Peoples</u>

Confused by the title, Desmond unsuccessfully tried the desk light, then anxiously turned to page one:

```
    ~~The Parasi~~
    A Parasite is any organism existing on
 or in another organism Wich derives part
 of its life necessities from a host W
```

ithout contributing anything to the host
and, in some cases causing damage to the
host. PARAsites that cannot survive With
out a host are called <u>obligate</u> parasites.
<u>Autoecious</u> parasites, pass the parasitic
stage of their life cycle in only one host

"What the hell is this?" Desmond glanced back to the cover page, then flipped about twenty pages ahead:

The larvae undergo partial ~~maturation~~ ma-
turity in the snail, then breaks out back
into the Water as mature larvae called
<u>cercariae</u>. At this stage they penetrate
the skin of the neW host, then migrate
through the blood vessels. There they mature and lay eggs

Practicing flipping his cigarette in and out of his mouth, Buzzcut apparently got bored standing outside so he ambled into the shed and peered over Desmond's shoulder silently for several seconds.

"Must be interesting," he finally uttered. "You ain't sayin' nothing."

Desmond didn't look up. "Interesting doesn't even start to describe this." Disgusted, he flipped another fifty pages ahead.

The larvae of the egyptian blood fluke
penetrate teh skin or mucous membranes
when a ~~hunan~~ human sWims in infested

>   water. Eventually the flukes rech the
>   capilaries in the bladder, Where the

Stunned, Desmond dropped the stack of papers on the table and just stared at it. Buzzcut stared at him for a second before he chuckled insincerely. "I'm not in the movies but that looks more like a book report than a script"

"That old man did not like my ideas for the script so he wrote this bullshit," Desmond spat. "He never worked in the movies either. He's an imposter and he's trying to toy with me."

"Well, maybe your man didn't know nothin' about scriptwriting," Buzzcut observed, scratching his buzzed head, "but he knows an awful lot about bloodworms." He turned and exited the stifling bunkhouse, leaving Desmond standing there alone, shocked and confused. An empty Wild Turkey bottle lay on the floor. It was coated in dust.

"Where is that son of a ..." Desmond mumbled as he looked anxiously around the shed, finding nothing but stacked garbage. He could feel his blood pressure start to boil his arteries. "Buzzcut! When was the last time you saw him?"

Buzz stuck his head inside. "I told you, Mr. Desmond, I never saw him."

"You had to see him! He's an old guy," Desmond insisted, "about this tall. White beard and glasses. Yellow shirt. Never lit his cigarettes."

Buzz shook his head. "Like I said there was never no Gerald on the crew register and I never saw anybody matching your description. I think your scriptwriter is a haint."

Gerald's "script" a crushing disappointment, Desmond abruptly picked up and threw the maddening document across the room in a blizzard of flying papers. "I want you to find him," he ordered Buzzcut as he turned to face him. "Find him and bring him back so I can start the paperwork to get his ass removed and back to wherever the hell he came from."

"Um ... I'll do my best Mr. Desmond, but ..."

Desmond exited the shed and stomped back to his cabin, staring at the ground. "Flaherty, my ass," he grunted, damning Gerald's credentials. "That worthless bastard didn't work on no Flaherty pictures. He had to have been over a hundred freaking years old to work on Nanook. He didn't do jack."

Furious and confused about the time he wasted over the Gerald and script situation, Desmond arrived back at his bunkhouse and discovered his new roommate Eric had gotten back from the replacement village and cleaned up the place. He swept and dusted, and hung little Christmas tree air fresheners all over. The most amazing thing was he took leftover wood and bolted together an upper bunk for Desmond. His own lower bunk was perfectly made, with clean matching Laura Ashley sheets and comforter – in stark contrast to Desmond's upper bunk, which was only a wrinkled sheet on a bare mattress with a single mashed pillow.

Wearing only a pair of short black, skin-tight Joe boxers, Eric wrinkled his nose at Desmond as he came in. "Mr. Desmond, if we have to live together you have got to be a better housekeeper," he complained as he folded and put away his remaining clothes in a plastic tub that slid under his bunk. "And stop ignoring personal hygiene. This place is pretty gamy. You're sleeping topside if you don't mind."

"Whatever," Desmond mumbled. He climbed the ladder and lay down his bunk as Eric walked around in a circle spraying a can of Glade Morning Breeze. He was surprised how sturdy it felt. "Eric, I had a scriptwriter here but he's gone, and I'm being led to believe he was not even here at all. Did you happen to see him? Older man named Gerald, white hair and beard?"

"Never saw him," Eric replied, stashing the Glade under his bunk.

"I must be losing my mind," Desmond muttered. "May I have a moment alone, please?"

"Why not," Eric sighed as he put on his flip-flops then stepped outside. "Please don't mess up anything."

Desmond lay still and stared at the ceiling after Eric left. Why did this have to be so complicated? The quarrels, the talent, the heat, the equipment, the villagers, the script ... my gosh, they've been on the set for five days and he only had about six seconds of footage, and most of that unusable. He was suddenly responsible for eight more people and a bus driver. It suddenly dawned on him also that he had never seen the footage Schuyler shot when the Afarkil elder supposedly "killed" himself. He was so bogged down in annoying nuisances he was forgetting to look at his own film or talk to the Afarkils. And worse, it seemed he may have hallucinated a screenwriter.

Desmond closed his eyes and remembered when he finally moved out of the truck stop at the advice of his television porn star friend, Loni Andersin. It was around 1977 or '78 or even '79, he didn't really remember because he was weaning himself off the junk and those days were all a blur. He only remembered a single specific incident as he entered the disinfect-smelling lobby to settle his bill ...

"Checking out of the craphole you call 211 for good this time," he stated as he slapped the room key on the counter to a Pakistani guy in a short-sleeve silk shirt, seated in front of a tiny oscillating fan. "Tell the hookers and the junkies goodbye for me."

The Pakistani desk clerk pulled Desmond's card from a file drawer. "That will be ... $140.57 with tax for the week, sir. My rooms are not crapholes, and there are no prostitutes here. I have a strict rule."

"Wait a minute, let me see that card," Desmond ordered, taking the card from the man's hand. This week's rate was over $20 more than it usually was.

"What is this $21 for in-room movies?" Desmond asked, pointing to a line item.

The clerk unfolded a cable television printout and silently read it. "Here," he said, pointing to a row of numbers beside number 211.

"You watched an adult in-room pay-per-view movie seven times in a row. Loni Andersin's Adult Pleasures. That is seven times $3.00. $21.00 even."

"You can't charge me for a movie that played while I was sleeping! This is total bullshit!"

At that point a security guard, probably awakened by the commotion, walked out from a little office hidden around the corner behind the counter. He was about 5'5" and weighed probably 250 pounds. He held a little package of nab crackers in his hand, like he was scared to lay them down. "Is there a problem here?" he asked in a gruff, cracker-filled voice.

Desmond tried negotiating the movie cost down to just one viewing, since he slept through six of them, but neither the clerk or the guard would budge, so the rate stayed, taking another precious $21. He also learned that he would have enjoyed one free in-room movie if he had gotten the discount card that was offered to him when he first checked in weeks ago.

That was where he was in life: from making Oscar-nominated feature films to arguing with a desk clerk over a $3 nudie flick in a truckstop motel. But life was going to get better – he was weaning off the drugs and going back to Chicago to dry out.

Then, he looked forward to getting back in the business.

After several minutes Eric came back in, probably concerned that Desmond was doing something to disrupt his sense of order. He kicked off his flip-flops and laid down in his bunk with a copy of Men's Fitness magazine, while Desmond lay in his upper bunk staring at the ceiling, realizing how much damn hotter it was next to the ceiling. After about fifteen minutes Eric whispered "lights out" and flipped off his light, leaving them both in inky blackness.

After several minutes Desmond whispered "Eric?"

Eric didn't answer. "Eric?" he repeated louder.

"Mmm?"

"You awake?"

"I am now," Eric mumbled from below him. "What do you want?"

"Can I ask you a personal question?"

"M-mm."

"Have you ever ... how do I ask this ... have you ever had trouble undressing?"

"Never myself, no." Eric replied. "Maybe others. What are you talking about?"

"You've had trouble undressing other men?"

The question seemed to jolt Eric awake a little more. "I don't believe you asked me that," he grunted, trying to ignore the query.

"Seriously," Desmond was adamant. "Before my heat stroke I couldn't seem to take my clothes off. It was like they were glued on. But then I had a heat stroke and they came right off."

"Mr. Desmond, if this is some sort of veiled request to get me to undress you, it is not going to work."

Desmond stared up into the thick blackness of the room. Even though the ceiling was only a foot or so from his face he still could not see it. He could have been lying outside, staring into an infinite sky. Somewhere outside the propane generator hummed, keeping the food pantry and freezer cold. Desmond had fond memories of his day yesterday lying in the cool comfort.

"I don't want you to undress me, Eric, I'm asking if you ever had trouble getting your clothes off, because I tried to take off my socks the other day and I started to pull off my skin with them."

"Mr. Desmond?" Eric clicked his light back on. "Are you having issues? Is this the start of another breakdown or something? You talk about a ghost scriptwriter named Jerry or Gerald or something and honestly, I don't know of anyone who has experienced what you are describing and I'm starting to wonder about you."

"It's over now, forget it." Desmond sensed Eric was not in the mood for listening to his personal problems. "Let me ask you another question. You think that Isaiah guy is good-looking, or what?"

Eric moaned. "The talent? What do you think?" he asked unenthusiastically. "You got the hots for him? You want him to undress you?"

"No, no," Desmond replied, looking back at the ceiling before Eric clicked the light off again. "Men don't do anything for me ... but honestly, women don't do much either anymore. It's weird. Maybe my testosterone is out of whack." Desmond was quiet for a minute, and Eric probably assumed he had gone to sleep.

"But you know," Desmond suddenly spoke up again, "if I were homosexual it would be for Isaiah. I guess. He's arrogant but a pretty good-looking man."

"Good for you," Eric murmured. "I'm sure he would be flattered. Goodnight."

Silence.

"Eric?"

"For ... yes, Mr. Desmond?"

"If you were straight, would you go for Mary or Schuyler?"

"What do you mean if I were straight?" Eric was obviously annoyed. "How can you be sure I'm not? Did I tell you I was gay? Because I blow-dry my hair, exercise and take care of myself you assume I'm gay? Aren't we stereotyping just a bit?"

"Oh come on Eric!" Desmond persisted, surprised that his bunkmate would neither confirm nor deny his sexual preference when it seemed so obvious to him. "You're sleeping on Laura Ashley sheets! Your entire body is waxed! You always smell like you fell in a bottle of Bulgari cologne! Come on, answer my question, which one would you go for?"

"Yes, I see you are indeed stereotyping," Eric acquiesced. "Neither. Neither one is my type. Mary's a headstrong showoff and I hear Schuyler likes to mate then devour like a praying mantis. I also heard she's bulimic, and that's a turn-off. Now I built most of an entire village today and I'm exhausted. Good night."

"Schuyler is bulimic? She looks great, not starved!"

"Anorexics are starved. Bulimics binge and purge," Eric explained. "They do a great job of hiding it. But you never heard about Schuyler from me – it's just a rumor. Let it go."

Desmond remembered both how much pork Schuyler devoured at the party, but also how flat her stomach was. It made sense. "I used to be a real horn dog over women myself," he admitted after a short silence. "Even when I was married. Cheated on my wife too many times to count, but she cheated on me just as much, I'm sure. But you know, in the film industry, you see all these filled out, over-developed groupies, with their makeup, collagen, silicone and saline. They're liposucked and implanted – then man, they just throw themselves at you ... It's not your fault – you can't help it."

"But then, I see a woman like Schuyler, and I think, man, she looks really good, and natural, and there is nothing artificial about her at all." He rolled over and partially hung over the side of his bunk, his hand absently swinging in the still air. "I remember the girls I grew up with were like that. Plainer than plain – no makeup, hair tied back, round and firm farm girls. I thought about them constantly. I knew this one girl, Debbie something-or-other. She and I had a thing for a while back in the late fifties. We would tongue kiss but that's as far as it went."

"In summer of 1959 my mother and I moved to Washington D.C. and I fell into the Beatnik crowd on K Street. Met a girl at a coffee shop there who said her name was Poppyseed. Talk about natural – hairy legs and all. Didn't dare tell my mom about her. She smoked clove cigarettes and drank hibiscus tea with honey. I was only fifteen but to me, she was beautiful. Man, she had no qualms about sex either. Then she found out my age, broke it off and hooked up with of all people, Jim Morrison, who read a poem one night at the coffeehouse. She was twenty I think."

"Then I got in the movie business and I saw how much female beauty there is manufactured. I guess what I'm realizing is that Schuyler reminds me of the girls I used to know, and even though Mary has not gone so extreme she does more remind me of the women I see there now."

Mentioning his mother and relationships made Desmond remember that awful day in the downstairs rumpus room, when he stumbled across Jerry, the Dr. Pepper Silver Dollar Man, violating and beating the first woman he loved. Then he remembered that Gerald the scriptwriter told him that he took a break from the movie business in the early fifties, around the same time. Gerald the scriptwriter – Jerry the Dr. Pepper man. Both regular guys who shared a similar name who popped into his life, tried to squash his dreams, then vanished. Now that was a coincidence.

Desmond was truly confused and more than a little suspicious. "What in the world is the deal with Gerald?" he whispered just as he drifted off.

CHAPTER ELEVEN

Desmond abruptly awakened and listened worriedly to what sounded like a very large helicopter passing very low overhead. He wondered if it was Mr. Haile-Selassie coming to check on his progress, then after seeing how badly things were going, force him to eat his own genitalia before shooting him in the head.

The boiling sun streamed in the bunkhouse window, heating the small room like a toaster oven. Sore, groggy and sloppy hot, Desmond swung his feet out of bed and, forgetting he slept in an upper bunk, abruptly dropped five feet straight down to the floor with a crash. He lay there on his back, stunned and checking if he broke anything. He noticed while lying there that Eric was already up, and his bed was perfectly made. It hardly even looked like he slept in it.

Once Desmond struggled back on his feet (and noticing his right knee was killing him), he looked in his mirror. The reflection that greeted him resembled more the Sunset Boulevard winos than the dashing young hit film director of several years ago. He was going to pot, if he wasn't already there. His disheveled, dirty hair was completely gray. His face was a mass of sun-scorched lines, making him appear much, much older than he really was. He had not shaved in a couple days, and his lips were a sun-scarred mess. He gritted and looked at his teeth, which were turning yellow. Were his gums inflamed? He stood with a stoop, since he couldn't straighten all the way from falling out of bed.

"This is a rather harsh and unforgiving environment," he reminded himself, trying to excuse his degraded appearance. He really just didn't care about looks when he had such an important job to do – a job that re-started today. Saving an entire culture of people was a tremendous responsibility, and one he did not take lightly.

Besides, he was literally a God to them. And he needed to get over there right away and beg them to let him film them.

It was almost 9:00 a.m. when he finally staggered outside after a moist towelette bath. The camp appeared empty, except over by the kitchen Bruny and Mary were loudly arguing. It seemed Bruny neglected to remove a yolk from one of the talent's egg white omelets at breakfast.

"You think your precious Amadi would be insulted if he also knew I ejaculated in his breakfast this morning?" Bruny casually asked.

"You sick bastard!" Mary almost screeched at Bruny's sarcasm, "If you ever ..."

"Oh, don't worry! My body fluids are high in protein and low in fat!"

"Mary, where is everybody?" Desmond interrupted by stepping between them, hoping to break up a potential fistfight.

Mary paused and looked up at him. "The talent is in their quarters but they tell me they have no direction. Do you plan to talk to them at all about what you want in case you need them?"

"I need to get to the Afarkils first before I can even consider dealing with them. I have no idea my status with them at the moment. I promise I will talk to the talent after that. Now, I repeat, where is everybody?"

"The crew is all at the replacement village. I'm supposed to take you there for an inspection at 10:00, then over to the real village so you can try to talk some sense into the Afarkils."

Mary looked around him to Bruny. "I better not ever hear you came in the talent's food!" she seethed as she turned again back to her director. "My God, Desmond, you look like somebody picked up the bed and dumped you out."

"That's pretty much what happened. I really hurt my knee."

"You should be more careful," Mary suggested. "By the way, before we go there are two people here to see 'the director,' so I guess that's you. I'll meet you over by the Humvee."

"Who is here to ...?"

"Mr. Kanayama? Yukio Kanayama?" An unfamiliar voice surprised Desmond from behind. "The name's Brad – Brad Steele. This is my assistant Mi Lin." Desmond turned to see a short, handsome, somewhat muscular man wearing aviator Raybans with a jet-black ponytail to the middle of his back, smiling very broadly with his hand extended as he approached. He was dressed in a Hawaiian sport shirt and expensive-looking safari pants, with casuals and no socks.

With him was a petite Asian woman with short, spiky pink-tipped hair under an enormous sun hat, wearing purple Capri pants, black platform wedges and round, white Cyndi Lauper-style sunglasses. She had on a loose-fitting jeweled halter-top that exposed her bony pelvis and tiny waist, which was punctuated by a large diamond navel ring. She carried an extravagant Louis Vuitton briefcase.

"Sorry Mr. Brad Brad Steele, you have the wrong person. My name is Tom Desmond ..."

"Oh, I do apologize." Steele dropped his hand when he saw Desmond was not going to shake it. "It's just one Brad, not Brad Brad. I was looking for the director of the Ethiopian documentary ..."

"Then you have the right man but the wrong name. I am the director of the Afarkil documentary."

"I apologize again." Steele held out a business card. "Mi and I are with Pittston Steele Marketing, and we have this concept to run by the director but Mr. Haile-Selassie said only this person named Kanayama could give a verbal okay ..."

"I'm the director here, and I have a civilization to save," Desmond insisted wearily, taking Steele's business card and losing patience. He hated mush-mouth marketing twerps. What the hell was this all about anyway?

"Hey okay, Mr. Desmond is it? Well, as you undoubtedly know this film has great buzz stateside already, and Mr. Haile-Selassie has taken on the role of executive producer while Mr. Carswell recovers. He loves American pop culture, and even though he is a little clueless on how things really work, his company, HSM LLC, contracted my company, PSM PC, to specifically address children's MLM, or what we call multi-level merchandising, specifically the 'toyability' of this Afarkil project."

He motioned to his assistant. "Mi, show him the goods. A little warm here, huh? Man."

Desmond perked up. "Wait, Mr. Carswell is recovering? I guess I kind of assumed he had died – news travels slowly in the Danakil."

"He didn't die, but after his heart attack he had a stroke," Steele explained as Mi popped open her briefcase and took out a flat piece of stiff colored die-cut paper. She displayed it briefly then quickly folded and snapped it together. When she was done, she held out in her hand a perfect miniature African hut, about six inches square. She displayed all four gaily-painted sides to Desmond before setting it on a table.

"He's non-verbal and kind of comatose so that's why Mr. Haile-Selassie is running the show, which also explains why our processes are kind of well, bizarre. But who's going to argue with a man who looks just like Idi Amin, with a dozen bodyguards, almost as many wives and a hundred medals on his chest. Am I right?"

Brad reached into his case and retrieved six plastic zip-lock bags full of plastic toys. He opened one, picked the figure out then quickly dropped the bag back into the case. "I now present to you ..." He snapped out his hand to display a three-inch tall, colorfully painted plastic African figurine. "The Afarkil kids meal action figure, available for a limited time only! Well, our proposal, anyway. This is Ungawa, the medicine man."

Desmond took the small toy from Brad and studied it intently. It resembled a replica of the talent Mary brought in for the shoot, complete with a cheerfully painted robe, dangling jewelry and perfect chocolate skin-tone. This one, Ungawa, had a large, exaggerated head and body features, and held a sort of stick with a scary painted mask on one end. It was more a deep African stereotype and looked nothing like an Afarkil.

"They don't have medicine men," Desmond uttered flatly. "They have ... sorcerers or something ..."

"That's exactly what we need from you, Mr. Desmond," Brad announced as he pulled each from their plastic bag and displayed them one at a time. "Real Afarkils to base our characters on. From the hip, we came up with Ungawa the medicine man; Molinda, the crusty but warm-hearted high Priest; Jadiba, the goofy and forgetful but loveable clan elder; Sh'niquwa, the clan 'babe,' well, that's what I call her anyway, I mean, look at those breasts, and finally ..." He held up two identical figures holding hands. "... there's Mola and Dola, the loveable twin scamps." He set them all down beside the painted kids meal hut.

"I know the medicine man figure is a stretch, but a 'sorcerer' wouldn't play at all in the south. We don't want Falwell's group on our case again. We actually started out with ten figures but our study showed documentaries don't have the staying power downline for that many consecutive figure introductions so we rightsized it to six. We're all kind of shooting in the dark here until we can get some real character development. We'll ship to an additional five percent more franchises to make up the difference, inner city locations specifically."

Desmond stared silently, almost stunned by this development. Since when was a documentary "toyable" anyway? He glanced at Mi, who had yet to utter a single word, then at Steele, who was smiling and nodding.

"I've been a little out of the loop here lately Mr. Steele," Desmond admitted slowly, looking down at the collection of little Afarkil natives on the table. "You say the film's got good buzz already?"

"Shit fire and save matches – I dare say Golden Globe-caliber buzz Mr. Desmond! The United States, Europe, hell, the world is talking about the Afarkil civilization! Mr. Haile-Selassie paid in advance for the Thanksgiving double-truck ad in Variety after Cher talked up the project on Carson last Tuesday. We wouldn't greenlight the kids meal lead-in if the film wasn't already bankable. Honestly, I have never seen this much activity this early in anticipation of a documentary, it's uncanny."

Desmond shook his head, feeling a peculiar, unwanted sickness welling as he studied the cardboard Afarkil kids meal hut and the six colorful action figures. While he was relieved Carswell's and Haile-Selassie's studios and money were behind him, it ramped up the pressure to deliver a spectacular documentary to almost unbearable heights. In light of the problems they were experiencing that thought suddenly dropped a lead ball in his throat.

"We're ready to ship 100,000 dozen units nationwide as soon as the studio confirms the December 1 release date," Steele continued in his rat-a-tat delivery as he punched a pocket calculator. "We're looking at a 24-day lead, tops, by opening in about 1,000 theatres. By Christmas, best case scenario, I can have a quarter million American kids playing with their Afarkil action figures under the family tree. Then, by New Year's our staggered rollout puts us in 2,100 theaters. Hey, and that's not all, Mr. Desmond – there's a great feel-good incentive on this: for every Afarkil kids meal retailed the franchises agree to donate one and one-eighth cents to Madonna's brand new 'Save the Afarkil Foundation.' The studio agreed to match what, Mi? Was it 18 cents on the dollar? We milk that for the first quarter of next year when the film goes to Laserdisc at $22.99 a pop. Same deal, but with director's cut, running commentary and outtakes. You are saving the outtakes for the Laserdisc, right?"

A hundred thousand dozen units? Save the Afarkil Foundation? Carson? Outtakes? Laserdisc? Steele's words washed over Desmond like a greasy wave. Nothing made sense, and everything made him sick. He couldn't even think in terms like those. The encounter was just making him anxious with stress. "So ... damn, I've got a headache. So the whole world is anticipating this movie? So much that it justifies making kids meal action figures? I mean, I can't ..."

"It's called merchentainment, Mr. Desmond," Steele explained, grinning. "And it's never been done with a documentary before. Hell, this puts us in the Empire Strikes Back leagues! Picture this: the kiddies get a cheeseburger, fries and small soda, and now with one of the rich, vibrant Afarkil action figures, packed inside this colorful Afarkil hut carry-all, which will get them to drag their parents to the movie at $3.50 a head. And we start marketing thirty days before the movie opens – November 1. Mr. Haile-Selassie assumes everything will be ready? He is very anxious to see this project through."

Hearing that Mr. Haile-Selassie and the world was behind the project and awaiting the results put Desmond in a gut-wrenching dilemma. His goal to get five million viewers was always an internal one; an almost abstract number that served only to satisfy his own ego. Now fast-talking marketing know-it-alls chattering about action figures and lead-ins and "merchentainment" made his pipe dream a terrible reality.

"I don't know ... if this film is worth all this," Desmond muttered, feeling a sickening and desperate need to tamp down expectations. "It all just doesn't seem to justify any of this."

"Doesn't justify it? Doesn't ... seriously?" Steele blurted with a surprised look. "Okay, how's this for justification – we are saving a race of people, right? We tie in this doc with a 10-minute intro from the president of Eco-Green, a multinational resource recycling initiative. He is getting these students from an American middle school who planted 150 trees on Earth day this past April to tape a message on how the Afarkils can improve their chances of survival by going green, planting and recycling and stuff like that, demonstrating with our action figures. They are thrilled about doing it!"

Desmond shook his head in nauseated amazement and set the action figure back down. It fell over. "Yea, sure. This already seems to be full speed ahead anyway. I fail to see how my opinion changes any of this."

Steele grinned as he and Mi packed up their cases. "Excellent. A verbal confirmation from the director was all Mr. Haile-Selassie wanted! See if one of your staff can get us some character sketches to base the final figures on – pictures would be great, but sketches and full descriptions will be fine too. Just fax them, the number is on my card," Brad chirped as he and Mi packed up the action figures.

"Take care, Mr. Desmond! The chopper's leaving, only one flight is going stateside until next Monday and we are not missing it."

"What's the rush?" Desmond asked. "You're not going to party over the weekend with Mr. Haile-Selassie?"

"Fuck no," Steele suddenly stopped, deadly serious. "First of all, between you and me, that fat bastard scares me – he speaks a little too casually of 'dispatching' people who don't agree with him. Second, that helicopter is on its last legs. Third he put us in a hotel on the outskirts of Addis Ababa behind one of his goat slaughterhouses. Apparently, he is the largest provider of goat meat in east Africa. You ever lay in bed and listen to goats being killed all night? They scream like children. I'll have fucking goat nightmares for life."

Desmond watched them turn to leave. He looked briefly at Brad's back, then with a sudden urge, he took a couple of quick steps forward, grabbed his ponytail and gave it a sharp downward tug. As expected, it popped off in his hand.

"It's a clip-on!" Desmond proclaimed with a badly-overdue sense of self-satisfaction, holding it up like a trophy as a horrified Brad grabbed the back of his head and spun around, "I once heard you marketing twerps wore clip-on ponytails, but I didn't believe it!"

Mortified, and trying to save face in front of his assistant, Brad held his hand out. "Ha ha. Good one Mr. Desmond. May I have it back please?"

Desmond dangled it high out of reach. "What's the magic word?"

"Just give him his damn hair back!" Mi suddenly exclaimed in, of all things, an Irish brogue. "Show some bloody respect!"

Shocked, Desmond stared at Mi as Brad snatched his hair out of his hand and shoved it in a pants pocket. "What, are you from Belfast?" Desmond asked sarcastically as they again turned to leave.

Mi sneered at him. "Galway, for your *fooking* information."

Desmond was suddenly sick of their presence there. The film industry was full of bloodsucking sycophants like them, looking only to make a quick buck off the sweat of others. "By the way," Desmond shouted in their direction as they walked away and disappeared behind a shed, "the magic word was ..."

He paused and looked down at the ground. Ever-present salt crystals glistened in the dry, sandy packed clay under his feet in the baking sun.

"The magic word is we don't have a fax."

CHAPTER TWELVE

After watching Steele and his assistant disappear behind the compound to their waiting chopper, Desmond walked thoughtfully over to the parking area where Mary patiently waited beside the Humvee. He could hear and see over the tops of the buildings just outside the compound the blades of the rather large helicopter roughly warming up.

"What did those two want?" Mary asked as she got in. "And why the hell are you always the driver? I'm just as capable a driver as you."

"They're making Afarkil kids meal action figures," Desmond grumbled as he slid in the driver's seat and turned the key. And, the air conditioning magically came on. "Damn, the a/c works. Glad something around here does."

"Go straight out here then veer left," Mary instructed, barely tolerating Desmond's comment and directing him to the replacement village as she lifted her sunglasses and stuck her face in the cold air vent. "Oh, that feels good. That's a good sign if the studio is doing marketing already. Maybe we can get those kids meals here so we don't have to eat Bruny's slop anymore. Drive around the stack of oil drums like you're going to the real village but keep going left, like a traffic circle."

"Bruny's not used to having talent nit-pick his meals."

"Now go straight and you'll run right into it. Well he needs to get used to it. And by the way, where's our shooting script, Desmond?" Mary suddenly asked. "Didn't you say you had one?"

"I have decided to shoot without a script," Desmond announced, choosing not to tell Mary the truth that the mysterious Gerald was either an AWOL incompetent or a figment of a heat-induced hallucination, both of which made him sound weak and rudderless. "I was wrong to depend on a script. This is a documentary, Mary, and a true documentary uses no script; it is true life recorded in real time."

They both suddenly ducked instinctively as the low-flying, garishly-painted giant helicopter roared overhead, with the words "Haile-Selassie Mynbou" emblazoned near the tail rotor. It backfired loudly and briefly sputtered right over them.

"What the hell?" Mary blurted, ducking then looking up. "Somebody in that chopper shot at us!"

"That's the marketing people, in what I guess is one of Haile-Selassie's pimped out helicopters," Desmond explained as the chopper disappeared in the distance, a contrail of black smoke trailing it. "They don't have time to shoot at us, they're in too much of a hurry to get back so they don't have to listen to goats scream all night. Anyway, we have no script."

"You know, back in the sixties, word on the street was you could not wipe your ass without a script," Mary remarked. "And I heard the rumor about what you did with the first draft of Pyro."

"Well, don't believe every Hollywood rumor you hear," Desmond responded petulantly, recalling the incident quite clearly. He had indeed taken the first draft of Pyro into the studio bathroom stall, then came out a few minutes later and handed the smeared script to the mortified young writer, telling him that he "marked up a few revisions." That was the kind of director he was back then.

"But you can bet the second draft was a whole lot better," he told Mary as they pulled up to the replacement village, parked and got out of the cool and into the desert sauna.

Desmond stopped – he was stunned to see that Donato, Schuyler, Eric and Ricky had, in less than thirty hours, done a magnificent job creating a replacement village, which formed a semi-circle around them. Eric constructed three complete, realistic huts, framed, coated with wet plaster and painted to resemble mud. He had also painted on realistic-looking art and symbols. He created thatch from scrub to make authentic roofs, then spray-painted it muted earth tones.

There was also a total of eight hut façades, all cut from plywood and realistically painted. When viewed from pre-determined perspectives they looked exactly like real 3-dimensional huts. Donato had painted a large canvas sunset backdrop, and real vegetation was added.

The cooking contraption centerpiece of the new village was a marvel of primitive engineering art, and made a grand focal point for the documentary. The center was a fire pit, about six feet in diameter and encircled with large, matched salt blocks found nearby. Directly over the fire pit was a huge tripod, almost twelve feet tall, built out of 2x4s but dressed up to resemble tree limbs. In the crux of the tripod was a primitive 2-stage block and tackle, with a surplus rope descending down through the center disguised with strips of found Baobab bark. A large black stew pot, provided by Bruny, hung suspended about three feet over the pit. The rope passed through the block and tackle and stretched to a pulley at the top of a wooden pole then to a lever at ground level. There was also a rotating spit over the fire pit, operated by a large crank handle. Eric told Desmond he found some tarpaper so he stained it to resemble leather then constructed a prop bellows, which pointed to the center of the fire pit.

"Donato you and your staff outdid yourselves," Desmond declared to the pale and shaky art director as he and Mary admired the crew's handiwork. It looked like a real movie set. Suddenly things seemed a little better. "I have to admit now, this was actually a good idea."

"Thanks, and I don't mean to rain on your parade but did you go to the village yet?" Donato asked in a weak voice as he wiped his mottled red face with a handkerchief. "The real village? Something's not right, there's nobody there. Me and Eric went by to make notes on the huts and it's like the Afarkils packed up and moved out. It's a ghost town."

"I can't believe they just moved out," Desmond responded to seemingly more bad news. "Where would they go? They're all probably out doing something. I was going over there and talk to them anyway. Donato, are you about done here?"

"Just a few touch-ups, but Mr. Desmond I'm not feeling at all well …"

Okay, take a Bufferin and you and Schuyler stay and finish up. Drink lots of water. Eric, you and Mary come with me to show a unified front. Rick you got your translation book? I need to find and talk to the Afarkils – maybe offer them something to get them back on board."

"Right here." Ricky pulled the book from his back pocket and held it up. "I'm much better now. I've been studying."

Desmond, Mary, Eric and Ricky got in the Humvee and drove just over a mile to the real village. Along the way both Eric and Ricky expressed concerns to Desmond of Donato's health – mainly that he wasn't eating or drinking enough water. "He seems to zone out," Eric noted, "like he doesn't know where he is. And he drinks an awful lot of that nasty gin. I don't know where he gets it all. It must have been all that was in his suitcases."

Desmond emptily promised to speak to him later as they parked and got out. As Donato had said, the village looked completely empty. "I'm telling you the place is vacant," Eric observed as he walked in between the trees and started looking inside every hut. "They bailed on us."

"Mr. Desmond? This may not be a good idea!" Ricky warned. "They don't clear out like this without good reason. It's possible the whole clan got infected with some sort of communicable virus or something and went off for care. There could be Marburg, or Ebola germs floating around here."

"This is such bullshit," Mary grunted, her arms folded near the Humvee. "What are we supposed to do now, start driving all over the desert looking for them?"

"Good Lord!" Ricky suddenly gasped. "Do you think it's possible Donato caught something here and that's what's wrong with him?"

"Ricky, will you please stop obsessing about diseases for one minute," Desmond implored in growing disbelief as Eric walked around inspecting the entire village for the second time.

"Anything Eric?" he called out, his voice cracking.

"There's nothing here, Desmond. They packed up everything. Every hut's empty. Even the UN crates are cleaned out."

Desmond suddenly covered his face at the sudden and horrible realization that he had no society to film.

"Tell me you're kidding," he moaned from behind his hands.

"Sorry, I'm not kidding."

"Look at the ground," Mary suddenly noted, looking down, then up at the trees, "All the leaves are falling off these trees. Is it autumn here? Maybe the Afarkils move when the season changes?"

"Baobabs shed their leaves in the dry season," Ricky added, also looking up. "But it's strange they are doing it all at once."

"You two do realize I have much bigger problems here than the leaves falling off the damn trees!" Desmond shouted, startling the two. He was truly in hell.

"We understand, Mr. Desmond, but like Mary said, maybe there's a connection between the leaves falling off the trees and the Afarkils leaving!" Ricky stated, trying to restrain his boss from having another breakdown or worse. "It's something we should consider! It may give us a clue where they went, and why!"

Desmond looked down and stared at the loose Baobab leaves that surrounded the village. Ricky bent down to pick one up – it was still green. "Now that really is strange," he observed, turning it over several times. "Baobabs especially don't lose their leaves when they're still green. And look at the monkey bread," he continued as he picked a piece of the tree's fruit off the ground. "It dried up before it even ripened." Dozens of pieces of undeveloped, withered fruit lay strewn under the trees.

"Wonder if something's killing these trees and the Afarkils knew it, so they left?" Ricky continued, staring at the numerous bare branches as he walked into the eerily silent village.

"This is giving me the creeps!" Mary shuddered, refusing to set foot inside the village. "If there's a disease or something here that can kill trees what will it do to us? The Afarkils were smart enough to get out but we're just standing here, soaking in the killer germs."

"Well, something is going on here ... Mr. Desmond?" Ricky pleaded nervously to his frazzled director, who was only staring straight through the empty huts at all the nothingness. "It might be something in the ground, or in the water or even in the air, like that lake in Tanzania that released trapped volcanic gas and killed all those people last year. Mary's right, we maybe ought to get out of here."

"... Stop being so paranoid, Ricky," Desmond suddenly snapped. "We're not doing anything until we find something, anything that will tell us where the Afarkils went and why." He noticed an odd odor when he walked to a certain spot. "They can't have gone far ... and they're on foot. We can fan out and go looking for them."

"Oh, that could be very dangerous," Ricky warned. "They have as much as a two-day head start, and we have no idea what direction they went in or if they split up. This desert is thousands of square miles, with white-out conditions in this heat, and riddled with bands of armed militia who are fond of such things as castration. They could be literally anywhere ..."

"Goddamn it!" At a breaking point, Desmond suddenly turned at Ricky, "I'm interested less and less in hearing your reasons why we can't ...!" Suddenly he stopped, and his demeanor dramatically changed, like he flipped a switch. "... What smells like kerosene? Eric, do you smell it over there?"

Eric was at the far side of the village, walking back. He carried a very old pipe wrench in his hand. "I only smell the stench of defeat."

"I don't need that kind of talk right now, Eric! You want to be confined to camp for insubordination?"

"Sorry. No, I don't smell kerosene." He held up the rusty pipe wrench up as he approached his director. "But I did find this in one of the huts. I guess they used it to loosen the valves on our fuel tanks and drain them. Sabotaging bastards."

"I smell it too." Ricky tentatively stepped beside Desmond. "It's stronger here by their water supply hole."

"Their water supply hole? Here?" Desmond asked, pointing at the tripod. He turned to Eric. "They drained our fuel tanks, Eric? With that? How do you know?"

"Yes, there's water under this village," Ricky quickly explained, eager to capitalize on his director's calm side. "When the Afarkil family, or clan, would move they always settled near a water supply – a pond or spring or something. They would look for a grove of trees or certain plants that indicated water nearby, and set up camp. That's obviously why they settled under this grove of Baobab trees, because of the underground ..."

"Shutup Rick," Desmond snapped. "What did you say, Eric?"

"I said I can't prove anything, but they sure could have used this," Eric answered, waving the pipe wrench, "It would have easily cracked those valves loose."

"If the trees start dying, then that would be a clue that ...maybe they ran out of water." Following a hunch, Ricky pulled the long rope out of the ground. On the end was a small hand-carved wooden bucket full of water. He lifted it to his mouth and took a drink. Shuddering, he spit it out.

"They didn't run out of water! Their water's gone bad!"

Desmond took the bucket from Ricky and took a sip before spitting it on the ground. "It tastes like gas!" Suddenly he paused. "No ... diesel!" he announced. "Diesel fuel!"

"Diesel?" Eric walked over and smelled the bucket. "You're right, but how did ..."

Ricky's color drained from his face when the terrible truth dawned on him and Desmond at the exact moment. "Oh, shit shit shit – oh no ..." Desmond cried out with horror as he cupped his hand over his mouth, as if that would keep his head from exploding right there. "Tell me we didn't ..."

"Didn't do what?" Mary asked as she walked over. "Desmond, don't flip out again! Keep it together!"

"The spilled diesel fuel from the damn bulldozer!" Desmond shouted as he turned to Ricky, who almost crumpled in fear for his life. "Remember, Rick, you and Buddy had an accident with the bulldozer, and the tank ruptured and you spilled gallons of diesel fuel down a sink hole ..."

"... and into their water!" Mary finished the sentence. "My God, Buddy and Ricky contaminated their underground water supply! No wonder they hauled ass away from here."

"It wasn't my fault!" Ricky protested, "Buddy swung the backhoe bucket into the dozer! I was just sitting there! It was all his fault!"

Desmond stopped and suddenly got very quiet before he turned and walked out of the village toward the Humvee. Mary, Ricky and Eric followed, still bickering but scared he would leave them there. The three crammed into the back seat, none of them wanting to sit in front beside their director, who started driving slowly back to the compound without uttering a word. They all silently feared he was about to have a heart attack. On top of that the air conditioning refused to come on.

"Desmond?" Mary finally asked, leaning between the front seats, needing to break the unbearable tension in the vehicle, "this is not the end of the world, you know."

Silence.

"You aren't going looking for the Afarkils are you? Because Ricky is right, it isn't safe for us to start scouring the desert for them."

More silence. Mary could see Desmond's jaw flexing in anger, chewing a sinewy wad of mounting frustrations.

"You realize we made preparations for something like this. You should be glad we planned ahead."

More silence as Eric and Ricky exchanged worried glances. They were more concerned Desmond would slowly drive them all off a cliff.

"Desmond ... stop being such a child and listen to me," Mary continued, her voice rising. "We have a spectacular replacement village already built, and a talented group of actors to play the roles of Afarkils. We can still pull this off."

"Wait ... those actors are here to play the Afarkils?" Ricky suddenly asked, surprised by her statement. "Are you serious Mary? Was this the plan all along? I thought they were going to be stand-ins, or play bit parts, like salt miners and stuff! This is a documentary, it would be dishonest to use actors to ..."

Mary turned to Ricky, smiling far too broadly. "Why don't you try shutting your mouth for once? You are not helping!"

Desmond finally pulled into the parking spot at the compound and just sat there with the engine running. Eric and Ricky quickly bailed out but Mary stayed in the back, trying to talk Desmond down.

Suddenly he turned to face her. "Mary, tell your talent to get out here. We got work to do."

She raised her hands in a sort of victory salute. "Well okay then!" She got out and went off, shaking her head in aggravation at Desmond's arrogance but seemingly thankful he seemed to have come to his senses.

Desmond sat silently in the Humvee as the cold air finally puffed on with a clank and a shudder and Mary disappeared behind Isaiah's bunkhouse. He noticed that it seemed one of the jeeps was missing.

Desmond knew this could happen, he predicted it. He was afraid from the beginning that variables beyond his control could wreak havoc with shooting on location, especially a location as unstable as this. He knew from day one that he needed to hold dictatorial control over the production to keep it on track, and he was disappointed that he had failed to do that. He made a promise to himself to be more assertive in keeping the production on schedule, to be more of the "old" Desmond.

After several minutes he watched Mary walk back alone. He rolled down his window only four inches and spoke through the crack. "Where are they?"

"They're not coming out today, Desmond," Mary reported, almost remorsefully. "It's almost noon – their motivation is gone for the day. The weather has apparently thrown off their timing, and they've had no rehearsal time. Isaiah said, and I agree, that by the time we costume it will be too late in the day to get into character."

They'll pick it back up in the morning, they hope, as long as there are no other distractions. We'll just have to wait and see."

Desmond blinked. He couldn't believe what he just heard – he had just minutes ago promised himself to maintain control, so he was damned if the talent was going to dictate his shooting schedule. He turned off the engine but he could still hear something, like a train rapidly approaching. "What do you mean ... not coming ... in the morning? Tomorrow?"

"Yea," Mary responded, "I know it's frustrating but talent can be a little temperamental sometimes. But you know, as director you need to schedule rehearsal time."

Desmond looked at the steering wheel as the inside of the Humvee started to spin, and that horrible roaring train that had started out of nowhere escalated in intensity. He had heard that train before, now he was stuck on the tracks and it was bearing down on him and him alone, and he was unable to get out of the truck to safety. Fumbling for the door handle, he glanced out the window and didn't see Mary, but a woman bursting into flames with a sickening wail, then flailing and screaming that she was on fire from the misfire of an explosive charge on her back.

Suddenly the entire compound thundered from the torturous heat, and people consumed in flames dropped from the doors of buildings like droplets of molten torch slag. Revolted by the sight, Desmond suddenly felt a jolt of pain in his right arm and holding it up, saw it was as shriveled as a dead Baobab branch. Dropping the malformed limb, he was stunned to see the floorboard of the Humvee spiraling down, like a maelstrom. Shaken and nauseated while instinctively lifting his feet to keep from getting sucked in, with the imminent groaning reaching an apex, the air conditioning flickered and sizzled several times before blowing out with a loud pop. There was suddenly no air in the vehicle.

"Keep it together, Desmond!" Somebody inside his head shouted, like a man in a rowboat believing he could weather a hurricane.

"HOLD IT!" He shouted as he finally grasped the door handle and fell out on the ground, gulping in life-saving but scorching hot air, his knee screaming in pain. His voice rang across the wasteland like a cannon report.

Mary flinched and spun around. "Don't you shout at me like that!" she admonished.

"Stop telling me what to do!" Desmond screamed, out of breath, as he scrambled to his feet and stomped up in her face. "Everybody is fucking telling me what to do, what I need to do, what I have to do! And look where it has gotten us! But this time I'm talking!"

"I have been very patient!" He shouted, an inch from Mary's alarmed face. "I have given all of you leeway on your jobs. I have tolerated egos, broken, stubborn and stolen machinery, substance abuse, an insane, trigger-happy security guard, nasty weather, toxic spills, maggot-infested food, wrecked equipment and worst of all, a subject matter that was, frankly, boring, and is now missing! But even with all of these liabilities I still have a huge responsibility to deliver a documentary that the entire fucking world is waiting for, so I expect my crew to go to work when I say go to work! And that includes your top of the line, state of the art talent! Now, if you are not willing to go get them, then I will go get them. And if they will not come willingly ..."

Desmond's voice rose in pitch, fury and intensity with every word, "... then I will drag their lazy, pampered black asses out of their cozy bungalows and I will hold Buzzcut's gun to their heads while they happily recite their fucking lines!"

Mary stood stunned and speechless. No director ever spoke to her that way before. Ricky and Buddy tried to hide behind the Humvee, hoping Desmond wouldn't notice them and then lash out at them too. Buzzcut, hearing his name shouted, stepped out of the bus he napped in to see what the commotion was. Bruny stopped shredding faux-hydroponic lettuce for someone's lunch long enough to look at the show between Desmond and Mary. Schuyler leaned against her bunkhouse and stared. It seemed the whole camp slogged to a stop with Desmond's outburst. The tension was as thick and heavy as the desert air.

Livid, Desmond stomped and cussed in a circle. "So what'll it be, Mary? Will you go get your spoiled babies or will I have to be the one to …"

He stopped when he saw Isaiah walking purposefully from his bunkhouse straight toward him across the shimmering ground. He and the crew stood rock still, breathless as the muscular giant approached. It was a showdown at the OK compound.

Isaiah stopped in front of Desmond and the two of them just stared at each other: a rumpled, sweaty, limping, rapidly-aging one-time epic director, and a strong, perfectly-coiffed imposing character actor. They were a study in opposites. Desmond wondered somewhere in his mangled mind if Isaiah was going to kill him – he could probably do it fairly easily.

"Mr. Desmond," Isaiah started in a calm, rational, French-inflected voice as he folded his muscular, hairless arms that sported badly-drawn tattoos, like prisoners gave themselves. "I understand you are under much pressure to complete this documentary. Ordinarily, me and my fellow actors would tolerate the poor living arrangements, your second-rate crew and the terrible food to help you accomplish this goal. But we will not work for an unhinged racist. As spokesman I am ordering a work strike. I will also file a report of your unprofessional and bigoted behavior directly to Mr. Haile-Selassie. I know one thing he truly hates is bigotry."

Suddenly to everyone's horror Isaiah quickly and expertly pulled a Glock 9mm pistol from somewhere in his pants, flipped the safety with his thumb, grabbed and spun Desmond with his other arm and placed the gun tight under his chin. Everything in the camp froze. He leeringly turned the pistol from side to side, grinding the barrel into Desmond's chin before placing his own face mere inches from his director's, who barely had time to think about what was happening.

"I regard your threat to drag out our pampered black asses as bullying, and the threat of holding a gun to our heads as assault and battery – criminal charges I plan to report." Isaiah laughed, pulled the gun from under Desmond's chin and almost lovingly stroked the side of his head with it. "Oh, and I gave our bus driver, Carl Haile-Selassie, permission to take one of your vehicles back to Addis Ababa for the parts he needs to repair the bus and deliver us out of this hell hole."

Isaiah swiped the gun across Desmond's forehead as he shot a look at each of the crew members – daring them to rebut him – before he flipped the safety, returned the gun to his pants and abruptly released Desmond. "Have a nice day." He turned and walked back to his bunkhouse. Everyone heard the door close with a deliberate and final "snap."

Desmond had soaked his pants. He had not done that in years. Here he was, the eminent film director, throwing a child-like temper tantrum, screaming and making wild, unreasonable, even racist threats then peeing his pants. Then, there was Isaiah – a mere actor, for crying out loud – calmly and rationally giving the performance of a lifetime, beating him into the ground with unrehearsed but perfectly-delivered lines Desmond prompted and prepared especially for him before out of nowhere threatening his life. Right in front of his entire crew. Desmond watched his project, his career, and his life dissolve into that maelstrom in the floorboard of the Humvee.

Mr. Carswell, Mr. Haile-Selassie (the powerful investor, not the hapless bus driver), a dozen celebrities, even Brad Steele and Mi Lin were going to be livid. The quickly expanding desert suddenly seemed huge, distant and lonely. The overhead sun broiled him alive. Everyone stood deathly silent, turned like Lot's wife into salt statues in a still-life tableau.

Suddenly all Desmond could think of was that woman on fire, and a wave of guilt and sorrow for her rolled over him. He was turning inside out – slowly and painfully.

"Desmond!"

Everyone looked except Desmond himself. It was too much work to raise his head.

"Desmond!"

He finally painfully looked up to see another surreal sight. A panic-stricken Bruny was running towards him. "Mr. Desmond!"

Everything was in slow motion. Desmond reeled so badly from the pitiless heat, Isaiah's death threat, the missing Afarkils and the deaths and turmoil he had caused years ago that the sight of Bruny running was an incomprehensible illusion, a mirage. He stared, his mouth ajar. Bruny's voice slowed to a crawl. Every ripple and bulge on him bounced with deliberate and thunderous intensity.

"*Des ... mond ...*"

Time stood still, as if the desert itself screeched to a stop. Bruny was nothing but a smudge on a frozen, torrid tableau.

"DESMOND!"

Desmond came back to life. "For God's sake, what is it Bruny?"

"You gotta come quick! It's Donato!" Bruny gasped between gulps of cooked, salty desert air, "He's gotta gun in the pantry, and he looks crazy!"

"Does everybody in this fucking camp own a gun but me?" Desmond shouted to no one in particular. Ignoring his question, the crew immediately took off toward the food pantry leaving Desmond standing by himself. He hesitated a couple of moments as he shook off his encounter with Isaiah and his brain slowly awakened. When time finally caught back up to him he, too, ran as best he could to the pantry, his knee throbbing in teeth-grinding misery. Only Bruny remained behind, puffing and blowing, his hands on his knees.

"Let me through!" Desmond got to the pantry and clawed his way through the crowd. He stopped in horror at the door. Sometime while everyone was distracted by the confrontation out front, Donato either brought his own gun or stole one from Buzzcut's belongings and carried it into the pantry.

And there he sat, naked on an empty green bean crate, in the dim light, with a tablecloth across his lap. He had the unlocked pistol jammed in his mouth, pointed straight up, his finger trembling on the trigger. His eyes were wild. Apparently Bruny discovered him like this when he went to retrieve something for the night's dinner.

Eric arrived with a wrecking bar he snatched off the dozer and jammed open the spring-loaded door. The entire crew stood at the entrance, watching in shock as Donato sat like a hirsute, suicidal Greek statue. An almost empty Gordon's Gin bottle sat at his feet.

"Donato please don't do anything!" Mary shouted, her voice shrill and panic-stricken.

Desmond calmed himself. This was no time to be hysterical – he had to set his own problems and fears aside and focus. He had been in the exact same situation; he knew how it felt to be pushed into an impossible corner by circumstances beyond control, then attempt something outrageous. It made him feel qualified to talk Donato down.

"Everybody calm down and let me handle this," he ordered as he took another deep breath, trying to forget his terrifying confrontation with Isaiah before taking a step into the walk-in pantry. "Mick I'm coming in with you if that's okay."

The cool air felt great. He felt almost guilty for basking in the fresh air before talking someone out of a suicide.

Desmond looked at Donato, smiled and took another step in. "Hey Mick," he announced in a shaky but friendly, let's-go-have-a-beer voice. He ran his hand through his hair. "Feeling a little off today, buddy?"

He winced at the awkwardness of own words. He suddenly felt inadequate at being sincere in the face of multiple crisis situations.

Donato watched silently as Desmond took another step towards him. The rest of the staff watched breathlessly. Mary, standing in the back of the crowd with her hand clapped over her mouth, couldn't bear to watch and turned her head.

"Life seems kind of rough sometimes, doesn't it buddy?" Desmond asked soothingly as he took another couple of steps closer. "But you know, there are ways of dealing with the rough spots. And really, if you think about it, this is not one of them. What you're doing creates big problems and a lot of pain – for a lot of people. Believe me, I know – you remember what I did taping an episode of Dick Cavett, right?"

He was almost beside Donato. "And I even fucked that up. I missed and had to go through all these horrible operations, which led to painkiller abuse and – damn, you know the story."

Donato didn't move, but his eyes did seem a little less crazed than they were a minute ago. Desmond looked over his shoulder at the rest of the staff, who stood motionless at the door. "Why don't you guys go on and do something else while Mick and I hash this out?"

They reluctantly drifted away.

Desmond was now one-on-one right beside Donato. Feeling connected, he sat down on some industrial-size cans of third-world chocolate syrup and pickled Namibian chili peppers, courtesy of Mr. Haile-Selassie.

"Did you knock back this bottle of gin?" he asked, nudging the near-empty bottle with his foot. Donato stared, then weakly shook his head yes.

"Take the gun out of your mouth and answer me, please."

Donato slowly lowered the gun. His voice was a choking whisper. "Yea."

"You do anything else, Mick?" Desmond continued, staring at the bottle. "Any cocaine, pot, angel dust, speed? Anything like that?"

Donato shook his head no. "Where did you get the gun?" Desmond asked.

"Stole it."

The two of them sat in silence.

"Things really suck for me too right now, Mick," Desmond drawled, looking at the floor. "You know the Afarkils seem to have moved out. Disappeared. I wanted to go find them and beg them to come back but the staff thinks the desert is too dangerous for us to go looking for them. Back home, Madonna – the most famous performing artist in the world – has started a 'Save the Afarkil Foundation' or something like that. Advertising has been bought and paid for by a shady investor who might be Ethiopian mafia and apparently looks just like Idi Amin and may be just as murderous. They have excited American schoolchildren making an animated Afarkil cartoon, and now we have kid's meal action figures, all to promote this film, which is supposed to open in a thousand theaters in three months. My talent – who was my last resort, against my better judgment – went on strike, and one of my actors just pulled a gun on me after I threw a racist fit and called him a pampered black baby. I pissed my pants when I thought he was going to blow my head off. And now I don't have shit."

Donato looked at Desmond almost like he felt sorry for him. He laid the gun in his lap, picked up the bottle and took a drink. Then he held the bottle out. "You need a snort."

"Hair of the dog that bit me, Lloyd," Desmond responded, thinking of that scene in The Shining when Jack Nicholson sat in the bar, talking to the ghost bartender. It had been years since he completed the twelve steps, and while he occasionally enjoyed wine and especially sangria, straight liquor was forbidden. Resigned, he shot back a swig anyway and shuddered – it was hot, straight rotgut gin, and it boiled his esophagus all the way down.

"Jesus. I thought you quit drinking lighter fluid, Donato," he shuddered as he handed the bottle back. "Weren't you in detox for this stuff?"

"I positively quit drinking before breakfast," Donato answered hollowly before taking another gulp. "I was in Betty Ford to get off the anti-freeze and shoe polish, not the booze. And the Percodans. Oh, and those Dexatrim diet pills, and what were those damn things, Vicodins? And, let's see ..."

Desmond may have been at rock bottom yet was simultaneously intrigued and repulsed by the candor of the other man at rock bottom beside him, and thankful he seemed to be establishing a connection. Addicts, obsessives and compulsives like them could always find an alcohol-fueled common ground despite their immediate hellish circumstances. "You drank ... wait a minute, you drank anti-freeze? And shoe polish? What the hell?"

"Got hooked outside Moscow, making one of those Matt Helm movies. It's a low-budget concoction some of those constantly shit-faced Russky construction guys made up. They had a name for it ... but I called it a 'Brezhnev sledgehammer.' They mixed the shit together, cooked it and added straight ethanol. Then they had to pour it several times through a galvanized pipe to make it slightly less poisonous."

The hot gin going straight to his head, Desmond countered Donato's war story with a half-hearted, barely-remembered tale of how he drank a half-gallon of drug store wine then threw up blood the night his wife walked out after catching him getting better acquainted with a young actress-to-be who later turned out to be only seventeen years old. He left out the part where she went to jail at age nineteen after pushing another actor off a cruise ship near the Florida coast while filming a porn loop. Funny how little details like that stick with you.

Donato started to say something as Desmond took another drink of his gin. "Mr. Desmond, I'm really hurting here, and if you want my opinion, I think you should ..."

"The Afarkils have blown out of Dodge, Mick," Desmond interrupted, his head swimming from the heat, the alcohol and the stress. "We killed their fucking trees, set fire to one of their huts, poisoned their water and shot at them for coming just to say hello. Guess I would have run away too. And I have no clue where they went. But look at my track record – I killed people on my last film. And I only worried about my own career and felt sorry for myself. Now here I am, handed an opportunity to redeem myself, and the world is waiting for a movie I can't make. All the shit I'm going through here is just payback for what happened on Pyro. I know it. Gerald was right, I was set up to fail here. Karma can be a royal bitch."

Donato stopped and stared at the pistol in his lap. Desmond knew he was dragging his friend down even worse, and suddenly both of their situations seemed equally desperate.

"And that unhinged motherfucker Isaiah let that bus driver take one of my jeeps back to Addis Ababa and I probably won't ever see that son of a ..."

"DROP THAT GUN!"

A shrill, breaking voice suddenly shattered the quiet as Buzzcut burst into the pantry in full fatigues, and stood pointing at Donato. His other hand was on a snapped holster on his thigh.

"Just what are you doing, you asshole?" Desmond hissed in a startled, quiet rage. "Mick and I are doing just fine, so get out!"

"That crazy fucker's gonna kill me," Donato whispered. He picked up the gun and held it twitching in his hand.

"Mr. Donato confiscated one of my weapons from my personal belongings, Mr. Desmond!" Buzzcut barked, taking an intimidating step forward, never losing eye contact with Donato, whose eyes resumed their wild look as the gun trembled in his hand. "It is registered in my name only! Not only is he a common crook, but he is obviously an unbalanced substance abuser and may pose a threat to the cast and crew of this compound with his reckless thievery of ..."

"For God's sake ..." Desmond angrily sputtered, trying to drown out Buzzcut but desperately trying to keep his composure, for Donato's sake. "Just calm down, he isn't posing a threat to anyone!"

"I cannot condone stealing firearms, especially by substance abusers, Mr. Desmond!" Buzzcut rapidly shot back. "I took an oath."

"I said he's not threatening the staff you idiot!" Desmond shouted.

"Mr. Desmond, please! I have to request you step away so he can peacefully transfer the weapon back to me!"

Desmond and Buzzcut's conversation degenerated into a furious and senseless dog pound-style barking match. Donato's eyes darted between the two, as he fingered the pistol in his lap. Desmond suddenly stood in frustration. "Buzz, yes, this man is mentally unbalanced! He is sick and needs help! And so help me, if he doesn't kill you with this gun, maybe I will!"

"Oh, he's not going to kill anyone if he pulls that trigger, Mr.

Desmond," Buzzcut mockingly responded as he rocked spastically back and forth. "How many bullets are in that gun, Mr. Donato? Did you check when you stole it?"

Donato looked confused as Desmond took a deep breath, regretting his empty threat. "Now let's just stop. Nobody's going to pull any triggers," he implored, "Are they, Mick?"

Buzzcut chuckled. "Well, let's see if he will or not! Tell you what, forget handing the gun back! You're a pretty snazzy art director, Mr. Donato, so instead, let's see what kind of a shooter you are!" He released his hand from his holster and held out his arms. "Care to take one at me?"

Desmond may have been emotionally suffocating and not thinking clearly – but did Buzzcut just dare Donato to shoot him? Was he that stupid? He looked at him. "Buzzcut, what in the fuck are you doing?"

Buzzcut stared at Donato. "I wanna see if this man's got what it takes. Well, c'mon, Annie Oakley!" Buzzcut taunted, "I'm gonna take that gun away from you in about fifteen seconds anyway, so here's your chance to tag me!"

Stunned, Desmond could only stutter. "Buzzcut, no ... don't ..."

Ignoring Desmond, Buzzcut walked right up to Donato, grabbed his right hand with the gun in it and placed the barrel right on the center of his own forehead.

"The gun's not loaded, Mr. Desmond!" Buzzcut laughed. "Mr. Donato never checked the chamber! Go on and pull the trigger, I'll prove it!"

"That's it." Out of ammo or not, Desmond saw no choice but to take Buzzcut down himself. And just as he was about to shove away the deranged security guard, Donato suddenly jerked the gun back away from Buzzcut's head toward his own just as an ear-shattering explosion and lightning-like muzzle flash briefly lit up all three of their faces like a thousand-watt flash bulb. A bullet that was not supposed to be in the chamber tore straight through Donato's upper teeth and lip, fragmented his nose and disappeared into the pantry ceiling. A geyser of blood shot straight up while the concussion simultaneously thrust his body straight down, crushing the crate he sat on.

The unexpected blast knocked Desmond and Buzzcut backwards, with Desmond rolling into a protective fetal position, like an armadillo. "Son of a bitch," he barely heard Buzzcut say, blind and deaf by the report and stunned by the realization that he could have easily been killed. "I could have swore that gun was not loaded."

Desmond slowly looked up, his eyes burning and ears ringing. Through the blue haze he saw Donato splayed out in a half-sitting, half-lying position beside him on the crushed crate, unconscious, with the bottom half of his face a bloody mass. Desmond was horrified that he planted the bullet in his brain, and was probably dead.

Buzzcut sat in front of Desmond, his mouth open in shock and surprise, just before he struggled to his feet, took the hot gun out of Donato's hand and stood over him. An uninitiated glance at the carnage at that moment seemed to indicate that Buzzcut shot Donato in the face, as he now stood in front of him, cracking open the pistol to make damn sure there were no more bullets chambered.

"Looks like he just blew his nose off," Buzz observed of Donato's face, closing the chamber and scrutinizing Donato's unconscious head. "No exit wounds."

But from outside, Eric obviously did not know that Donato "just blew his nose off" as he burst into the pantry, blind with rage, centering the top of his head directly into Buzzcut's lower back. He slammed the security guard brutally from behind, sending both of them flailing face-first like a runaway locomotive into a wall of heavy cans. They hit the shelves with a terrible clamor, with boxes and cans falling all around them and the unconscious Donato. They tussled on the floor briefly before Eric managed to get on top of Buzzcut then blindly reached around for anything he could clobber him with.

"But I didn't shoot him!" Buzzcut screamed, on his back with his arms pinned by Eric's knees as Eric grabbed a large can of pork and beans that rolled past him on the floor. "I didn't ..."

He was silenced when Eric slammed the heavy can with both hands across his face. In shock, Desmond could only squint out-of-focus as Eric – sitting on Buzzcut's chest and completely out of control – beat him viciously with the heavy gallon can. Blood popped from Buzz's mouth and nose as the crazed Eric, screaming unintelligibly, rained one nasty blow after another to his face and head.

The pantry was raging chaos before Desmond could even think to act. "Eric! He didn't shoot Mick! It was an accident!" he finally yelled as he stumbled to his feet. "Eric! Stop! You'll kill him!"

He stumbled over to grab the heavily dented can out of Eric's hands just as the side of the can burst open, dumping brown, syrupy pork and beans over the two men and the floor.

Ricky and Schuyler raced into the pantry to try to stop the violence. Blood from Donato's head and Buzzcut's face blended with a gallon of pork and beans, creating a slimy, sugary bean-filled bloodbath. Ricky got in first but both feet flew out from under him on the slippery floor and he went down hard, crying out as his ankle made a sickening pop.

Desmond grabbed Eric's arm and stopped him from inflicting any more damage on Buzz's face with the jagged can, then he and Schuyler manhandled him off the prone security guard, who lay helpless on his back on the floor, his face a bruised, bloody mass. Both of his eyes were swollen shut, and his nose looked broken. He was practically beaten beyond recognition.

"Get Eric outta here!" Desmond yelled to Schuyler as she in an adrenaline-filled rush shoved the furious young man out of the pantry.

With Eric out of the way, Desmond was horrified to see the unconscious bodies of Donato and Buzzcut laid out among cans and boxes in a viscous, sticky puddle. It was a war zone scenario straight out of Vietnam-era issues of Look magazine.

Or worse, right out of Pyro.

Dazed, half-blind, mostly deaf and syrupy, he put two fingers on Donato's neck and felt a strong pulse. "Apparently he just missed major damage," he told Ricky, his own voice muffled and indecipherable as he helped him limp out the door on an eggplant ankle. Outside the pantry Desmond saw Schuyler ordering Eric to sit as he stomped and ranted that Buzzcut killed Donato. Finally, he sat down on the bare ground.

Before Desmond went back inside the pantry to drag out Donato and Buzzcut, he told Schuyler that Donato seemed to not be seriously injured after all, and instructed her, Mary and Bruny to care for the wounded outside the pantry. Since Schuyler had a year of medical school, she showed Bruny how to quickly dress and bandage Eric's cut hand and wrap Ricky's ankle. Meanwhile, Desmond was unable to muscle Donato out by himself, so he dragged an unconscious Buzzcut by the feet, leaving a bloody, bean-riddled skid mark all the way to the door.

Once outside, Schuyler helped him lay Buzz beside Ricky. She went to work on his face, which brought gasps from the others who did not realize the extent of Eric's merciless thrashing.

Mary calmed herself, then got up and tiptoed over to Desmond, purposefully avoiding looking at Buzz. "Is Mick really dead?" she tearfully asked, fearing the worst but asking anyway.

Desmond looked at her and shook his head, then put his hand on her shoulder. "I can't hear you."

"I said is Mick dead?" she asked louder, her voice cracking.

"Dead? No, Mary. I thought at first he killed himself but he missed. The gun went off by accident right in our faces and the bullet just nicked him. But I need some help getting him out of there, I can't do it by myself."

Overwhelmed, Mary suddenly burst into tears.

Suddenly decompressing, Desmond started crying also. He hadn't cried in years. He and Mary took a minute to hug each other and let it out.

Desmond and Mary's moment had a ripple effect. Suddenly realizing the gravity of the situation, Eric started weeping as he sat on the ground, his cut hand throbbing badly. Schuyler's lower lip quivered but she kept a straight face as she cleaned Buzzcut's face and set his nose before walking over to look at Donato in the pantry. Ricky was a horror-struck, weeping mess. Bruny could only stare at the ground in shock, clutching his chest, looking as if it were about to burst.

Inside the pantry it appeared a bomb had gone off; cans, torn, overturned boxes and demolished crates littered the floor, all splattered in a thick coating of bloody, molasses-saturated brown beans. In the center of the chaos sat Donato, the last man standing but splayed over a flattened crate.

"Desmond?" Schuyler called from the doorway.

Desmond tore himself away from Mary and walked over to her. "What is it?" he sniffed, wiping his eyes with a bloody handkerchief.

"Even I don't like seeing that asshole all alone in there," she whispered, her voice breaking and eyes welling as she motioned to the unconscious art director with the missing upper lip and destroyed nose.

"He's as much passed out drunk as injured," Desmond explained, "but you and I can get him out …"

Desmond suddenly felt close to Schuyler, and wondered if he should put his arm around her at that moment. Despite the altercation with Isaiah by the Humvee just prior to this disaster, and despite all the problems over the last few days, he felt no anger toward anyone, only overwhelming sadness and paternal compassion – traits that were missing back in 1970 at the accident on his last film.

He had grown, matured. He was now a thinking, feeling human being, and that warm realization swept over him, making him appreciate that no matter how bad things get, nothing was so bad that he had to abandon simple human decency. He was surrounded by breathing, emotional human beings, not workers, crew members, talent, union, essential or nonessential personnel, mush-mouthed marketing twerps or any of the other labels he attached. They were family, united by a horrendous shared experience that affected them all the same. Even Schuyler was upset over Donato, something he would have never imagined.

He suddenly felt closer to this group than he ever had before – except maybe Buzzcut. But he would deal with him later. First he had not an art director, but a friend to get out of the pantry and help, and several other friends who needed his friendship, comfort, and leadership.

CHAPTER THIRTEEN

As Desmond stepped back into the pantry, he thought he saw Donato's eyes flutter. "Schuyler?" He observed, "I think he's waking up."

She stepped inside the blood and bean-spattered storeroom. "Thank God," she whispered before the two of them walked carefully into the pantry across the slippery floor and knelt down. "Donato?"

Donato blinked a few times, and then slowly raised his head and looked at Desmond and Schuyler. His shattered lip and nose were ragged and bleeding, there was a splash of blood down his hairy chest and a bloody streak that pointed up between his eyes to the bullet probably embedded somewhere in the ceiling.

"Mick? Can you hear me?" The hair stood on Desmond's neck as he spoke. It was like witnessing a dead person come back to life. And although Donato's injuries did not seem life-threatening, he realized the concussion of a gun blast so close could have killed him.

He opened his mouth a bit. "I ... I need a drink," he whispered.

"Mary!" Desmond jumped up and ran outside, skidding in the mess on the floor. "Mary! Come quick, we need some help in here!"

"Bring some water!" Schuyler shouted, "we need ... forget it, I'll get it myself!" Schuyler followed Desmond out, ordering someone, anyone for some water that she could take inside.

Showing up with two one-liter water bottles, Mary audibly gasped in shock. Desmond and Schuyler heard her and spun around to see a bewildered Donato standing at the door of the pantry, holding the bloody tablecloth haphazardly around his waist. His face was mostly a crimson mess, and his teeth were unnaturally visible – Lazarus, back on his feet.

"I can't hear a fucking thing," he whispered in a sandstone voice.

Desmond, Mary and Schuyler turned the kitchen into a makeshift hospital for the wounded, which included Donato, Eric, Ricky and especially Buzzcut, who turned out to be the most injured of the four, thanks to Eric's thrashing with a 12-pound metal can. It was truly a miracle that neither the gunshot nor the exploding pork and beans did not kill anybody.

Donato remained mostly conscious while Schuyler shot up his mouth with Novocain, then sewed and bandaged his upper lip and his nose as best she could with what skin was left. He even weakly joked with her about how he was a much worse shot than he thought. When she was finished Desmond asked him several personal questions to rule out a concussion, but Donato shook his head, claiming he had no hearing.

"Good thing I'm a lousy shot," he joked in a hoarse whisper. "If I'd shot John F. Kennedy, he'd still be president today."

Schuyler half-laughed and half-cried as she fixed him up. "Shutup, ya stupid Brooklyn Greaser," she virtually shouted to the side of his head. Donato only looked confused at her – he seemed to be completely deaf. "We'll get you to a real doctor as soon as we can."

By 11:00 that night, swollen and in self-described "screaming pain" around his nose and mouth, Donato rested as comfortably as possible.

With things finally settled, Mary pulled an exhausted Desmond outside the kitchen hospital. "I'm really worried, Desmond. We can't get any outside medical help – I tried to raise someone on the radio for over ninety minutes to get an ambulance or a doctor sent here, and finally someone in Mr. Haile-Selassie's office picked up. According to them there was an assassination attempt, now there's some sort of military operation going on in Addis Ababa involving the Eritrean Liberation front or something, and the whole city is under lockdown, nobody in or out. They said sending a doctor is out of the question."

"Call the American Consulate there," Desmond suggested, suddenly worried.

"Nobody picks up – just a fast busy signal."

Desmond leaned back against the door frame and lowered his head for several seconds. "The hits just keep on coming, don't they?" he finally asked, lifting his head. "Since no help is coming, we have to fend for ourselves and make do with what we have. Tell Schuyler to inventory our medical supplies and use them as sparingly as possible. I'll keep an eye on the injured. Keep trying on the radio – call anybody you can find, and tell them to send a doctor the minute they can."

Eric's nasty deep cut he received on his hand when the metal can burst open required twenty-three stitches to close. Resting on a mattress on the kitchen floor, Desmond squatted down beside him as he made his rounds. "You know Buzz really didn't shoot Donato," he whispered. "The gun went off accidentally. But that doesn't mean your beating was not entirely justified."

Eric looked up at him with baby seal eyes. "I'm so sorry, I fucking lost it. I spent two days working with Donato on that damn village. I saw what a true talent he really is, behind the drinking. Then when I heard a gunshot and looked in that pantry, I would have bet a paycheck that security guard just shot him for no good reason. I couldn't take it."

"I can see your mistake."

Eric paused, then motioned toward Buzzcut. "I was half-afraid too I had beaten that asshole into a coma. What all is wrong with him?"

Lying nearby on a bare mattress with an ice bag on his swollen ankle, Ricky overheard and answered for him. "Schuyler said Buzzcut has a possibly fractured lower jaw, a broken nose, a concussion, at least one missing tooth and a bunch of cuts and abrasions."

Desmond struggled to his feet, grunting and groaning. "Thank you for the update Ricky. I can always count on you." He turned back to Eric and squeezed his shoulder. "Take care of that hand, young man. We're going to get you some real medical attention as soon as possible."

"I'll be fine, Mr. Desmond, I'm more worried about Donato." Eric then nodded in the direction of Buzzcut. "And him too, I suppose."

After checking the wounded, Desmond thought he smelled pot smoke as he walked unsteadily back to his bunkhouse. Only one outside pole light was burning since the gasoline supply was so low. The familiar sweet odor led him to Isaiah's bunkhouse, where he heard laughing and loud, drunken French-Arabic conversation from inside.

Desmond stopped, took a deep breath and knocked. The building went quiet. He knocked again. "It's Tom Desmond. I know you're on strike and you're pissed at me, but I need to ask you something. It's an emergency."

Quiet. Someone giggled, and there was some whispering, thumping and banging. Finally, Isaiah called out. "What do you want?"

"Do any of you in there have medical training? We had an incident while you were partying and we could sure use a doctor."

Isaiah cracked the door open. A hot cloud of marijuana, burned hash and alcohol burst from the opening. It seemed all of the talent was squeezed inside this one building, fogged in smoke. Desmond could see Isaiah's eyes were blood red. "Mr. Desmond, we are pampered black baby actors, not doctors! Remember?" The door closed to an explosion of muffled laughter.

Exhausted and angry, Desmond turned and on his way to his bunkhouse thought he heard someone throwing up behind the editing shed. He remembered Eric's admission that Schuyler was bulimic and started to walk over, but changed his mind. It was none of his business, and it would embarrass her. Or piss her off.

Arriving at his bunkhouse he laid down on Eric's immaculate lower berth. He felt as if he was the one beaten with that gallon bean can, as he replayed the day's events over and over, wondering what he could or would or should have done differently.

This was no longer a documentary about a vanishing way of life inside an embattled, famine-wracked African nation, it was a world war. He was not a filmmaker but a hapless trench captain, commanding a battalion of bloodied and shell-shocked soldiers, measuring success in inches only to be brutally pushed back by a much more powerful adversary. Every strategy up to this point had failed, and he had no idea what the next move would be. He even had a squadron of enemy combatants squatting in his own trench and was helpless to do anything about them. Meanwhile he was being peppered with fragmentation grenades, each one dropping more and more reminders on him that the world was eagerly awaiting a film he couldn't even manage to start.

Finally, he drifted into a deep sleep.

Sometime during the night, he sensed someone in the bunkhouse with him.

"Mr. Desmond?"

"Hm? Eric is that you?" Desmond thought his bunkmate's voice sounded much different. "You can sleep up top tonight."

"Mr. Desmond?"

Desmond opened his eyes and blinked. It was very dark but he could tell it wasn't Eric at all – it was a strange man in what looked like an outdated and muddy military uniform. One of his trench soldiers, maybe? Here to tell him that he was disobeying his orders by refusing to launch another suicidal assault on the story of a vanishing society? The soldier's head was blocked by the upper bunk.

"Mr. Desmond, I need to talk to you."

Desmond rubbed his eyes. Was this real or a hallucination? "Who are you?" he asked as the strange uniformed man kneeled down beside him.

"It's me, Desmond. Wake up." Christ, Desmond realized, it wasn't a soldier, it was Schuyler. His angel from the pantry. "I know you don't want to hear this right now but I overheard something really bizarre."

Desmond struggled to a seated position and grabbed her arm. In the dimness filtering in from the single outside pole light she was hazy and indistinct. "Schuyler? God, it really is you. What is so important?"

"I have reason to believe that these actors we got aren't really actors at all," she whispered. "I was outside the editing room a minute ago and overheard Isaiah and two of the other men talking near the porta-john. One of them sounded British and they were speaking a weird English-French-Arabic hybrid, I could only make out about half of it, but honestly they sound like homeless drug addicts Haile-Selassie rounded up and sent here. And they sound scared shitless of him. I'm afraid too they might be spies or even worse."

"I got the same impression when Isaiah pulled the gun on me today. But they came with such good credentials ..."

"They didn't come with credentials at all, they only came with Haile-Selassie's assurances to Mary they were actors," Schuyler countered. "It seems to be a big scam – those guys were talking about how they could buy a year's supply of crank or khat or some shit with the money Haile-Selassie was paying them. They're all stoned off their asses."

"Did you hear them say why they are so scared of Mr. Haile-Selassie?"

"Like I said I couldn't understand most of it," she answered. "But I thought I heard them call him 'monstre fou,' which if my French still works is 'mad monster.' That can't be good."

Desmond wiped his face with both hands. Now his camp was filled with desperate junkies who were probably spies. "We need to lock down everything that can possible be stolen."

"Especially the vehicles," Schuyler added. "Who has the keys?"

"I had Eric hide all the keys after Isaiah let that bus driver take one of our jeeps. Look, Schuyler, we have to act like we don't know about any of this," Desmond insisted, now wide awake. "Don't tell anybody – we don't have the manpower to throw them out. Mary said they got paid whether they worked or not, so maybe Isaiah was serious about them getting a ride out of here, and the sooner the better. Why would they want to hang around if they were getting paid anyway? Maybe that damn bus driver will come back for them soon."

"I assume we are going to abandon this project?" Schuyler asked, almost pleading. "We don't have any villagers and we got these scary imposter actors in our own compound. It's gotten pretty impossible to continue."

"I'm not abandoning anything yet," Desmond answered. "I have seriously injured people under my care and my first priority is to get them well again. They sure as hell cannot travel. That will buy me some time to figure a way to get those fake actors the hell out of here and then what to do about this documentary – if I can even pull it together at all."

"Those people worry me, Desmond – I think they're dangerous."

Desmond thought for a minute. "I don't understand something: Mr. Haile-Selassie supposedly wants this movie made at all costs, more I suppose to enrich himself than save the Afarkil society, I'm sure. He has put a ton of money into marketing and advertising. So I don't comprehend his motivations for sending fake actors here. I can't imagine him allowing them to sabotage the project or threaten the staff. That makes no sense."

Schuyler stood. "Maybe they're all his family and he thought this whole clusterfuck was a way to enrich his leeching in-laws as well as himself." She turned to leave. "In any case you need to come up with something. I'll see you tomorrow. Lock your door after I leave." Desmond watched her leave. It never occurred to him to accompany her for her own safety – she seemed so self-sufficient.

"Hey Schuyler …" She turned to him. "What were you doing behind the editing room at this hour anyway?"

She fumbled the question. "I was … throwing, throwing some stuff away. In the dumpster." Her voice suddenly got cross. "Why does it matter anyway?" She then hurried out.

"Christ," Desmond muttered as he watched her make it safely back to her room. He turned the deadbolt then laid back down. "Everybody's fighting a demon."

Desmond lay in Eric's bed until about 9:30 the next morning, and when he finally got up, he couldn't do much more than sit and stare. Wretchedly sore, he suffered a blistering headache and grinding tinnitus from the close gunshots, and actually felt that Donato came out of the episode physically in better shape than he. He was also worried sick about what Schuyler had told him about the talent as he walked to the porta-john then to the kitchen.

He met Eric inside the kitchen/hospital, and they both walked over to Buzzcut as he finally awoke. Desmond nudged Eric. "Go on, tell him."

Eric bent over him. "Mr. Desmond has asked me to apologize to you for beating you to within an inch of your life."

He stood up as Buzz seemed to drift off. "Okay, I did my job," he muttered before walking off to get some breakfast.

Desmond knelt beside Buzzcut and shook him back awake. "Okay, Eric apologized and now it's my turn. I am recommending your permanent removal from the shoot." The battered security guard grimaced then faded back into unconsciousness.

After breakfast Desmond asked Schuyler to assist Bruny in cleaning the pantry. A lot of food had to be pitched, because even though it was in cans and boxes there was blood splattered on it and no one wanted to keep anything with Donato and Buzzcut's blood on it. While cleaning, Schuyler found the bullet embedded in the pantry ceiling. She pried it out and threw it out onto the sand as Eric tossed bags of discarded food into the dumpster behind the compound.

The disposal of much of the food created a major meal challenge for Bruny; however, since the talent was "on strike," (a situation Desmond elected not to contest in light of Schuyler's revelations), Desmond ordered him not to cook for them, freeing his time to concentrate on just the crew. The talent, meanwhile, was informed by Mary on Desmond's orders that they had to prepare their own meals when it was convenient for Bruny and the staff. Desmond also ordered a padlock be kept on the pantry door.

Desmond remained at his desk most of the day, not planning the documentary but preparing a survival schedule just to coordinate all the setbacks and keep them from running out of food, water and fuel. He tried to strategize medical care for Donato and Buzzcut especially, as well as prepare a speedy exit of the talent off the property.

He figured propane, gas and diesel rationing, the food shortage, the disappearance of the Afarkils, and all the other disasters he was dealing with, including at dead last the restarting of the documentary, a goal he found virtually impossible at this point. In fact, the thought of giving up and driving away was one option he would eventually have to consider – but how would he explain that decision to Mr. Haile-Selassie and everyone else who was counting on him to bring this story home?

He left his door open in a futile attempt to get some air stirring – even though it had gotten dark the outside temperature was still about 100 degrees and even worse inside his bunkhouse. He realized as he worked that he had stupidly forgotten about the maternity hut, and wondered if the three pregnant women inside had also left with the other Afarkils. He made a note on his spreadsheet to go back there as soon as possible.

Eric stepped inside without knocking. "Hey Mr. Desmond?" he asked with some concern, "There's something weird out here you need to see."

Desmond never looked up. "Eric, where is Mary?" he asked, remembering his conversation with Schuyler.

"She's right out here. Hey Mary," Eric called out from the door.

After a minute Mary stepped inside. "What do you need?"

Desmond lowered his voice. "What exactly did Mr. Haile-Selassie tell you about this talent he sent us?"

Mary shrugged. "The ones you pissed off? Just what I told you. They're actors, Ethiopian mostly. I think one was born in England but apparently lived most of his life in Addis Ababa ..."

"So all you know about them is just what Mr. Haile-Selassie told you?"

"Well, yea. I don't know their specific credentials. None of them had resumés, and no Ethiopian films or TV shows play in America. Why?"

"No reason. And what exactly did you tell him we needed actors for?"

Mary rolled her eyes in frustration. "Desmond, forget that ..."

"Just humor me. What did you tell him?"

Mary exhaled a frustrated breath. "First of all, he thought we were Japanese for some reason. After I got that straight, I told him we needed stand-ins and long-shot doubles. Trust me, I told him nothing specific and gave him no hint that we were having problems."

Desmond sat back and rubbed his eyes. His vision was still blurred from when Donato's gun went off inches from his face. As he stood his back temporarily locked and he had to promptly sit back down for a minute. "Ah ... damn, I feel a hundred years old," he mumbled as Eric helped him out of his chair when his back loosened.

"What's so weird?" Desmond asked, remembering what Eric told him. "We're not being visited by those marketing people again are we?"

"What marketing people? And by the way," Eric continued, "Consider washing or changing your clothes – you still got Donato's blood on your shirt."

The three of them stepped outside and limped around back of the bunkhouse. "Take a look, Mr. Desmond," Eric observed, pointing with a bandaged hand to the southern horizon, "Looks like the Afarkils came back and built a soccer stadium."

Desmond was stunned to see the southern horizon awash in an eerie whitish-blue glow from mysterious lights that appeared to emanate from the original village.

Eric held out a pair of binoculars. "Here." Desmond looked through them and despite his temporary blurring could see far off in the distance what looked like the tops of large tower floodlights.

"What do you think it might be?" Eric whispered as they all stood and stared open-mouthed at the village. This was yet another alarming development that Desmond would have to add to his spreadsheet.

"... I don't know," he replied after a long pause as he watched the lights through the binoculars, "But by golly, we're going to find out, right now. Get Schuyler. Ricky is unable to travel so Buddy has to go with us as translator."

Buddy suddenly showed up at Desmond's side, as if he were listening from around a corner. Desmond turned to him. "I'm lifting your confinement – even though I should kick your ass for being Isaiah's servant boy."

"It wasn't my idea," Buddy explained. "Isaiah told me to be his assistant or he would set me on fire."

Desmond stopped at Buddy's revelation while Mary seemed hesitant. "Do I need to go Desmond?" She asked. "I don't see any reason for me to …"

"Yes, Mary, for God's sake you are as invested in this as I am. Let's go."

CHAPTER FOURTEEN

Desmond, Mary, Schuyler, Buddy and Eric got into the Humvee and drove toward the village, watching the artificial light on the horizon grow brighter and more focused. In fact, Desmond was so focused on the approaching lights as he drove around the base of oil drum mountain that he accidentally dinged the Humvee into an empty drum.

"Careful, Desmond!" Mary admonished, "Watch where you're driving ..."

She paused when a noise like thunder just behind them literally shook the vehicle. Desmond slowed to a stop and listened. "You hear that? What the hell?" he asked as an empty black drum bounced past them, then another. One struck the side of the Humvee. "Are we in a fucking earthquake now?"

"Drive Mr. Desmond! Fast!" Eric shouted, looking out the back glass. "Oil drum mountain is collapsing!"

Suddenly the Humvee was deluged in a thundering hailstorm of flying steel drums and waves of slopping dirty black oil. In a panic, Desmond fumbled to drop the vehicle into four-wheel drive and stomped the gas just as several particularly heavy drums slammed the back of the vehicle and shattered the rear glass while several more bounced heavily off the hood, smashing it badly and temporarily blocking the windshield. Everyone covered their heads and cowered low in their seats as drums bounced off the top of the vehicle, rocking it wildly and mashing the top down even lower with each raucous hit, the lids sailing off like flying manhole covers.

It was the end of the world outside the Humvee and pandemonium inside of it, with everyone screaming at Desmond to get the hell out of there. In a panic, and tightly gripping the steering, Desmond sharply jerked the wheel and gunned the truck in a zig-zag motion, rolling the drums off the hood while everyone held their ears against the deafening bombardment of hollow metal around them.

"Get us the hell out of here before they fucking bury us!" Schuyler screamed over the din of pounding and exploding drums. Desmond could barely control the vehicle as one almost full drum slammed the driver door like a runaway truck and sloshed viscous tar-like crude all over the windshield. Unable to see anything, he tried the wipers but they only smeared and made it worse.

Finally escaping the boisterous hell of flying drums, and with the thunder behind them abating, Desmond drove several hundred more feet, then drifted to a stop when he sensed they were out of danger. Once stopped, they all sat stunned for several minutes, thankful they were still alive and not entombed under a prison of steel and oil as the engine stuttered and a lone windshield wiper impotently flopped back and forth.

"Fuck me," Desmond whispered after a minute, before he tried to open the driver door several times, but it was hopelessly smashed shut. "Damn. Let me out Mary." Mary opened her door and got out in a daze so he could crawl over and exit out the passenger side. Buddy, Eric and Schuyler forced their doors open and also got out.

"Ah damn it." Desmond was crestfallen when he saw the vehicle. The body was mangled from front to back. There did not appear to be one square inch that was not dented, crushed, scratched or had something missing. The rear bumper, window and spare tire were completely gone. The front bumper dragged the ground, with only a single bolt holding it. The front quarter panel was crushed against the tire, and had already shaved a substantial amount of rubber away. One headlight was shattered, the other was pointed up at a stray angle and the driver door was mashed in so far Desmond was surprised he wasn't injured by it. The roof rack lights were smashed flat like pie pans.

Suddenly as he stood there the windshield simply collapsed into a thousand tempered shards.

"Is everybody okay?" Desmond asked as an afterthought, looking at the glinting glass pieces on the ground. He was slathered in dirty oil.

Schuyler plopped down on the ground, shell-shocked. A drum slowly rolled to a stop near her, one of a thousand spread out like a solid black steel sea behind them. Buddy could only stare.

"I thought we bought the farm back there," Eric whispered.

Finally, Mary spoke. "Nice driving, Desmond." Suddenly Desmond started laughing, not at what Mary said but how he heard it.

"What's so damn funny?"

"Nothing, Mary," Desmond chuckled as he wiped the oily windshield with a rag he found on the floorboard. He started zoning out, his wiping slowing to a stop. He was then outside his body looking in when he suddenly dropped the rag, looked up at the black, starless sky.

"I am Vishnu, destroyer of worlds!" Desmond shouted into the void. "I single-handedly drove a society into exile in the desert and brought down oil drum mountain! I am God, I am Sonto!"

He laughed, lowered his head and looked at them. "Well let's get going," he finally announced.

"Are you okay, Mr. Desmond?" Schuyler timidly asked.

"I am now," Desmond answered. "Come on, we need to go." They all got back into the mangled vehicle and continued their slow, creaky voyage to the village, just after the front bumper broke completely off and they ran over it with a jolt.

As they approached the village, they saw portable stainless-steel floodlights, set on tall telescopic arms with eight clustered halogen Klieg bulbs on each arm. They were movie lights, and they lit the village like daytime. Desmond stopped about 100 yards back, in the darkness. As they sat, they all could hear the drone of portable gas generators drowning out the erratic stuttering of the Humvee motor.

"We appear to have company," Desmond mumbled as he shut off the engine and they all gingerly got out of the vehicle, with Desmond again having to slide over to the passenger side. From his vantage point he could see in addition to the dazzling floodlights two large non-descript late model panel trucks, a van and two jeep-like SUVs parked just outside the ring of trees.

The group could also see quite clearly in the harsh white light that all the surrounding Baobab trees seemed completely dead, their leaves on the ground and their bark brittle and flaking. The light shining on the dead, skeletal branches cast eerie, jagged and elongated shadows across the desert floor.

Desmond suddenly saw movement inside one of the huts. He and his crew watched in silence, hidden in the protective blackness behind the lifeless trees and the glare of the lights, as three men, each wearing identical white long-sleeve coveralls tucked into shiny black boots, white cotton gloves and white hard hats with chin straps stepped out of the largest hut. Desmond was stunned also to see the Afarkil man they called Harvey – with the characteristic three stripes shaved into the side of his head – emerge behind them.

The three strange men and Harvey stood in front of the hut talking, their voices drowned out by the generators running the lights, as yet another man dressed in similar white coveralls came out of the back of the paneled truck outfitted with what looked like a gyroscopically-balanced, state-of-the-art video camera with a bright halogen light mounted on the front.

"Are they United Nations?" Desmond wondered out loud.

"Whoever they are they have the new Sony Betacam," Schuyler whispered. "I saw one at an electronics show in Vegas – totally digital, high-def, anti-shock, multiple zoom and extremely expensive."

Desmond suddenly realized something. "My God – the lights, the camera – they're filmmakers!" he exclaimed.

They watched the four men in space suits stand and talk to Harvey for a few more minutes before Desmond's patience ran out. "And I'll bet a paycheck they're planning to steal the Afarkil story away from me!" He stood up, seemingly getting angrier by the second. "This is my project, dammit! Come on, we're putting a stop to this!"

The others exchanged worried glances. "Desmond are you sure?" Mary asked. "We don't know who they are or why they're here. Do you think it's safe? I think we should just go back."

"Look how small they are, and I don't see any weapons," Desmond observed as he started walking into the village. The others stood and obediently but cautiously followed him into the Afarkil compound. Mary hung back at first, but not wishing to stay by herself in the blinding darkness hesitantly joined them.

As Desmond – with his crew bringing up the rear – approached the group from behind he said "excuse me" to make his presence known. The strange men were so engaged in animated conversation with Harvey they did not hear the group approach, just as the Afarkil men had surprised Desmond's group days earlier.

"Excuse me!" he exclaimed again, much louder this time. Still they did not notice. He stopped and crossed his arms, suspecting they were ignoring him, which he hated.

"Hey!" He shouted. They all stopped and turned around.

The white coverall men were Asian. The one with the Betacam turned and kept filming, his spotlight blinding them.

"Excuse me!" Desmond pronounced again, "Who are you men, and what are you doing here?"

Harvey's eyes grew large and fierce at the sight of Desmond and his crew. He pointed accusingly at him. "<click> So-ahma Beo, tua soa moa deeb!" Desmond heard him say. "Soa! Moa-deeb!"

One of the Asian men turned to the agitated Afarkil man and spoke to him softly in seemingly fluent Khoisan as the one with the camera continued filming. "Mea so-ahma <click> Seo moah de-ahma so?"

"So-ahm, me-alla <click> de-ahm, soa!" Harvey answered, nodding accusingly and pointing at Desmond.

The man turned to Desmond and took a step toward him. They sized each other up for a second before the man spoke.

"My name is Yukio Kanayama. I direct films for the Kodanoguchi company in Tokyo." Up close Desmond verified an insignia on his coveralls as "Kodanoguchi Films." "My crew and I, as you can see," he pointed out, gesturing to the other three unsmiling Japanese men, "are here to produce this documentary for our company of the Afarkil people. And you must be Tom Desmond."

"Yes I am, and I am here making the documentary of the Afarkil people," Desmond declared flatly. This was another goddamn problem he was going to have to add to his fucking spreadsheet. His staff exchanged more concerned glances.

"Yes, Tom Desmond. Many of us thought you were dead, but we are not that lucky." Kanayama motioned to Harvey behind him, his voice rising in anger. "According to our friend, the Afarkils have abandoned this village because of you. You came in claiming you were saving them by making a documentary, then you pointed a gun at them, poisoned their water, killed their trees, desecrated the dead and ran them out."

Kanayama's anger suddenly climaxed. "You also killed my project I have been planning for two years! This your twisted definition of saving?"

Desmond did not appreciate Kanayama's condescending and frankly untrue comments about his films or his relationship with the Afarkils. "Listen, Mr. Kanayama, I don't know what you heard but the Afarkils did not leave solely because of me ..."

"Oh, yes indeed, Tom Desmond," Kanayama furiously interrupted, taking a menacing step forward. "They have relocated several miles south of here, hidden inside a refugee resettlement camp with 2,000 other Eastern Ethiopians, just to get the hell away from you!"

Kanayama pointed to Harvey behind him. "This man, by the way whose name is not Harvey but Mobuto, told me all about their experiences with the American film director and his crew of misfits and weirdos who insisted they were saving their society! I planned this project for two years, Mr. Desmond! And now if I cannot negotiate a deal with Mobuto to rebuild their village and get them back, all my plans will be ruined because of your idiotic and clumsy interfering!"

"I do not know or even care who sent you or assigned this job to you," Desmond continued, angry and jealous that this man found his villagers and seemed poised to take over his project. "But you need to know that I have been in this desert seven days preparing my documentary of the desperate plight of the Afarkil people. I have gone to hell and back, Mr. Kanayama, and I am far better qualified to tell the world the plight of this tragic society, than, quite frankly, a bunch of no-name, Johnny-come-lately Japanese."

Kanayama shook his head in disbelief then angrily motioned to the empty village around them. "You say you have grown to know the Afarkil people? What do you call all this? Mobuto told me that you think you are the God Sonto, coming to save them, but you appear with weapons, bringing destruction to their people! Who is responsible for the burned hut with the Ethiopian man inside, who by the way died of dehydration in the desert after his truck broke down and was carried by hand three kilometers by two Afarkil men, just to give him a decent burial? And the poisoned water, and the dead trees? Know the people? I now have to beg the Afarkils to return and try to salvage what's left of my documentary because of you second unit idiots!"

"What second unit?" Desmond interrupted, hearing enough from the smart-mouthed director. "Where do you get off relegating us to second ..."

"You ignorant American asswipes are second unit!" Kanayama articulated almost in a shout, pointing at Desmond, his patience exhausted. "Your job was to shoot landscapes and sunsets! I am first unit! You were working on my documentary! This is my project! For over two years! I told Carswell I did not want or need a second unit, but he insisted! He said he would make my job easier, and besides he had to give his bimbo girlfriend a job!"

Mary's face dropped. "Hey, now wait a minute ..."

"And the entire point of this project was not to save the Afarkil society, but to show the world how they were saving themselves!" Kanayama pointedly continued, his voice furious but measured.

"They are not stupid and helpless, Tom Desmond! They are a smart, imaginative and resourceful people who, despite huge obstacles, wanted to return to their traditions and were actually making a comeback here – until you and your low-expectation bigotry arrived!"

"Hold on!" Desmond's voice cracked. "Mr. Carswell gave Mary a faxed copy of the project and nowhere did it say we were second unit! Did it Mary?"

Mary hesitated, just long enough for Desmond to suddenly think she had not been entirely truthful with him all this time. "Mary?"

"Tell him Ms. Semper!" Kanayama continued, interrupting Desmond. "What would possibly qualify you to be first unit on a documentary that the whole world is waiting for? Carswell's not an idiot! You haven't made a film in years! You don't know Afarkil culture, the language, or even the point of this entire project! Tell us Mary Semper! Tell us the truth!"

Mary grabbed Desmond by both hands and turned him away from Kanayama. Her hair stood almost straight out. "Okay I was positive at first we were first unit but after a while I thought it was weird that Wallace handed such a highly visible and important job to me with absolutely no preparation," she blurted, her terrified eyes filling with tears. "I entertained the idea that we maybe, maybe might be second unit, but since Wallace had the heart attack and never told me otherwise, I just assumed … dammit, Desmond, I really needed this job! You did, we all did! I really needed to show I could do this!"

Desmond put his hand on Mary's shoulder. "No, no, calm down Mary. Kanayama has you tied in a knot. If Mr. Carswell wanted me to direct, I'm sure we were picked as first unit." He turned back toward Kanayama. "I have never second unit directed anything in my life. And I want Mr. Kanayama to know that we took this assignment so seriously that we were poised and prepared to tackle it head on! We read every piece of literature we could find on the Afarkils. And …"

Kanayama listened in disgust as Desmond continued. "… And, and maybe I personally don't know their language, but we cared enough to bring a first-class translator, right here!" Desmond grabbed Buddy by the back of his shirt and dragged him up beside him. Desmond did not want this know-it-all Kanayama to get the best of him.

"First class translator? Him?" Kanayama reacted incredulously, staring harshly at Desmond. "Mobuto tells me this punk kid knows nothing of their language!"

Desmond was guarded, but eager to show that they were indeed in touch with the people and the project. "You're bullshitting, Mr. Kanayama – you are just trying to save your own ass. Buddy studied African languages and is an excellent translator. I can prove it. Go ahead, ask him something."

His eyes darting with anxiety, Buddy looked at Desmond nervously as Kanayama took a step forward and faced him. "Okay, young man, you are indeed a linguistic genius if you can translate to English what I am about to say in Afar Nilo-Saharan northern dialect Ongota: '<click> Kahn-me sua bo-ama <click> soa, mu-boa to mea.'"

He stepped back and crossed his arms. "We're waiting."

Buddy stood silent. "Well, go on Buddy," Desmond acknowledged, dead serious as he impatiently crossed his arms. "Humor Mr. Kanayama. Translate what he just said."

"Uh ..." Buddy stuttered, "Would you repeat it please?"

"Of course! Anything for the clever American translator! You ready?"

"Yes."

"You sure? You don't look ready!"

"Well, actually ..." Buddy stammered, staring at the ground.

"Of course he's ready!" Mary broke in impatiently, "Just repeat it!"

"<click> Kahn-me sua bo-ama <click> soa, mu-boa to mea."

All eyes were on Buddy. Even Harvey/Mobuto stared curiously at him. Buddy darted his eyes toward Desmond and licked his lips nervously. "Um ... you said ..." Buddy's eyes dropped to the ground and his whole body slumped. "Actually I have no idea what you said.

I don't know their language. I'm sorry."

There was about five seconds of stunned silence. "Then which Ethiopian language do you know?" Kanayama asked. "Tigrinya? Gafat? Mesmes? Which one?"

"I don't know any languages." Buddy glanced up at Desmond, then at his co-workers, all of them staring slack-jawed and fuming. "Again I am sorry. I'm so sorry everybody."

"Yes sir, you got a top of the line translator there, Tom Desmond," Kanayama declared after an awkward silence. "Best money can buy."

Desmond, as well as the rest of his crew continued to glare disbelieving at Buddy, their collective anger building like a volcano.

"Buddy," Desmond hissed, his forehead a deep purple, "Are you seriously telling me that you ..."

"You know what I really said to him?" Kanayama interrupted, turning to put his arm around his Afarkil friend. "Maybe Mobuto will translate for you – or Harvey, as you call him. His English is actually pretty good. He learned from one of your missionaries."

"Mr. Kanayama said," Harvey translated in a bizarrely American southern accent as Desmond and his crew stared in shock, "for ya'll rebels to pack ... your saddle bags ... and return back to the ... lunatic asylum from where you come from."

The Americans were thunderstruck. Desmond pointed at him. "... You speak English? What the hell?"

"Not fluent. Conversational," Harvey explained in a New Orleans southern fried drawl. "An American... Southern Baptist missionary lived with us ya'll ... some time ago. Yep."

"Why ... why didn't you fucking tell us?" Desmond pleaded, furious at this double-barreled revelation that the Afarkil spoke English and Buddy spoke nothing but English. Ricky had been right after all.

"I declare ... ya'll just needed to ask me. Ain't that a shame."

Desmond turned to Buddy, ready to tear his head from his shoulders. "It's his fault, Mr. Desmond," Buddy stammered, pointing to Mobuto. "If he would have told you from the get go he spoke English, I could have been just a PA and you wouldn't have even needed a translator."

Sensing a nuclear meltdown, Schuyler approached Desmond and put her hand on his shoulder. Desmond winced. "Mr. Desmond? The longer we stand here the worse this is going to get," she whispered over her director's shoulder, "We need to go back and re-group. This situation here now is not going to end well."

"Yes, maybe you're right," Desmond stated resolutely, his voice a furious hiss. He was enraged at Harvey, or Mobuto; at Buddy; at the anonymous Southern Baptist missionary who taught the Afarkils English; and at the Japanese for making him and his crew look like idiots. He was angry at oil drum mountain for trying to kill him.

He took a step toward Kanayama, although the Japanese director never budged. "Mr. Kanayama, first unit or not, I have the rights to this people and to their story, signed by Mr. Carswell himself." He glanced at the other Japanese guys, who stared back menacingly.

"You show me this signed agreement," Kanayama ordered.

"You ... you have to take my word for it because the fax has faded out. But you cannot make this documentary, so I strongly advise you and your white-suited flunkies, to pack your equipment and get the hell out, right now. I will not be held responsible for the consequences of you staying here."

"Mr. Tom Desmond." Kanayama was suddenly deadly serious at Desmond's overt threat. "You must know that we are here, to not just film the tragic history of the Afarkil society but their comeback, and now, their near-devastation at the hands of the clueless Americans with the white savior complex. But I am just as tough as you. I too know, without a shadow of a doubt, that you and your ..." Kanayama motioned frivolously to Mary, Schuyler, Eric and Buddy, "... your low-rent gofers and toadies, played deliberate roles in the collapse of this Afarkil society and the loss of my original project. These facts shall not go overlooked in my new updated documentary, for all to see and the truth be told. Mr. Haile-Selassie has been informed of this travesty, and I implored him to come here and witness it firsthand. I suspect he will not be amused."

Kanayama turned to walk away, a move that infuriated Desmond. "You waste my time, Tom Desmond," Kanayama shouted over his shoulder. "Got a story to tell."

Kanayama, Mobuto and the Kodanoguchi crew walked out of the village and disappeared in the darkness behind the larger panel truck.

Desmond was so angry he shook. "This isn't over, Kanayama!" he yelled. With a furious roar he turned and stormed through the lifeless village back to the totaled Humvee. He grabbed the driver's side door and yanked on it twice before remembering it was stuck. Even angrier, he stomped around the vehicle, threw open the passenger door and beat his way over into the driver's seat. No one dared laugh or get in his way. Mary, Schuyler and Eric gently got in the vehicle after he did, with Buddy climbing in the middle of the back seat between Schuyler and Eric.

Everyone sat on eggs as Desmond just stared over the steering wheel through the missing windshield across the battered hood, silently simmering like the desert landscape that loomed in front of him. Schuyler and Eric slowly scooted away from Buddy – they seemed to sense that Desmond was about to blow, and that Buddy was in his crosshairs.

But he suddenly turned to Mary, seated beside him. "First unit or second unit, Mary?" he shouted. "And don't lie to me!"

Mary jumped and shrank back in her seat. "Stop yelling! I'm, I'm positive we were supposed to be first unit. I'm positive. But you are right, Kanayama is lying! About everything! He wants this project so badly, I think he will say anything to get it. The papers were sent over and Wallace never clarified one way or the other because he had that fucking heart attack! He said he had a job for me and that was the one that showed up! Christ, Desmond, would I have gone through all this if I believed for a minute we were only second unit? I'm not stupid!"

Desmond paused for a moment after Mary's explanation. "So our investor, who really wants this documentary made, and who is overlord of the Ethiopian mafia, and murders goats in his spare time, is on his way here," he recounted in a voice barely a whisper. "I cannot wait to explain this to him. 'Sorry, Mr. Haile-Selassie, there seems to be a huge misunderstanding.' That bastard will turn me one limb at a time into goat sausage at one of his slaughterhouses."

After a minute of terrifying silence Buddy leaned forward. "Say, Mr. Desmond, that Afarkil could speak English after all – and can you believe he has a southern accent … I mean, he sounded like he was from Mississi …"

He never got to finish. Quick as a flash Desmond spun in his seat, grabbed Buddy by the collar with both hands and jerked him up nose-to-nose with himself as the others cowered in fear.

"Desmond!" Mary warned, "Don't do something you'll regret!"

"You never did know their language, you pathetic lying little shit!" Desmond growled at Buddy through clenched teeth. "You've been making it all up haven't you!"

Buddy licked his lips nervously. "Mr. Desmond. I am sorry. This job meant a lot to me … my Uncle Billy …"

"What exactly did you study at UCLA?" Desmond shouted.

"Um, actually I went to San Jose Community College … for a semester …"

"Fuck! I was warned about you!" Desmond shrieked, his crackling voice a cannon report inside that vehicle, as he jerked Buddy's head back and forth by the collar. "Ricky told me you were a fraud, and I didn't believe him! I trusted you and you made me out for a chump in front of an Afarkil elder and the Japanese, you ass-kissing idiot bastard!"

"But Mr. Desmond!" Buddy protested, "Mary told me when she hired me I wouldn't need to speak directly to them!"

With a fierce burst of strength, Desmond physically pulled Buddy from the back seat by his collar, over the seatback, across the dashboard and completely out the missing windshield, where he dropped him, kicking and flailing, across the hood into the dirt.

"Stay away from me and this project!" Desmond screamed as he turned the key and the engine cranked helplessly until after several tries it finally started and he turned to drive away, leaving Buddy in the middle of pitch black. "I never want to see your sorry ass again! You're off the shoot for good! Maybe Oromos will come and kill you quickly!"

Desmond gunned the gas and tore away toward the compound, the damaged vehicle rattling and jerking horribly and starting to smoke from under the hood.

"Desmond, you can't leave one of our crew members in the desert," Mary nervously warned him.

"The fuck I can't." Desmond turned to face Mary. "And you would be going out right behind him if I didn't think for a second that little shit was lying about what you told him."

"Of course I never said that, but if he dies out here it would make things even worse."

"Worse? Worse? Watch me."

With only one mis-directed headlight, he involuntarily played low-speed pinball in the dark with several errant drums trying to get around what used to be oil drum mountain but was now oil drum ocean, his passengers wincing and holding their ears with each jarring strike.

"Seriously Desmond, you need to go back and get him," Mary repeated.

Desmond ignored the request.

By the time they arrived at the compound the engine was spewing steam and Desmond was out of control. He sputtered to a stop, somehow knocked open the crushed driver's door and scrambled out. He was so mad that when he tried to slam the door it caught the side of his already injured knee. In stomach-churning pain, he grabbed the door with both hands amidst a rushing cloud of hot fog from under the hood and threw it open once, twice, three times – so hard it rocked the vehicle. Finally, on the fourth throw the door snapped from the hinges and spun across the ground like a giant, crumpled square Frisbee.

"You know what really makes me crazy?" Desmond shouted to Mary and Schuyler as he limped in a frenetic circle, "Even more than our brain-dead goddamn top-of-the-line translator? Kanayama and his men were wearing long coveralls and gloves! In this heat!"

"Yea, so what?" Schuyler answered, "And who cares?"

"But they looked cool!" Desmond yelled.

Everyone stood confused for a second. "Cool?" Mary repeated, "You mean ... what DO you mean?"

"Air-conditioned!" Desmond clarified as a shout. "Like they didn't even feel this overbearing, goddamn soul-sucking heat! How did they do that?"

"How do you know that?" Mary responded, "Besides, who gives a shit about what they have? We don't have one of our crew members because you left him in the desert!"

"Who indeed gives a shit about any of that!" Desmond screamed at Mary as he put the finishing touches on his meltdown. Kanayama had state-of-the-art equipment, a talented staff, air-conditioned coveralls and the cooperation of the Afarkil people. He had everything Desmond did not have ...

He stomped into his bunkhouse and slammed the door so hard the whole building shook, muttering "... including a reason for even living."

CHAPTER FIFTEEN

Desmond seethed in his bunk until around 5:00 a.m. with Kanayama's words swirling in his head. He did not buy the position that the documentary was supposed to be about the Afarkils saving themselves — would they have considered him Sonto if that were the case? I mean, they saw him arrive on the Rhino with the glowing eyes, right? They even called him Sonto, right?

Right?

Something had to be done. If Kanayama kept his word and made a documentary about his missteps on this project, his life and career, as well as all of his crew's, would be over. He would be back at the truck stop.

There was no way that would happen.

Around 8:00 it became too hot to stay in his bunk, so Desmond stumbled out to get coffee and try to eat something.

He looked and felt positively wretched. His matted hair, which had not been washed or combed in days, stood straight up. His face was a scorched moonscape of untrimmed, gray stubble. In the mirror his eyes were so bloodshot the whites appeared completely red, and they still burned from the gunshots the other day. His lips were a blistered mess. His knee was swollen and throbbing. His clothes were still spotted with caked sweat and dried blood.

In the breakfast line, Mary watched his hand tremble as he picked up a Styrofoam cereal bowl and spooned in some tepid generic cereal and reconstituted powdered milk.

"I was going out to look for Buddy, but Eric said it wasn't safe," she explained crossly. "I think you need to go get him before the temperature gets too high and he dies out there."

Desmond stopped. He had forgotten all about leaving his top-of-the-line translator in the middle of nowhere. He looked at Mary. "He can find his own way back."

"That's bullshit Desmond, and you got to pull yourself together, apologize to the crew, admit this project is over and get us the hell out of here," she finally declared in a combination of disgust, anger and pity. "You look like ... well, I won't say it. And you stink."

Desmond looked around and spotted Eric at another table with Ricky. "Eric, after breakfast go out and get Buddy please before he dies."

Eric nodded. "Shouldn't I go now?"

"When you're up for it. No rush."

Desmond turned back to Mary as Eric got up to leave. "Mary, I am assuming that talk of Carswell telling you he wanted two million viewers was also a lie."

Mary winced at the memory. For someone as unbalanced and rough-looking as Desmond he still had a good memory. "Not so much a lie as a motivator," she answered. "It did spur you to up it to five million, right?"

"Make an announcement," Desmond whispered in a rasping voice, "general staff meeting after breakfast. All essential and nonessential personnel. Attendance is mandatory."

"I hope you're proposing an exit strategy."

"For once just do what I fucking say without question. And no more lies or motivators."

After everyone spooned down their bland cereal, juice and coffee, they gathered around Desmond's podium under the awning, muttering their dissatisfaction with everything in general. Even Buzzcut – his face swollen and purple – was able to hobble over. Donato was unable to join them, and Eric had gone out to fetch Buddy. Desmond came over last, and as he stood at the podium one of the legs gave out and the whole thing fell over on its side, breaking off the top. Desmond just stared at it, then kicked the pieces away from him.

"People, as all of you know by now, our project has been overrun by interlopers," he asserted in a dry croak, knowing full well a mutiny was probably brewing. "They are a documentary team from the Kodanoguchi Film Company, out of Tokyo. They are respected world-wide for their films, especially those they produce for Japanese television. Their director, an egocentric fucking motherfucker smartass named Yukio Kanayama, studied under the legendary director Akira Kurosawa, and then worked in advertising for several years making commercials. His docs and commercials have won too many awards to count."

He shifted uncomfortably – his feet ached horribly, his knee was killing him and the sand flea bites seemed to be particularly vicious. "Anyway, they are talented, they have superior film making equipment, they seem to have a larger budget, they have the respect and cooperation of the Afarkil people, and, most importantly of all ..." Desmond took a breath. "They have these air-conditioned spacesuit coveralls."

Everyone exchanged confused glances. "How does this development affect our mission?" Desmond continued. "First, the Afarkils will not cooperate with us, so they and their village are temporarily off-limits. Only the Japanese know exactly where they are anyway – some resettlement camp south of here. Second, our talent is on strike, therefore we cannot use them, nor do we have any use for the set we built, because we have no villagers to populate it. As you can see, these developments stonewall our project and leave it wide open for the Japanese to appropriate. Now, I made a promise that I would deliver the world the tragic story of the Afarkil people. And that is a promise I will keep, regardless of the obstacles placed before us and whether or not I am first or second unit or goddamned dead last unit."

He took a deep breath and looked up at the cloudless sky. "Plus, I am determined to find out how those coveralls work, whatever that takes."

Mary stood up. "Seriously, how do you plan to do anything, Desmond? I mean, with Kanayama here, and with the Afarkils AWOL, and with the talent on strike, I mean – what's left? I wanted this project as badly as you, but we really have no reason to be here anymore. For God's sake I don't see how we can recover from this. We should swallow our pride, pack it up and get the hell out."

"Agreed, Mr. Desmond," Ricky concurred, to the mumbled wishes of the others. "I say it's time to admit that this documentary attempt is over, and for our own safety ..."

"Quit?" Desmond interrupted, visibly perturbed and holding up his hands to quiet his crew. "You want to quit? You want to tell Mr. Carswell and Mr. Haile-Selassie you're quitting? After everything they've put into this, all the money and sacrifices they made? All the endorsements they got? Anyone who wants to quit can leave now, but you must personally inform Mr. Haile-Selassie first! Then we will all try to attend your funeral in one of his goat pens."

He stepped back, folded his arms and waited several seconds. No one dared move, fearful not so much from Desmond's threat but that he would fly into a frenzy. Frustrated, Mary sat down.

Desmond realized, too, that he may have had an edge on the Japanese; he knew the location of the maternity hospital. He thought this was the time to announce it to the staff, just as Eric suddenly showed up.

"Look, whether we make a film or not, we aren't going anywhere soon," Eric announced in a loud voice. Everyone turned to face him as he walked into the meeting.

"Eric did you find Buddy?" Desmond asked.

"No, I didn't find him but I know where he is. Two of Kanayama's buttboys stopped me a few miles from here and said they have him and will deliver him back here shortly after what they called an interrogation."

Desmond exhaled in guarded relief. "Well, that's ..."

"But we have even more complications to deal with," Eric continued. "The Humvee has a cracked water pump and a leaking radiator and will never make it more than five or ten miles, max. Don't you all remember the closest gas station? It's south of Berhale, more than 150 miles from here. Even if we all crammed into the other vehicles, we don't have enough gas or diesel left to get us more than fifty miles at best. We would be sitting ducks along the Assab road, in 110-degree heat, out of gas and with no protection."

"We'll call Mr. Haile-Selassie to send transportation," Schuyler suggested in a trembling voice. "And what will they do to Buddy?"

"Mr. Haile-Selassie has been fed a load of shit by Kanayama," Desmond interrupted. "According to him he is already on his way here to investigate his claims. I would not count on him to pee on me if I was on fire."

"What does this mean for our food? Our water, and our safety?" Mary asked.

"We have enough propane to keep the freezer and pantry cold another four or five days at most," Eric continued, "but we're down to our last thirty gallons of potable water, which should last two days, three maybe four if we ration. But thank God we are swimming in bottled water."

Desmond stopped. "Thirty gallons of water? That's like a 500-gallon tank, and it was topped off before we got here! Where the hell did our water go?"

"There is what looks like a bullet hole about halfway down the tank, and we lost a lot through it," Eric reported.

"Who would shoot our water tank?"

"All due respect, it was probably when you were wrestling that gun away from Buzzcut the day the Afarkils showed up," Ricky interjected. "It went off four or five times, remember?"

"No one will be calling anyone just yet," Desmond announced in a loud voice, ignoring Ricky's speculation and changing the subject. "And, I admit it does look bleak for us right now – however, we have to realize that a documentary is still about to be made."

There was some confused murmuring. "But ... the Japs are now making the movie, right?" Buzzcut mumbled through a swollen and bandaged mouth. His nose was a big purple Easter egg. "Not us."

"Exactly, Buzz. Currently the Japanese are making the movie, not us," Desmond continued. "Some of you heard what Kanayama said –

that he will make sure to tell the story of how we, the ugly bigoted colonialist American white saviors, forced the Afarkils from their own village, where they were making a new life. He will tell of how we burned a body inside a hut, and we tried to shoot them for making a peace offering, and we poisoned the water, and we killed their life-giving trees, even though most of that was not directly our fault. I see what he is going to do – compare us to the nineteenth century miners who exterminated them over a hundred years ago. Who knows what other lies he may add? 'Look,' the viewers will say, 'Times haven't changed; the white people are still oppressing and killing the Afarkils.' So I ask you, is that what we want? Is that what we came and endured six or seven days of living hell for?"

There was universal agreement that no one wanted to be accused of repeating the roles of white conquering colonialists of the past, mostly in fear of what is would do to their careers.

"... so," Desmond continued, "so, I'm of the opinion that Kanayama's film must not be made, under any circumstances." There was more silence; Desmond was met with blank stares. "Is anyone in agreement?"

"We need to get Buddy," Mary ordered flatly.

"We will, Mary, bear with me a minute here."

"What are you suggesting? Sabotaging their project?" Schuyler asked, "Because I won't sabotage someone else's work, no matter how obnoxious ..."

"No one's using the word sabotage, Schuyler," Desmond insisted. "This has been a very problematic shoot. I think anyone who comes here would encounter the same challenges and difficulties that we have. I just want to ... make sure that those challenges and difficulties are spread equally. The Danish documentarians gave up, right? And the British?"

He remained quiet as his words sunk into the gathered staff. "My end goal is very simple: I want Kanayama's crew out, and I want that village back. And I want to know how those spacesuit coveralls work. I'm willing to make these things happen, as well as finish our project."

Buzzcut slowly stood. "I'm with you. Mr. Desmond," he muttered with a wink through a bandaged jaw.

"Thank you Buzz. Anyone else onboard?"

"Hey Desmond," Mary suggested sarcastically, "wouldn't it make more sense to let the Kodanoguchi team go ahead and make their documentary, then when they're done kill them and destroy their film?"

Desmond was aghast. "Mary! Please! That is outrageous!"

"How is it worse than whatever you're suggesting!" she cried, seemingly distressed with Desmond's relentless determination in the face of abject failure and even irate that he considered her mocking idea somehow more unethical than his own.

Suddenly Desmond caught a glimpse of Isaiah walking quickly away from the porta-john between the buildings. He waited silently until he saw him go back inside his bunkhouse and gently close his door. Good God, did he hear anything?

"Don't misunderstand me people!" Desmond continued in a normal voice, thinking that he was not getting his point across. "This is absolutely not a call to violence." He then quickly lowered his voice even more and pointed toward his crew for emphasis. "But the world is waiting for a documentary that everyone has failed to make. Think of the rewards if our version gets made, but more importantly consider the consequences if the Japanese version gets made! Where will your careers be after that? Who would hire you? You will be where I was in 1980, begging for a part-time job at Woolworth's. How about we pool our talents to get Kanayama to abandon this project so the Afarkil allegiance will revert back to our team? Then we'll have our movie back and we won't have to content ourselves with living in truck stops and working for Woolworth's."

"They find out you dropped a crew member to die in the desert we'll all be there anyway," Mary blurted.

"Please Mary, we know where Buddy is. Besides," he added, about to drop his surprise, "I have something the Japanese don't ..." He held his breath for a second. "Donato and I found the secret maternity hospital a few days ago, and there are three pregnant Afarkil women there."

No one seemed impressed, except for Ricky. "So it's true."

"Is it a real hospital Desmond?" Mary asked, "Because I'd like to admit myself."

Schuyler raised her hand. "Why the hell haven't we gotten a doctor from there to look at Donato?"

"There are no doctors there, and you can't admit yourself, unless I guess you're a pregnant Afarkil," Desmond explained, a bit disappointed by the team's reaction. "It's basically a large hut, hidden under some trees about a mile away from the regular village. It's very clean and calm inside, and it does offer a ray of hope for the survival of the tribe – I mean, clan. And I intend to capitalize on that."

"How can you be so positive the Japanese don't also know about this?" Ricky asked. "I mean, they seem to be one step ahead of us about everything else."

"Kanayama is a braggart, and he said nothing to me of the hospital. I'm sure he would have rubbed that in my face if he knew about it. And even if they did know about it, the women would not leave, or even let them inside. They are very cloistered and protective. But the quicker we run Kanayama and his guys out, the less likely they will get a chance to exploit what I consider to be my discovery."

Desmond saw the maternity hospital as his final ace, and he was not about to let it go.

Eric tentatively raised his hand. "So, you're saying that ... um ... if we can get the Afarkils to think the Japanese are the ones that ..." His voice trailed off and his hand went back down. "... I'm sorry. I don't understand crazy."

"It's not crazy! And I think you know what I'm saying, Eric," Desmond responded. "We just need to convince the Japanese that the conditions here are just too demanding for them to continue. Use your imagination! Maybe you and Ricky can slip over to the village after dark to see what you can figure out and check on Buddy.

Meanwhile, let's meet back here first thing tomorrow morning with some fresh ideas of how to insist Kanayama's team abandon the project. Frankly, this is our last hope, people."

"What about Buddy?" Mary asked.

"Eric, exactly what did Kanayama's goons say about Buddy?"

"Only that they found him, he was safe, and that they would bring him back after an interrogation," Eric answered. "They did not elaborate on that. I'm assuming too, for Buddy's sake, they have moved beyond their World War II interrogation methods. But Rick and I will go after dark and see what we can find out"

Desmond paused. Interrogation? What could Buddy possibly reveal to Kanayama, anyway?

"Buzz?" He asked as he concluded the meeting and everyone got up and wandered off, confused and talking to themselves. "I know you have been under the weather, but I would like you to continue your search for what happened to Gerald Camber, our scriptwriter. He couldn't have just walked away from here. And I'm worried what he may report to Kanayama."

Buzz stared for a few seconds. "Wouldn't you rather I go rescue Buddy?"

"No!" Desmond ordered, "I cannot risk you taken hostage too. I don't like that scriptwriter loose, he seems to know too much."

"Can do, Mr. Desmond."

CHAPTER SIXTEEN

Desmond thought as he lay in his top bunk, oblivious to the searing mid-day heat, that sometimes it was difficult to decide which reality was the authentic one. He realized his impeccable reputation as a successful film director and the very real accomplishments he enjoyed in the 1960s was now more authentic to him than the escalating surrealness of the 1984 desert in which he now found himself.

He thought of the time his mom – in one of her many reparations for his broken arm after getting involved with Jerry the Dr. Pepper Silver Dollar Man – took him to Disneyland shortly after it opened in 1955. The rides and attractions were themed so authentically that he was immersed in the experience, which made it real. He remembered feeling as if he really was floating down a night river through a flaming village taken over by Pirates. He really was at one point inside a haunted castle; another time really riding a jungle cruise past live animals. It was a thrilling, yet temporary experience. When it ended he would just walk out.

The present that stretched out in front of him was no different. It was as if he was inside a Disney attraction called "Danakil Desert 1984," painstakingly themed so authentic that he was immersed in an artificial experience, not what he considered a full reality. He wondered if there was a door somewhere off in the salt flats that lead into some more realistic time and place from his past. Which reality would then be the false one? The pleasant one he recalled from twenty years ago or the one presented to him in all its terrible, sadistic glory right now?

He recalled while filming Normal Paul that he became one with the sets and the story. While on the motel room set, he lived the environment and the action. He actually slept in the room where the film was made for the entire shoot.

Maybe today he was on the greatest set ever built, topping even the colossal constructions of the 1962 Cleopatra and the silent 1925 epic Intolerance. He was in a magnificent desert constructed on a little-used Los Angeles back lot out of thousands of tons of salty sand, government surplus bunkhouses, Quonset huts, foam lava formations, cement trees and leftover military vehicles. No expense had been spared. A union-operated crane took days to stack hundreds of barrels to create oil drum mountain, and a remote-controlled hydraulic piston triggered the recent avalanche when the Humvee hit its mark. Thousands of heat lamps replicated the scorching desert sun. Everyone was under strict studio order to maintain character 24 hours a day. It was a brilliant production, masterfully planned and executed.

So why was everything going so damn wrong? Who was really in charge, anyway? He wanted to stop the Japanese crew from accomplishing their task, but who was conspiring to stop him? Someone somewhere was pulling the strings.

"Mr. Desmond! You gotta come out here!"

Desmond slowly opened his eyes at the shrill voices outside the door. Thinking about Disneyland reminded him when his mom rushed him out of there prematurely when she was positive she saw Jerry lurking behind a life-size Donald Duck character, watching them. It wasn't the last time either – After they moved to Washington D.C., he could recall his mom suddenly hustling him out of grocery stores, post offices and department stores always for the same reason, gripped in a paranoia that she was being followed by a man who may have vowed some sort of revenge that day in the hospital room.

Her obsession got so bad she never bought Dr. Peppers out of fear a real silver dollar man would show up. She freaked out when someone knocked on their front door, and she even eventually had to go on anti-psychotic medication to deal with it. Desmond remembered when her paranoia bled into his own subconscious, and even he started to imagine seeing glimpses of Jerry until they moved near Chicago when he went to film school. The obsessions stopped after that; he assumed he and his mom both just outgrew them.

He suddenly realized it was dark – had he been asleep all day? He could have, he only dozed two hours last night. Was his long nightmare over? What was on the other side of the door? Would he walk outside and find himself in Los Angeles, on the set of a successful motion picture production? Or would he be on the breezeway of a truck stop, dealing his next narcotic hit with an acne-scarred pusher at the advice of Loni Andersin, the surgically-enhanced porn actress with her arm in a cast who seemed to know him personally?

Climbing down from his bunk, he watched himself in his mirror emerge from the shadows, like Max Shreck making his ominous appearance in the castle doorway in the silent film Nosferatu. He was a mess – his startling appearance even stopped himself cold for a moment.

"Oh no ..." he muttered, losing his train of thought. He struggled to get back on track. Where was he? What day was it? Was he really still in the desert? What was he supposed to be doing?

"Desmond, come out, we have something we have to tell you!"

Hearing the voice of his crew member outside made him compare himself physically with them. Mary, Schuyler, and Donato were all about the same age as he, within only a few years, but they seemed downright young and sprightly compared to him. They were brand new Corvettes, racing through the sunny California countryside on a brilliant Sunday afternoon. He was a 1973 diesel dump truck loaded with medical waste on a freezing Tuesday morning in Buffalo.

There was frantic knocking on his door. "Mr. Desmond, please!"

Desmond opened his bunkhouse door and stepped outside. He saw he was still on the Disney ride, still trapped in the immersive experience. The giant Klieg lights were shut off, and the set was dark. Then what was providing the stifling heat? Giant portable kerosene salamander furnaces maybe? The dark sky was a hazy backdrop behind the lone camp light, perhaps painted by a drunk Donato before the accident. He was met by Ricky and Eric and their long, jagged shadows. They were in full character.

"Mr. Desmond, we were just near the village and we saw Buddy," Eric wheezed, out of breath. "He was in a chair, outside one of the huts, holding a water bottle, with his left ankle zip-tied to the chair leg."

Desmond gazed curiously at him. "How did he look?"

"He looked kind of beat up but okay," Ricky sputtered, "but you need to know that something's going down with Isaiah and the Japanese!" Desmond's eyes grew wide as smothering reality returned. "Me and Eric saw Isaiah talking with Kanayama over at the village. Then we saw him get in one of their panel trucks and leave! And we think all the talent was with him!"

Desmond shifted his curious gaze to Ricky. "Why were Isaiah and Kanayama at the fake village?"

"Not the fake! The real village! You told us to go! Remember?" Eric interrupted. "After it got dark, Rick and I took a jeep over to check on Buddy and look for opportunities to, well … you know, influence their production," Eric admitted. "We saw Buddy in the chair, then I saw Kanayama between the trucks, and we could both make out another man as well – but not dressed like the others."

"He was black, but too tall to be an Afarkil," Eric continued. "We saw him briefly pass through under the light before he got inside the panel truck. That's when we could tell it was Isaiah!"

"Are you sure of this?" Desmond asked, his curiosity turning to irritation.

"No question," Ricky jumped in, "and I'm sure the whole worthless bunch of his fellow actors were in that truck …"

Desmond looked away. It appeared as if one of his problems was taking care of itself. "I'm glad they're gone. They weren't really actors you know."

"Wait … they aren't actors?" Eric asked. "Then who are they?"

"Schuyler overheard them talking. They seem to be drunks, addicts and gang members. But not actors."

"Well, whatever they are, they're also blabbermouths," Eric exclaimed. "I bet that asshole Kanayama now knows about your plans to screw up their documentary, thanks to them."

Desmond looked up at them. "What plans? How do you know that?"

"Kanayama himself told us. While we were crouching in the dark behind the trees watching the truck pull away all the floodlights shut off," Eric claimed. "We were suddenly too disoriented and frankly too terrified to move, and we heard someone walking towards us. It was so bloody dark Ricky and I couldn't see shit but we could tell someone was very close."

"Kanayama?" Desmond asked.

"Right," Ricky answered. "He said he had on some kind of night-vision goggles, and could see us perfectly, but we couldn't see him."

"What did he say?"

"He said he knew all about our plans to disrupt his project, and for us 'flunkies' to put our tails between our legs and run back, and tell you to stay away," Eric explained. "He said if we all packed up and left he promised next time not to mistake us for hostile terrorists and kill us. He sure as hell could have killed us there. You can't see shit in this desert after dark."

"Isaiah must have heard me today, although I don't ..." Desmond admitted after a pause, staring at the ground. "I saw him go back to the bunkhouse from the porta-john during our meeting ... wait a minute!"

Desmond Suddenly pushed his way past Eric and Ricky over to Isaiah's bunkhouse and tested the doorknob. Finding it open he burst inside and flipped on the light.

"Son of a bitch!" he shouted inside the trash-strewn cabin. "Eric! Check the other cabins!" Eric quickly ran to each of the bunkhouses previously occupied by the talent.

Not knowing whether he should laugh, explode, cry or all three after Eric announced they were all empty, Desmond just turned in a circle inside the stuffy cabin. The worthless talent was gone, but worse, they told Kanayama everything on their way out. And surely Kanayama would also tell Mr. Haile-Selassie, the "mad monster." Major shit was hitting the biggest fan in the whole world.

Desmond came out of the cabin and met Eric in between the houses as Ricky hobbled up a moment later. "Well, Mr. Desmond," Eric revealed, "It looks like we're the victims of ..."

"Looking for something, Tom Desmond?"

Desmond's blood suddenly boiled at the familiar voice. A moment later Yukio Kanayama himself, flanked by two of his crew members in identical air-conditioned coveralls appeared arrogantly into the light in the center of the compound, half-dragging a nearly unconscious Buddy between them. Their cameraman followed, panning his state-of-the-art Betacam around the camp.

They stepped over the battered Humvee door on the ground then stopped in front of Desmond, Ricky and Eric.

Buddy looked as if he had taken an old-fashioned schoolyard beating – his right eye was black and swollen shut, and a trickle of blood ran from his left nostril. He was covered in dust, and seemed to be hardly able to stand.

"Mr. Desmond, you look worse every time I see you," Kanayama observed, looking him up and down. "You know there's a new thing out, it's called bathing. You may want to look into it."

He suddenly pointed to Eric and Ricky. "Strange things happening at night in the desert! Last night I found your top-notch translator, wandering around in the dark like a crazy nomad. He claims you threw him out of the car like an empty gin bottle on the L.A. freeway! Then tonight I put on night vision goggles and catch your two toadies here snooping around the village."

Kanayama reached down and grabbed Buddy by his shirt collar and shook him. "I did you a favor and brought your stupid translator back safe. He could die out there!"

"Looks like he almost died at your hands," Desmond growled, noticing Buddy's injuries. "What did you use on him? Water torture? Nunchakus?"

Kanayama grabbed Buddy's face in his powerful right hand, squeezing his cheeks until his battered lips puckered. Buddy put up no resistance whatsoever. "Tell your boss Tom Desmond what happened to you!"

"They beat me up Mr. Desmo ..." Buddy moaned through a split lip as Kanayama and the bodyguards suddenly let go and let him drop face down in the dirt.

"You're full of horse shit!" Kanayama barked at the back of Buddy's head as he laid face first in the dust. He looked up at Desmond. "Oromo marauders – bad, bad people, high on Khat, roam this desert at night. I assumed he was one of them when we saw him in the dark so we immobilized him. Better we catch him than the Oromos – they would cut off his penis with a dull jile and leave him to bleed to death."

"You didn't just come here to rescue my translator's penis, Kanayama," Desmond snapped. "What do you really want? And I bet you are nice and cool inside those goddamn coveralls."

Kanayama took two deadly serious steps closer to Desmond as Buddy struggled to a seated position in the dirt. His face was covered with sand, and he was too beat up to brush it off.

"You know why I came here," Kanayama retorted pointedly. "I am fully aware of your plans to sabotage what's left of my Afarkil documentary – what you haven't ruined already. Be warned that any attempts to further interfere will be considered hostile, and will be dealt with most severely with no reservation. I suggest you leave this desert, before you do something even more stupid than everything else you've already done here."

Kanayama again bent down close to Buddy. "Hey, translator, translate this: I am an example of what happens to chicken shit spies." Kanayama looked back at Desmond. "I hear you are so disorganized your art director tried to kill himself just to get off this shoot."

"That's a lie, and Mr. Donato's condition is none of your business," Desmond snarled, his patience and goodwill at the breaking point. "That talent was a bunch of liars, too. I'm glad they are now your responsibility."

"I don't think they were lying when they came to me and made me a generous offer for transportation back to Addis Ababa. Tomorrow the giant will be relaxing in a hot tub, laughing at Tom Desmond and his pathetic flunkies still jacking off out here in the desert, thinking they are making an 'important' film."

Apparently awakened by the loud, animated conversation outside, Mary and Schuyler emerged from their respective bunkhouses to see what was going on. They both groaned when they saw who was paying them a surprise visit.

Kanayama watched as the two women approached. "Good to see you again so soon, Ms. Semper. Any more transportation deals you want to make?"

He motioned to his cameraman. "Get a good shot of the two Hollywood has-beens before they start walking back to America because they have no rides."

Mary was mortified. "Has-been ...!" she sputtered, too angry to finish her sentence as she wrapped her robe tighter while eyeing the cameraman, who dropped to one knee and leeringly pointed his camera straight at her and Schuyler.

"Leave our compound, Kanayama," Desmond ordered. "Now. Or face the consequences."

Kanayama looked incredulously at Desmond. "You're ordering me out? Seriously. May I offer a final warning to you, Mr. Desmond?" He turned to leave. "I suggest you find a way back home, or this desert will turn even uglier."

"That reminds me," he added as he turned one last time, "there was a significant development with the women at the Afarkil '<click> ma-jahna jen-a.' You may want to go take a look. Don't know what I just said?" He pointed at Buddy, still sitting in the sand. "Ask your top-of-the-line translator."

Desmond's jaw dropped in shock. He didn't need translation, he knew Kanayama was referring to the maternity hospital, a revelation that just robbed him of his last remaining incentive.

"Son of a ... who told you about the maternity hospital?" he shouted at Kanayama's back. "How did you know about that? What happened there? Answer me!"

Kanayama never answered as he and his thugs walked away into the darkness back to their jeep. The engine started and they watched two headlights drive off into the darkness toward the glow on the horizon.

Desmond turned back and looked at Mary. "Mary, what did he mean when he asked you about transportation deals you want to make?"

Mary looked as if she were about to cry. "How the hell would I know? Probably he was talking about when we first saw him at the village."

She paused, seemingly between tears and fury. "Did he really call me a has-been?"

CHAPTER SEVENTEEN

Despite the 2:00 a.m. hour, the compound was left in an uproar from Kanayama's visit – everyone was awake and furious, except for Mary, who let their predicament and the Japanese director's condescending words upset her so much she seemed to be falling into a state of depression.

A frantic, frustrated wreck, Desmond set the filthy and battered Buddy at a picnic table under the awning to find out what happened, hoping to capitalize on any improper behavior toward him by Kanayama. "Buddy I should not have dumped you out in the desert, and I regret if I caused you any harm. Now what happened to you under Kanayama? Did he beat you or torture you in any way? It's important."

Buddy took a long drink of water before he slowly looked up and made eye contact with his director. Desmond noticed his eyes were unnaturally red and bloodshot. The purple corona around one was visibly spreading. His bloody lips trembled for a moment before he answered.

"With all due respect, fuck you Mr. Desmond." He quickly looked down at the ground.

"I told you I regretted what I did," Desmond answered. "Can you please answer my question?"

Buddy never looked up. "You heard me."

"So that's how it will be?" Desmond stood and stomped off looking for Buzzcut, finding him lying on his mattress in the pantry nursing his throbbing bean can-inflicted wounds. Desmond pulled up a nearby chair and sat down beside him. He remained silent for a minute as he just stared at Buzzcut's maimed, bandaged face. More and more of his crew were beat to shit.

The documentary was now low priority against Desmond's

dogged determination to repel Kanayama's crew from the desert and regain control of the village and the Afarkils. This was pure survival instinct kicking in. His life, livelihood and even his crew were too wounded and defenseless against the Japanese and their threat to expose what happened here, and there was no way he was going to stand for it. He was also sure Kanayama had tortured Buddy for information. Water, food and fuel supplies be damned; he was willing to go to any lengths to get back on top. The trick was to convince his crew that he had a plan, and to hold out just a short while longer also. But how?

"Yes, Mr. Desmond? What did I do wrong this time?" Buzz finally asked, in obvious pain, peering suspiciously up at his distracted director through the bandages. "I can't find any trace of that scriptwriter you keep talkin' about, if that's why you're here."

"You didn't do anyth-" Desmond's chair suddenly burst into three pieces, sprawling him on the floor. He angrily kicked and shoved the fragments out of his way and struggled to a seated position on the floor, a chore more difficult for him than he expected. "You didn't do anything wrong – this time," he answered, his ass suddenly in pain from his stupid, sixteen-inch fall. "Goddammit. Listen, forget about the scriptwriter. Confidentially, how many guns do you have here?"

Buzzcut's eyes darted away from Desmond then back to him. "One."

"Don't lie to me," Desmond answered sternly. "Everyone has been lying to me since we got here. I suspect you have at least two. How many more?"

Buzz looked away. "Okay... I got three guns. I had four but you busted one up with a hammer."

"Three? Good. Now, where are they?"

Buzzcut looked confused. "What do you want with my guns?"

Desmond took a deep breath. He needed Buzz as an ally, so he decided to share his plan with him, however ill-formed at this point it was. He got down close and whispered. "I need your guns because

I need to put a permanent stop to Kanayama's project."

Buzz perked up but was still quizzical. "Put a stop to them ... how?"

"Buzz, you must understand," Desmond implored warily, "I have no plans to shoot, maim or kill the Japanese film crew in any circumstance, and I will severely reprimand anyone who even attempts to do so."

He leaned in closer and lowered his voice. "I think they beat and tortured one of my crew members and I cannot stand for that. I believe that my threats to report that to Mr. Haile-Selassie and his bosses back in Tokyo, and seeing we have weapons will convince them to leave, that's all. I believe that will give me the upper hand, because I need control of this desert back. Is that understood?"

"Sure, sure," Buzz agreed with a wink, "Loud and clear. The guns are in my suitcase in the bus."

Desmond struggled upright to leave. "I will get back to you as my plan moves forward. Now this was all very confidential. Not a word to anyone, understood?"

"Mr. Desmond?"

"What is it?"

Desmond watched curiously as Buzz fumbled deep in his pants. "I'll keep this confidential, but in return you drop your complaint removing me from the shoot. Deal?" He pulled a mini-flashlight from a zippered pocket and held it out. "And you'll need this on the bus. It's dark over there."

Desmond thought for a second as he took the flashlight from Buzz. "If you help me out, and keep your mouth shut, sure. I'll drop the recommendation."

Desmond left Buzz and discreetly crossed the compound toward the bus, noticing most of his crew were still huddled in the dining area, too hot to sleep, moaning and complaining about Kanayama's visit. Buddy was still seated at the table, and Schuyler was dabbing his bloody lip and black eye with a wet cloth. The lone overhead pole light flickered, casting the compound in dramatic, almost black and white strobe lighting.

Desmond quietly opened the bus door, clicked on the flashlight and crept through the dark interior. It was stuffy and hot, and reeked of old clothes and pot smoke. He found Buzzcut's 1960s-era battered Samsonite suitcase and retrieved from among several pairs of black socks, MRE's and year-old copies of Swank magazine three pistols: the .38 snubnose Donato had used to shoot off his nose and lips, a .45 that Buzzcut had in the pantry, and a brand new .38 Colt that seemed to have never been fired. Packed nearby were several boxes of ammunition for all three weapons.

"Wish I hadn't hammered up that AK-74 now," Desmond mumbled as he rolled the weapons and rounds in a sheet and carried them inconspicuously back to his bunkhouse, where he stashed them under his desk.

Once Desmond deposited the guns and ammo, he retrieved the hammer out of his drawer that he had used on Buzz's assault rifle and went back out and called Ricky, Mary, Schuyler and Eric together under the awning. Mary just sat down and stared sadly at the ground. Everyone else couldn't seem to take their eyes off the hammer in their director's hands.

"Listen, folks, I know you are frustrated and want Kanayama away from here as badly as I do ..."

"I'm at the point where I want out of here even more," Eric moaned. There was much agreement about that.

"Well, I have a plan. First – "

"I hope your plan does not involve our emergency radio," Mary revealed, almost as an afterthought. "Because it's missing. Somebody went in my cabin and took it sometime between yesterday and just now. Along with several pairs of my underwear."

Desmond paused as collective groans rose from the staff. "Wait – our radio is gone? Why didn't you tell me?"

"Jesus Christ," Schuyler muttered, dropping her face in both hands.

"That damn Isaiah took it, I'll bet," Eric pleaded. "We are really screwed now. We have no communications!"

"We still have those emergency smudge pots, right?" Ricky almost begged, looking from person to person, realizing they had been left cut off from the outside world. "We can signal aircraft with them. NATO planes fly over here all the time, don't they? Right?"

"I'm afraid we used all the smoke pots at the pig party," Eric replied with much resignation. "I said we should save some for an emergency, but you and Donato thought it was more important to burn them then go bowling with them, remember? Plus we are underneath a no-fly zone. No aircraft."

Desmond was getting sucker-punched by these revelations but he had to get his team back on track. "Sorry about your personal items, Mary, but forget the radio and smudge pots for now. We are not screwed. I have a plan."

Most of the crew scowled at Desmond's flaccid pronouncement.

"We need to first go see what happened at the maternity hospital," Desmond continued. "Then, we are going to visit Kanayama and his crew at the village. And Eric? I'm asking Buzzcut to go with us – he's very contrite about what he did, and we need to show solidarity. You're just going to have to put aside your differences."

"I have no memory of bowling with our emergency smudge pots," Ricky mumbled. "I'm an idiot."

"Schuyler, grab the good camera, some tapes and whatever critical lenses you need. Bare essentials only. Mary? When we get to the village, I would like you to go in and strike up a conversation with Kanayama and his crew for a short time, say, five minutes ..."

"Conversation? You mean distract them? What are you planning to do, Mr. Desmond?" Eric asked suspiciously. "I don't want anything to do with violence, and frankly that is where this seems to be going. And I feel naked and alone here without a radio – I think instead we should make peace with Kanayama so he can get us the hell out of here. He's our only chance."

"No violence," Desmond answered quickly. "I'm just going to convince Mr. Kanayama that it is in his best interests to leave, that's all."

"But Eric's right, the Japanese may be our only ticket out of here at this point," Ricky continued, to the agreement of the others. "Instead of distracting them I think Mary should beg them for a ride back to civilization."

"Distract them?" Mary suddenly asked, looking up at her director. Her eyes were red, like she had been crying. "You're certainly not suggesting using my body for bait, right? The whole idea is sexist and insulting. After all, I am just a Hollywood has-been. And Ricky's right – without the radio we're too vulnerable. Time to pull the plug, Desmond."

"No, no, first you're not a has-been, Mary. Kanayama was jerking your chain," Desmond pleaded, trying to soothe Mary's wounded ego. It was the first time he had seen her so defenseless and it concerned him – he was afraid he was losing her. "And I'm not asking to use your body for bait of any sort, and we are not pulling any plugs just yet. I have a great plan for us to stop Kanayama and get out of here, and we will do so when our objectives are completed, but right now I have a point to prove. I just need to distract them somehow, Mary. Mary are you listening?"

"Yes, yes I'm listening," she acquiesced.

"I need you to go in and give them a long-winded story about why you need to immediately leave the Danakil or something. Tell them that you have information that you need to pass along. Tell them that we need medical help for Donato, and explain our vehicle and gas situation ..."

Desmond paused. "... How is Donato, anyway?"

"He has an infection, and he's still in quite a bit of pain, but I gave him antibiotics and Percodan, so he'll live," Schuyler answered. "Nice of you to notice. And Buddy by the way has a broken nose. I gave him enough morphine to keep him down several hours. But they need real medical care – most of our medicines are out of date."

"Okay, so while Mary is distracting Kanayama, I, along with Buzz, Eric and Ricky, will go into their equipment and editing truck, destroy their equipment, then get out – without anyone knowing."

Buzzcut approached the group, dressed in full security regalia. He had on fewer bandages but his face was still a battered mess.

There seemed to be universal belief that Desmond had no plan at all. "Whoa, wait a minute," Eric interrupted, only glancing at Buzz, "I don't like this half-baked shit one bit. How do we know exactly where their equipment is? And exactly how are we supposed to bust it up quietly without them knowing it? This is insane."

"I know the biggest panel truck is a dorm with sleeping tubes inside," Desmond explained. "I've seen pictures. The slightly smaller Toyota truck is a mobile sound and video editing studio as well as an equipment truck, and I know those trucks are padded and completely soundproof. A bomb can go off inside and no one can hear it. Plus," Desmond added, "there's a toolbox in the back of the Humvee. It has some tools in it we can use to quickly render their equipment useless. With no equipment they have no movie, and will have to leave."

"Desmond ..." Schuyler spoke up, obviously confused and worried, "I don't care how good Mary is at distractions, she can only hold those guys off for so long before they find out the rest of you are destroying their stuff, I mean, come on! This plan sucks at best! These guys could be martial arts experts, or worse. They could kill all of us inside that bombproof truck and no one would ever know it!"

"If the equipment truck is unlocked, which I'm sure it will be, it should take no more than half a minute for four men to permanently render their equipment useless. Besides, like I said, they won't hear a thing. We can be in and out without any of them suspecting we were there, as long as they are distracted."

"But even if we get in and destroy their equipment, then get safely out and back here – they'll discover it sooner or later, and they will know it was us," Schuyler continued. "Then they'll come after us with a bloody vengeance."

"I thought of that, Schuyler," Desmond disclosed, taking a deep breath. "And I got the solution – before we leave, we destroy our own equipment."

This terrible idea was somehow getting even worse.

"Hear me out!" Desmond shouted, holding out his hands to quiet the protests. "Kanayama will never suspect us of doing such an insane thing to our own stuff! That's why I asked Schuyler to carry with us only the barest essentials! We blame the destroyed equipment on Oromo marauders, and he is forced to admit the same. This is genius, people!"

Desmond was losing his crew. This concept was too hard sell. "Look, remember we are doing this to save our own reputations. None of us, especially me, can afford for the Japanese to spread lies about what happened here. Right now, making our documentary is less important than preventing Kanayama from making his. I would rather commit myself to a mental institution than let their movie get out, so we must stop the Japanese at all costs, get that village back, and disable those damn air-conditioned coveralls. Then, with Kanayama out of the way, we can re-focus on what's important – replenishing our supplies, making the documentary that will save the Afarkils, and leave when we are done."

Desmond looked over everyone's heads to Bruny standing in the back, leaning quietly against an awning post with his arms folded. "Bruny, how are we on food?"

He shrugged. "We can make it another three days on basics, then maybe another two after that on rations. But that's it."

"Eric, if we ration gas and propane how long do we have?"

Eric thought for a minute. "If we cut the electric generators six hours a day and severely restrict driving, we might have two or three days on gas. We can always switch electricity to the propane generators in a pinch, but the trade-off is that will shorten power to the freezer and pantry ... but Mr. Desmond ..."

Mary stood, suddenly looking more confident than she had in days. "Mr. Desmond, I want to go on record that I officially think you have lost your mind. And I feel it is likely we may never get our documentary made or even get out of this desert alive. But goddamn it, at the same time, I realize I cannot afford to have my film career stopped dead by what that wild card Kanayama may say about what happened out here. That would make that little freak absolutely correct – I would then truly be a has-been."

She scanned the crew around her. "We would all be has-beens at best, and criminals at worst, in the eyes of every single person who watches his film."

The crew listened to her without a sound. "But none of us are has-beens," she continued, commanding everyone's attention. "Wallace entrusted me, he entrusted all of us, and I think we owe it to him to recover from this, because as a group we have no other options left. We are a talented collection of film professionals who encountered less-than-ideal conditions, and we let ourselves get overwhelmed by them. I'm as guilty as anyone. We can make excuses all day long about how circumstances prevented us from accomplishing our goal, but we will be hard-pressed to excuse or explain away anything Kanayama says about us that ruins our careers. Personally, I would like to see that little shit dead, but that's my problem to deal with."

She pointed at her director. "Desmond, if you can guarantee our safe passage out of here when this is over, I'll do whatever I can. But please, please, tell us how you plan to do that!"

"Thank you, Mary," Desmond nodded in appreciation of Mary's support. "I happen to know that the bus driver is on his way back with parts and fuel to repair the bus. I overheard it from one of the talent before they high-tailed it out of here. He should be here tomorrow. I anticipate once we force Kanayama out, I can focus on somehow getting the Afarkils back to the village and wrap the film in two or three days, tops. Then that driver will take us back."

"You're positive he's coming back here?" Ricky asked.

"He has to, he told me he has another job with his bus, Rick. He's not going to leave it here."

Seemingly appeased by the prospect of both stopping Kanayama and getting a ride back, the crew hesitantly stood and got ready to leave. "I hope you're right, Mr. Desmond," Eric noted as he stood. "I don't want archaeologists finding my skeleton out here in a hundred years."

"I guarantee it, Eric. Schuyler?" Desmond asked, holding up the hammer, "This is for you."

Schuyler stopped, confused. "What do you mean?"

"After you remove your camera, you need to use this to destroy the rest of the equipment. Don't be gentle. Make it look like Khat-crazed marauders did it."

Schuyler took the hammer and looked sadly at it. "I never thought my film career would come to this," she muttered as she turned to go to her editing room.

CHAPTER EIGHTEEN

After Eric pumped five gallons of their precious gasoline into the battered Humvee (leaving according to the stick a priceless six gallons inside the storage tank), and topped off the leaking radiator with water, Desmond retrieved the rolled sheet with the guns and ammo and discreetly stashed it in the back.

Shortly after that six of them got in and, using the glow from the village, drove the struggling vehicle out into the scrub far around the ocean of oil drums to look for the stand of Baobabs that concealed the maternity hut.

The desert all looked the same through only one stray headlight. Desmond clicked the light on and off high-beam, driving around seemingly in circles, anxiously searching for the tell-tale trees. Not only was he sandblasted in the face by the open windshield, but he also regretted tearing off the driver-side door, as sand ripped his side as he drove. The erratic engine noise was almost intolerable.

"It's the only stand of trees out this way," he shouted over the noise after almost a half hour of wandering aimlessly around, with his wind-whipped crew pleading that they should wait until daylight. "It can't be but so hard to ... wait ..."

The lazy-eye headlight briefly illuminated what appeared to be a stand of three or four trees ahead to the right, just past a lava formation. In the darkness, however, this stand loomed much, much larger and taller than the stand Desmond was looking for. In fact, it looked horribly different. And the closer he got he saw stuff littering the ground that he did not notice before.

Squinting ahead into the desert blackness at his vaguely defined target dead ahead, he braced when the Humvee suddenly ran over something big and soft, bouncing everyone out of their seats. "Careful, Desmond!" Mary shouted over the roar and the wind, "Watch the damn road!"

"What road? I can't see squat!" he shouted back, noticing more and more unrecognizable objects littering the desert the closer he got. Whatever it was, he apparently just ran over a huge chunk of it, and their vehicle seemed to run even worse than before.

Approaching the stand of trees, Desmond stopped the Humvee, shut off the coughing, hissing engine and left the lonely light on high-beam. Lying all around them were ugly shrapnel-like objects.

"Something's not right," he muttered as he looked out his missing door, getting sick to his stomach. He noticed also some of the junk littering the desert appeared very out of place: to his left lay what looked to him like a chunk of fiberglass hot tub. Many fluffy white monogrammed towels – some of them scorched and torn – littered the ground, as did several broken wine and champagne bottles.

"There are a couple mag flashlights back here," Eric suggested, retrieving them from a storage box behind the back seat. Desmond still had Buzz's mag light so he turned it on and shone it toward the trees. What they illuminated once everyone was out of the vehicle stunned them beyond belief.

A huge helicopter had inexplicably dropped out of the sky smack into the maternity hospital, utterly demolishing it. The chopper smashed into the trees and sat nose-down, its tail rotor almost straight up, precariously balanced, leaning slightly to the left. The entire front end was crushed, with the front cockpit compressed flat. Debris was scattered in a huge radius out from ground zero. The rotor blades had apparently roared through the tree tops on impact like a wood chipper, as shredded branches and millions of leaves littered the ground around the crash site. The maternity building was obliterated, pounded into dried mud chunks no bigger than a fist. Desmond's powerful flashlight illuminated the fuselage, where to his great shock and sorrow he read the familiar sign, "Haile-Selassie Mynbou."

"Oh, dear God!" Desmond cried out loud at the unspeakably horrifying, deathly silent scene dramatically lit only with dancing flashlight beams.

"It's a Sikorsky S-58," Ricky sadly observed, staring at the illuminated wreckage. "Looks Vietnam-era."

All six of them stood outside their hissing vehicle with their mouths ajar. "Desmond this isn't the helicopter that flew over us when we were driving to the replacement village the other day is it?" Mary asked. "The one you said had marketing people inside?"

"Yes ... this is it," Desmond moaned in the face of what appeared to be the one overwhelming catastrophe that surpassed all the others. He could barely speak. "There was ... a peaceful little hut, right here between these trees ... with three young pregnant women inside. There was fruit, and fresh water, and candles ... it was positively idyllic."

Buzz stood with his hands on his hips surveying the damage. He could only grunt. "What a mess," Schuyler mumbled, kicking a scrap of black metal.

The carnage was too much to take in. Desmond fell to his knees in anguish and placed both hands on the top of his head and squeezed, as if he were trying to press some sort of rational explanation out of this, the final shocking scene of a steady series of shocking scenes. "I swear, this place was just fine the other day when Donato and I found it!" he shouted in desperation, his voice breaking with emotion while fat, watery tears flowed down his face. "Somebody dropped a fucking helicopter right into a maternity hospital! Someone please explain how something this horrible happens!"

Mary placed her hand on Desmond's shoulder. "Desmond, I'm ..."

He looked up at her, like a child pleading to his mother. "There is no God, Mary! A merciful and loving God would never allow something this terrible to happen!"

"I know Desmond ... but please ..."

"Can things possibly get any worse than this?" he begged, clutching to Mary like a prisoner about to be executed.

Buzz stepped over and looked down at Desmond. "You said there was three pregnant Afarkil women inside. Is it possible they had their babies in the last couple days and left maybe before this happened?"

Desmond knew in his anguish that if the pregnant women were inside when the helicopter crashed, they would certainly be dead underneath that razor-sharp debris – and that thought made him want to curl up and die ...

But he paused – Kanayama obviously knew about this accident, and would not have been so off-hand about telling him about it if that were the case. Kanayama knew something about the women, and he prayed that maybe they got out before the crash. It was a long shot, maybe, but a scenario to which he desperately gripped. After all, so far there was zero evidence they were here. Perhaps Kanayama himself got them out.

"Look for survivors, people!" Desmond suddenly shouted, hoisting himself up and limping into the crash radius, his flashlight beam dancing all over the wreckage. "If those pregnant women or our marketing people are still here, we have to get them out immediately! Come on! Fan out and start looking! Our documentary depends on it!"

The crew walked half-heartedly around the wreckage, shining their lights into the debris. No one really wanted to look too closely, terrified of what they may find. "I don't think I can handle seeing any mutilated bodies here, Mr. Desmond," Ricky warned in a wavering, sickly voice as he tip-toed around the rubble.

The horrific reality of the situation becoming more and more acute, Desmond soon could only walk back and forth in a daze, staring open-mouth at the disaster unfolded in front of him. The passenger side of the chopper was utterly ruined, mashed flat and layered with jagged, twisted steel and aluminum shards. Someone strapped in there would have been positively annihilated. This was the worst possible development, and dwarfed all the other problems they encountered. He knew that if those pregnant women were dead, it would guarantee the death of the Afarkils, of his project and all their careers.

But worse, how would Mr. Haile-Selassie react to this? Or the world, who was waiting to see the film that would save these people? How do you make an announcement like this? "Sorry everyone, but it appears that a snooty marketing team in a wheezing luxury helicopter snuffed out the last remaining hope for the clan – but don't worry, we still have kids meal action figures to remind us of them."

"I honestly don't see any sign of people, Desmond – dead or otherwise," Eric reported as he peered with his light through the wreckage, breaking Desmond's concentration. Buzz, Mary and Schuyler all searched a little more earnestly as a group, sharing a flashlight, and they, too, reported seeing no bodies.

"I don't even see any blood," Eric added, squatting down and staring into the center hold. "Just helicopter stuff. I do see a bunch of loose condoms in here."

"No blood?" Desmond asked, his spirits buoyed just a bit. "How about the rest of you? Anything?"

"I don't see anything except a few clothes and some shoes." Mary called out from the other side. "Nice shoes. Manolos and Farragamos. And condoms."

"I see what's left of some beds in here," Eric called out, his voice muffled as he lay on his stomach through a gap between the fuselage and the ground. Desmond held his breath as he crawled out. "No sign of anyone in them, though."

"Same here," Schuyler agreed as they walked back around, "But I can't see back inside the bulk of the fuselage. At this angle it's too dangerous to get in there."

"It's almost like nobody was here, Desmond," Ricky observed in a cautious voice. "Are you sure we have the right place?"

"Ricky's right," Eric agreed. "Either there was nobody here when the chopper crashed or Kanayama's crew got them out already."

Desmond was heartened by these observations, clinging to that hope they all made it out. "Perhaps the women did get out and the crew jumped to safety," he speculated. But he wondered, who wrecked the helicopter? He never met the pilot – was it one of Haile-

Selassie's men, or a double agent? This was dangerously suspicious – it seemed as if somebody intentionally piloted the chopper straight into the only inhabited building in several square miles. Fifty lousy yards in any direction would have crashed it harmlessly in the scrub. Was this a terrorist act, a suicide bomber? Was it an attempt to stop the documentary, or worse, put an end to the Afarkil legacy? What sick human being would do such a thing?

As Desmond tried to piece the circumstances of this accident together, Eric walked up to him from around the chopper. "What do you suppose this is?" he asked, holding aloft what looked like a small black horse tail. Desmond took it from him and grimaced in recognition.

"That Eric, is a clip-on ponytail. I know a guy who ..."

"Sshh! What the hell was that?" Schuyler nervously asked, pointing her flashlight out into the desert.

"Was what?"

"I heard a moan, I think, over there," Schuyler repeated, her light dancing in the scrub. "It sounded like a moan. Maybe a wounded animal?"

Desmond's hair stood on end when he also heard a moan drift from somewhere in the darkness. He spun and looked frantically in all directions, before his flashlight fell on what looked like a half-full garbage bag lying in the sand just past the debris field, about 25 yards away. He watched it for a second. Then it moved.

"People! I think there's a survivor over there!" Desmond limped in the pitch-darkness in its direction, his flashlight beam bouncing off and on the dark lump, with his crew following closely behind.

Finally, he got close enough for his light to illuminate the mangled body of Brad Steele, the marketing guru, lying on the ground on his back, still alive. Even in the dark Desmond could see he was a battered mess; his stylish clothes were scorched, bloody shreds. Both his shoes were missing. His assistant Mi Lin was nowhere to be seen.

Desmond knelt beside him. Brad blinked up at him, almost unconscious. "Mr. Haile-Selassie ...?" he whispered.

"It's Tom Desmond, Brad." The others arrived and surrounded them, astonished at the finding of a living human amongst such carnage. "What the hell happened?"

Steele's breathing was ugly and rasping, like he had a chest wound. "I don't know," he gasped. "Engine blew ... spun out ..."

"Where are the pregnant women, Brad?" Desmond ordered, holding Brad's head in his hands, "the ones inside the hut? What happened to them?"

Steele coughed, and labored to speak. Desmond leaned in close to hear him.

"I saw aliens..." Steele whispered, "Short, white ... big round white heads ... black feet ... I hid from them."

"Those weren't aliens, Brad," Desmond whispered. "Those were bastard air-conditioned Japanese filmmakers."

Steele coughed. "In the crash ... wasn't hurt bad..." Desmond was suddenly horrified to notice with his light that Steele's legs and torso seemed to be crushed. Blood suddenly gurgled from his nose as he struggled to speak. His breathing was even more labored and noisy. Desmond leaned way in close to listen.

"... I was okay ... until I think ... a tank just ran over me."

"A tank? That's ridiculous," Desmond whispered. "Brad, there are no tanks out ..." he grimaced at his painfully ironic realization – Brad Steele, marketing genius from L.A., who survived a horrific helicopter crash, then endured three days alone in the brutal desert, just got squashed by a 3-1/2-ton SUV. He must have been the big lump Desmond ran over.

Oh my God.

"Desmond what did he say? We can't hear him," Mary timidly asked.

"I asked if he saw the pregnant women," Desmond divulged, suddenly very sick. "Brad? Stay with me!" Brad's eyes went cold, his mouth drooped open and his head suddenly slopped lazily to one side. Desmond lifted and gently shook his limp head. "Brad! No! Stay with me!"

Eric, Ricky, Buzz, Mary and Schuyler somberly gathered around Desmond and Brad. Unsettled by the sight of Brad's mangled body and shredded clothing, Ricky held back a choke, turned and walked a few steps away.

"Who is that, Desmond?" Mary asked in a whisper. "Is he dead?"

Desmond lay Brad's head down gently, placed two fingers on his carotid artery while he made up a story, then stood. "You didn't get a chance to meet him. He was our Marketing Director, Brad Steele. It appears the helicopter crash killed him." The crew looked down sadly. "It seems he bravely crawled from the wreckage in an effort to find and save his assistant. He is a hero."

They observed an impromptu moment of silence while Desmond covered his face and squelched his urge to throw up.

"What are we going to do with him?" Schuyler finally asked, a tear creeping down her cheek and her voice cracking in the eerie presence of a dead fellow American found in the middle of a foreign desert hell. "We can't leave him out here."

Desmond thought a minute. Schuyler was right, and he certainly owed Brad something for running him over – a secret he would have to carry to his grave. "I have a sheet in the back of the Humvee to wrap him in. There's no room inside but we can tie him to the roof. I think there's some rope back there too. We'll get him back to camp later and ... I don't know, put him in the freezer maybe."

"The roof?" Mary asked in astonishment. "The freezer? You aren't serious! You can't put a man on the roof!"

"You have a better idea, Mary?" Desmond blurted. "He certainly doesn't care at this point! And his body won't last a day in this heat!" He stopped and took a cleansing breath. He needed to keep it together – he was on his way to meet Kanayama and he couldn't tolerate any more stressful confrontations.

Mary just shook her head. "I guess not. It just doesn't seem right."

Eric walked back to the Humvee, cranked it started and drove it up beside Steele's body. Desmond reached through the broken rear window and in the darkness gently unwrapped the guns and ammo before pushing them under the seat. Seeing the coiled rope, he grabbed that also.

After wrapping and binding Steele's body, and after five of them wrestled it to the top of the vehicle and tied it as securely to the damaged sheet metal as they could, the crew took one last look for traces of humans in the wreckage.

"This is the only thing I found," Mary announced when she got back, holding up what Desmond recognized as Sh'niqwa, the Afarkil kid's meal clan "babe" as Brad Steele had called her. He noticed she was in pretty good shape, only slightly melted around her huge elaborate, gaily-painted headpiece. Her plastic breasts were perfectly intact.

Leaving the crash site, Desmond very slowly drove in rattling, stony silence around the debris field back toward the lights of the village with the single headlight off and with Brad Steele tied to the mangled roof.

As they got close, he killed the engine and drifted before stopping in the dark behind some gnarled scrub. As he pressed the brakes, Steele's badly-tied body slid halfway off the top, and his lifeless face peered upside down through the window right at Ricky, Eric and Schuyler in the back seat. They tumbled out fast.

Desmond convinced himself he did not run over Steele as they wrestled him back up on top and re-tied him. There was no way. It was a piece of helicopter junk he ran over. Yes, it was.

The village was awash in the brilliant floodlights, which cast the village in stark high-contrast German expressionist black and white. The harsh, direct lighting looked more like a theater set than an actual village. A single Japanese walked through, looking ghostly not only in his white coveralls and hard hat, but with a clear oxygen mask over his face, connected via a clear tube to a small tank on his back. No wonder Steele mistook them for aliens.

The "dorm" truck and smaller equipment truck were plainly visible to the far left of the village. From Desmond and his crew's angle, however, they couldn't tell if the back was open or not. The rest of the crew was nowhere to be seen.

"Look at him," Desmond grumbled as he watched the man walk through the village, "running around like he owns the place with his oxygen and air-conditioned suit. They're not interested in saving that village or its people – they only want to ruin my career and make a name for themselves."

"You know, I could swear I saw headlights way out in the darkness just now," Schuyler whispered softly, looking behind them. "But now they're gone. Maybe I'm cracking up too."

"It's common to see mirage lights in this desert," Ricky responded before turning back to his director. "Mr. Desmond can you please be a little more specific about what we are doing here?" He seemed to want this whole thing over.

"Desmond?" Mary asked in a nervous voice, "I can't do it. I can't go in there."

Desmond winced and looked at her with pleading eyes. "But ... why not, Mary? I need Kanayama and his men distracted so we can get unnoticed to their equipment truck!"

"Well ... Kanayama and I have sort of a history, I think," she admitted. Desmond glared at her and held his breath – what the hell was she going to drop in his lap now? "He was introduced to me by another producer at an Inoshiro Honda festival in Tokyo sometime in the late seventies. We had drinks and poppers in one of those bizarre strip clubs where the servers dress like school girls, then we wound up sleeping together. It was a stupid one-time thing. I did some embarrassing stuff, and it's really weird now."

Desmond was as confused as he was infuriated. "What ... what do you mean you think you have a history with him?" He demanded.

"I mean I'm pretty sure it's him. He was the same arrogant little piss he was in our compound a little while ago. It clicked then."

Desmond threw up his hands and turned around. "Hell of a time to tell me, Mary," he announced as he stomped toward the back of the vehicle. Mary just sat in the passenger seat, staring, nervously chewing her fingernails.

"Did he call you?" Desmond suddenly asked Mary as he reached into the back.

"What?" Mary asked, turning to look at him.

"Did Kanayama ever call you after that one night?"

"Hell no he never called."

"Then you're the spurned lover," Desmond suggested, walking back and looking through the missing door at her. "You need to confront him. Hold it over his head. Tell him some bullshit of how you thought he loved you then abandoned you. And he fucking owes you now."

"Tell him you had a kid nine months after the Honda Festival," Eric suggested, overhearing the conversation. "An imperious, beady-eyed little shit of a kid."

Mary stared out the missing windshield. "I'm not going to tell him about a kid – that makes me sound desperate. But you know ... he should have called. And he said he would. And he didn't. I hate that. It's so cliché."

"Of course it's cliché. And I think he at least owes you an explanation," Desmond prodded, walking back toward the rear of the vehicle and knowing he was manipulating Mary into confronting him. "You deserve better. I mean he thought enough of you to sleep with you then, now here he is today calling you a second unit has-been. He used you, now he's a sexist asshole, in my opinion. He acts like he doesn't even remember you. You apparently meant nothing to him. Yet another easy American broad to take advantage of."

"Buzz?" Desmond asked, intentionally leaving Mary to chew on his inflammatory suggestion. "Can you help me out here?" Buzzcut walked around back, and found Desmond producing his three guns from the back. Schuyler, Ricky and Eric saw what was going on also.

"Whoa! Wait a minute!" Eric blurted, "What's with the guns? Nobody said anything about guns!" Ricky also backed up a step, his mouth open in astonishment. The underhanded equipment-bashing spy stuff seemed to make him nervous enough, but the addition of loaded weapons bumped his nervousness to panic.

"These are just for our own protection," Desmond answered calmly. "Buzz will carry one, since he obviously has some practice. I will carry one with me and ..."

"Desmond?" Mary asked as she got out of the Humvee. She seemed angry. "You're right, I've got to confront that sexist SOB. He owes me. At least maybe I can get an apology while I 'distract' him. But I want a weapon as well."

"You know how to use this?" Desmond asked as he handed Mary the .38 Colt after Buzzcut loaded it. "And by distract I hope you mean you won't shoot him. For defensive use only in an emergency."

"I took shooting lessons from the same guy who trained Mel Gibson for Road Warrior," Mary claimed in a blank voice as she pushed the gun in the rear waistband of her jeans.

Buzz gladly loaded the .45 and snapped it in a thigh holster built into his cargo pants, and Desmond tucked the .38 caliber snubnose in the back of his pants and pulled his shirt down over it. Schuyler got the camera out, hoisted it onto her shoulder and turned it on.

"How's the camera?" Desmond asked. The sun was breaking on the horizon. He looked at his watch – it was almost 5:00 a.m., and the temperature was starting to climb. "I'm committed to capturing something on tape here."

"So far so good," Schuyler answered, looking through the viewfinder. "What am I shooting?"

"We will need just a minute or two to circle around to their trucks, then Mary goes in first," Desmond told them in a low voice, pointing toward the smaller truck on the other side of the village. "When she gets their attention, me, Buzz, Eric and Ricky will go inside that truck without being seen. We just have to make sure Mary has the crew's attention before we go in."

Buzzcut saluted Desmond. "Boo yah!"

"And grab a few tools," Desmond added as he secured the pistol in the back of his pants and tugged his shirttail even lower in the back over it. "Schuyler, find a good angle where you can see the entire village and document everything. Maybe behind the Humvee.

Mary, give us two minutes, then whenever you're ready."

She took a deep breath and stared into the village.

Eric turned to Buzzcut as he opened the toolbox in the back of the truck and took out a claw hammer, a ball peen hammer and a pair of lineman's pliers and handed them out. Desmond watched them speak briefly then shake hands before he suddenly noticed Mary walking way too soon into the village. She was a shadowy figure against the harsh lights, eerily framed on both sides by the still-screeching branches of the dead Baobab trees.

"Mary! You're too early!" Desmond whispered as loudly as he could. She kept going. "Dammit! Come on let's go guys!"

From a safe point near the Humvee, Schuyler zoomed and filmed Mary walking into the village while Desmond, Buzzcut, Eric and Ricky jogged stealthily in a very wide path through the dark around by the side of the village where the trucks were parked. They noticed a patch of scrub about fifty feet away from the smaller truck so they jogged over to it and regrouped. The sun was rising in the far eastern sky, and they were losing their cover of darkness. They had to work fast.

"This sucks," Ricky moaned, out of breath and sweating profusely in the smothering early morning humidity as they crouched in the brambles and peered at the trucks a short distance away. They could see that the large truck had both back doors open, but the smaller equipment truck next to it had both its rear doors shut. They briefly saw one of the Japanese in his coveralls and oxygen mask emerge from the larger truck and disappear somewhere between a Baobab and the village.

Buzzcut pulled his pistol from the holster. "Listen," he instructed as clearly as he could through his swollen mouth, "I'll go in first, secure the objective, and open the truck doors. Then when I signal, you all come, okay?"

Desmond agreed. He was glad to let Buzzcut take the lead. He seemed to have experience in breaking and entering.

"Guys?" Ricky asked, his voice shaking, "What if the Japanese catch us? We would be sitting ducks in that truck! They could ..."

"They ain't gonna catch me, I guarantee," Buzz muttered, never taking his eyes off the truck as he double-checked his weapon and flipped off the safety. He rose to his feet, staying crouched behind the scraggly bushes. No Japanese were in sight. "Watch for my signal."

"No shooting!" Desmond ordered as Buzz took off running in the open to the smaller truck. When he reached it, he pressed his back to the side and hesitated a second. He then dropped and rolled underneath, maneuvering around a dozen or so 10-gallon gasoline cans stored there.

"What's he doing?" Eric whispered as they watched Buzz pull himself hand-over-hand by the truck frame on his back toward the rear. When he reached the rear he rolled out and crouched behind the rear bumper, which doubled as a step, looking into the center of the village.

Watching from the scrub, Desmond assumed Buzz could see Mary in the camp, and hoped he had the good sense to make sure the Japanese were fully distracted by her before he stood and opened the doors.

From behind the rear bumper, Buzz looked from the village up at the doors. Apparently, they looked unlocked and the coast was clear. He waved the other guys over.

"It's go time." Desmond scrambled to his feet and took off running in the open toward the truck, his knee screaming in agony and the pistol jostling in his waistband until it bounced out and landed on the ground. "Dammit." He stopped to pick it up and shove it back when he noticed Eric and Ricky still crouched in the scrub – they didn't follow him. He waved them out, turned and kept going to the rear of the truck, where he met Buzz. They both crouched down behind the oversize bumper.

"Eric and Ricky failed to follow instructions," Desmond wheezed between deep breaths, trying to sneak a peek over the bumper. "They're panicking. We have to do this without them."

"So you have the hammers and pliers to destroy the equipment?" Buzz whispered.

Desmond winced. No, Eric and Ricky had them. Dammit. He waved and tried to get their attention but they were ducked down in the bushes, hiding, and with no apparent intention of ever coming out. "Screw them. We'll just have to do it ourselves."

Desmond turned and peeked between two Baobabs up over the bumper inside the village. The burned hut was on his left, and in the center stood Mary, talking to Kanayama. They were surrounded by the other Japanese crewmembers.

Desmond was horror-struck. Mary was holding her gun to Kanayama's head.

CHAPTER NINETEEN

Mary was under strict orders to use the gun only in an extreme emergency. Good Lord, Desmond prayed she would not shoot Kanayama. He would never be able to explain that.

Meanwhile, noticing the Japanese were fully distracted by Mary's gun, Buzz hissed "Let's go Mr. Desmond!" With his distracted director right behind him, Buzz quietly hopped onto the bumper step, grabbed both door handles and deftly unlatched them. Looking briefly into the village, and seeing Kanayama and his men were still preoccupied, he gritted his teeth as he slowly turned up the right-hand door handle with a mild squeak. The Japanese never heard a thing.

Suddenly Desmond noticed from the truck bumper that Mary, Kanayama and the rest of Kanayama's crew were being watched in the early dawn from behind the Baobabs by five or six strange African men, all wearing short sleeve plaid shirts, shorts and brand-new Nike sneakers.

Further to his left, behind the men, he glimpsed an older model Jeep and an SUV, all surrounding a late model black Mercedes-Benz, complete with little flags on both front corners. Like a diplomat, or an Ethiopian Mafioso, would drive. There seemed to be people everywhere, for gosh sakes, and he panicked.

"Christ almighty, there's other people here! Abort! Abort!" Desmond sputtered, just as Buzz swung open both truck doors. Though it definitely was the equipment truck, with rows and rows of expensive, brand new, gleaming filmmaking and sound equipment lining the walls and floor, Buzz and Desmond were again very surprised to encounter face-to-face three sweat-glistened Ethiopian men inside, in their shiny new Nike sneakers, seated on the floor around a stainless steel table playing some kind of complex card game.

"Goddammit!" Buzz yelled to them in surprise. "There was no way anyone was supposed to be in here!"

The three men looked up at the same time. For a brief instant time froze for the five of them as they stared at each other —as if each were rendered unable to comprehend what they were looking at.

Suddenly the three men all at once pushed away from their card game and scrambled to their feet just as Buzz instinctively and without reservation reached into his thigh holster, grabbed the pistol there and in one swift motion pulled it around front and pointed it at them.

Forgetting about his own weapon, Desmond could only stand in a stupor and watch as Buzz, with both hands on his gun, started firing randomly into the truck. One shot went through the ceiling. Two more exploded a row of sound amplifiers and speakers. It was as if Buzz was just shooting with his eyes closed, hoping he would hit something.

Caught flatfooted, and seemingly unprepared for a shootout, the men lurched in a panic, trying to dodge Buzz's errant shots while grabbing and prepping their own AK-47s, which were stacked nearby. One of them stumbled into a stack of about a dozen waist-high oxygen cylinders, and in his alarm stared at Buzz, as he repeatedly smacked the magazine of his gun in his attempts to load it.

His ears ringing from the shooting, and realizing the danger, Desmond turned and dove from the truck bumper in a desperate moment of self-preservation just as Buzz fired two more quick shots.

Without warning everything went silent and white.

Tom Desmond tumbled slowly, as if being gently rolled through the soft hands of a whispering giant. There was no gravity, no up, no down, only forward motion. He was thrust uninhibitedly through a milky void, like an untethered astronaut, not knowing what was left behind him or what lay before him.

He recalled when he finally left the truck stop, sometime in the late 1970s, in a fucked-up daze much like this. His mom sent him bus money and he rode to his home outside Chicago, and he slept for what seemed like weeks. He then spent two entire years eating home-cooked food, trembling, sweating, drinking sweet tea, going through detox, visiting rehab and sitting and staring at nothing at all on her plaid sofa, bought from Ford's Furniture Mart on Route 9 almost twenty years earlier.

He also barely recalled the thunder of another event while surrounded by suddenly unemployed idiots as a fireball billowed straight toward him.

Am I dead, he asked himself in a child-like voice? Am I flying to heaven, propelled upward by what had become a deafening, hot roar? He couldn't tell either time. He seemed to have no senses, only the dreamy motion of either plummeting or sailing somewhere fast, between two trucks in the Ethiopian desert, from a fireball on a movie set hatched by some incompetent, or to a couch near Gurnee, Illinois, in a time and place he had trouble recognizing.

He barely felt slamming into the dining room table (or the rear bumper of another truck), falling to the floor (or to the ground) and instinctively rolling underneath, as the equipment truck – fueled by several gas storage cans and accelerated by compressed oxygen cylinders – detonated in an earsplitting, hurricane-like eruption that propelled thousands of jagged, disintegrated chunks and shards over the entire village and surrounding area, lighting it up like noontime.

Two oxygen cylinders with shattered valves discharged into the sky like wayward SCUD missiles before sputtering out of gas and plummeting back to earth. One cylinder screamed like a ground-based torpedo under both trucks right past Desmond into one of the Japanese Jeeps, where it ruptured the gas tank. The force of the compressed air mixed with igniting gasoline blasted the Jeep almost twenty flaming feet into one of the Baobab trees, where it lodged, upside down in the crotch of two stout lower branches.

The soundproofed truck roof – ripped almost completely in one piece from the truck body and blown straight up into the air – landed with a boisterous crash somewhere near Mary and Kanayama, who cowered on the ground while hot, flaming carnage rained down around them.

***

It could have been a minute, an hour or a week to Desmond, but the next thing he realized was that he was being hauled in confusion across the yard and through the front door of his mom's house near Gurnee by two men he did not recognize. Maybe they were policemen or ambulance drivers. His ears rang horribly, his right arm was killing him, and his eyes burned and watered from an explosion. He had trouble making his legs work, like he had forgotten how to walk. His clothes were burnt and tattered from the force of ... what? Was it a bus crash?

Finally, they stopped and he presumed his angry mother threw cold water in his face. He shook his head and blinked.

Through the fireworks in his brain he saw the short, stocky, infuriated Japanese man standing in front of him with a half-full water bottle in his left hand. His right hand was tucked under his arm. He also had an oxygen mask, although he had lowered it down around his chin.

"Why did *mmff* Tom Desmond was *mmff* my truck exploding?" he angrily declared, his voice muffled and mistuned like the midnight radio shows child Desmond once listened to.

Desmond could barely hear through the screeching inside his own head. "What?" he sputtered, his own voice scratchy and inaudible. "Why are you inside my mom's house?" Why was the heat turned up so high? Christ, it was burning up in this place.

"$85,000 *mmff*," someone screamed, "*mmff* the value of the truck and equipment *mmff* destroyed. Nice job."

"Who ... who are those other people?" Desmond asked, remembering in his mangled memory seeing other men just before everything went white. Christ, his arm hurt. He looked down and saw his right elbow was on the inside if his arm.

The man leaned over and grabbed Desmond's cheeks into a pucker, like he had seen someone do to Buddy. Desmond studied his face, trying to comprehend what he was telling him through the raging confusion and tinnitus in his head.

"*Mmmff mmff* a special guest, *mmff* anxious to *mmff* with you, but his bodyguards *mmff mmff* back to his car to *mmff* when the shooting *mmff*."

Desmond blinked – slowly the words became more distinct. "I'm sure *mmff* is even more anxious to talk to *mmff*, especially since you probably killed three of his men who were *mmff* guarding the truck."

Desmond then recognized Kanayama, who let go and turned. "Go get your boss," he ordered two men standing nearby. "Tell him we have Tom Desmond out here now – what's left of him." Desmond watched them turn and walk quickly out of the village toward the parked vehicles.

Desmond took another minute to gather his wits before croaking out a few words. "Sorry about the bus and …"

Kanayama stared furiously down at him. "… especially the men," he continued, "but my … personal security guard did that, not me." His speech and reasoning were confounded by the nightmarish effects of being six feet away from an exploding vehicle. "But I tried to tell you … that village, and that project, were mine … and I welcome an opportunity to explain my story to your guest … whoever it is, and apologize … for the actions of my security guard."

Desmond took a deep cleansing breath, trying to clear his brain before continuing. "So why don't you all just have a seat," he asked. "Maybe mom can bring in a few more chairs. I can write you a check for the damage."

As Kanayama stared, impatient and obviously confused, Desmond looked up in a dream at what was left of a large vehicle. The entire bed and rear body were grotesquely splintered – only a few shards of mangled sheet metal rose from the bent frame like the skeletal branches of the dead Baobab trees. A fire burned within the bed. The force of the blast blew the cab forward on its front hinges, exposing the ruined engine. Chunks of metal littered the entire village, just as around the maternity hut.

He had trouble processing the extent of the damage done. He looked back at Kanayama, his face swimming in a lake of wretched pain, pounding ears and abject bewilderment.

"Is that what's left of the bus I took here? My God, what happened?" Desmond asked. "... Mary was with me. Is she okay?"

"What bus? What are you talking about?" Kanayama asked. "And your production manager is right behind you." Desmond turned, and saw Mary being held by both arms by two powerful men in those new sneakers. She seemed more angered than dazed by the explosion.

"It seems she is upset about some deal she claims she made with me," Kanayama continued. "She pulled a gun on me but you Hollywood fat cats are sloppy with weapons – she dropped it when my truck blew up."

"This is none of Desmond's business, Yukio!" Mary yanked against the two toughs holding her. "Let go of me you assholes!" At Kanayama's nod they let go and she stormed over, stopping between the two directors.

"I told you, Miss Semper, my truck left right on time," Kanayama explained. "It was your fault you didn't show up."

Hurting and confused, but slowly returning to real life, Desmond looked at Mary, then at Kanayama. "What is this all about? What deal?"

Kanayama pulled his injured hand out and looked at it briefly. His right index finger was badly injured, and bleeding profusely. It must have happened in the truck explosion. He tucked it back under his arm.

"Everybody turned on you Tom Desmond! You dumb American redneck! Your giant talent friend came to me and paid me cash for a ride out for all his friends. Then Mary came to me, said Tom

Desmond is a loser, asking for a job on my shoot. I refuse to hire her, so she wants to leave the desert with your talent. I say only one truck goes out, you be on it – but she was a no show!"

Mary was furious. "He's lying Desmond!"

"Your talent showed up on time!" Kanayama explained, looking at Mary. "Perhaps the giant, Isaiah? Maybe he told you an incorrect departure!"

Despite the rolling fog of his injuries and rapidly declining vigilance, Desmond could see crystal clear what had happened. "Mary is this true?" he asked, shocked and saddened at her desire to leave. "Did you really ask this man for a job? And a ride out of this desert? How could you do that?"

Kanayama laughed. "Ask for a ride out? No, no – talent paid me cash, she had no cash, had to pay another way for a ride!"

"Kanayama! Not here!" Mary warned, literally stomping in frustration.

"I told her for a ride home she had to sweeten the deal, tell me something I wanted to hear about Tom Desmond to verify what the Afarkils told me," Kanayama continued, ignoring Mary's warning. "She came here and became my number one source of information. She told me all about you driving the Afarkils away and how you poisoned the water supply with diesel fuel! Burned a hut with a man inside, killed their trees! She told me how the Afarkils showed up at your compound to make a peace offering and your security detail shot at them! Damn, they're better off with the Ebola than having Tom Desmond around."

"I'm warning you Kanayama, shut your fucking mouth ...!" Mary cautioned again, her face red and furious.

"Wait, I thought the talent told you my plan to force you away!" Desmond stupidly blurted to Kanayama, returning closer to reality. He suddenly felt queasy, like he was going to pass out. He was astonished it was Mary who sold him out, not the talent.

"Once your talent made arrangements out of here, they kicked back smoking hash. They wouldn't tell me anything. No, it was all your production manager," Kanayama explained. "You need better personnel screeners for your productions, you asshole second-unit loser."

"You may have screwed me over, Mary, but then Kanayama screwed you twice, and I can't say you didn't deserve it the second time," Desmond slurred, furious at Mary and trying to keep the story straight in his foggy, scrambled brain. "Maybe you deserved to be forgotten by him after that Tokyo Honda Festival. You seem to have no loyalties of your own."

"What Tokyo Honda festival?" Kanayama blurted.

"Okay! So there was no Honda festival!" Mary shot back. "I made that story up, hoping I wouldn't have to confront this bastard. But dammit, I was so mad at him for leaving me here ... now look where it got us."

"But ... why all the lies, Mary? Things were just getting productive for us!" Desmond cried, stunned by the revelations. "Our project was coming along so ..."

"Coming along so what? So well?" Mary interrupted, stunned at Desmond's stubbornness as tears streamed down her cheeks. "How can you possibly say that, Desmond? You are in charge of the worst film project of all time! Look around you! Does this look like a productive and successful shoot? Cars, villages, equipment, careers and lives destroyed? There's a jeep in a tree and a fucking dead marketing guy strapped half-ass to a car that was practically destroyed by a million metal barrels! My God, what world do you live in?"

Desmond was going down the rabbit hole, and wasn't going to be able to stand much longer. He was crushed, professionally, physically and emotionally. The one person he depended on most on this entire shoot turned out to be nothing more than a backstabbing, deceitful liar.

He staggered and fell backward on his ass and didn't feel a thing. Just like on the Cavett show. Good thing he was back home on his mother's living room carpet, which was soft and clean. He was collapsing under the crushing weight of the catastrophic realization that the project was really over. He had failed in the most spectacular ways possible. This was not another Pyro – this was far worse than Pyro.

Then, as if things could not possibly get any worse, that man showed up.

At first, from his vantage point on the ground, Desmond was only aware of a group of men from the neck down returning from the parking area. He heard Kanayama trying to introduce one of them to him but his voice had become just farting sounds.

He slowly raised his head. He saw a guy in the middle, surrounded by five or six guys in those brand-new shoes.

They had apparently protected the middle guy, rushing him back to the safety of their vehicles until the bus crash was over. Now that the coast was clear, they brought him back. And in his exhaustion Desmond recognized that guest of honor – the one man he thought at one time he would never see again.

To him things were suddenly sparkling clear.

Standing less than fifty feet away from him was Gerald. Gerald Camber. His missing scriptwriter. But Desmond knew he was more than just a pathetic scriptwriter – much, much more. And he was angered beyond belief that this man was suddenly back inside his mother's house – right where all the trouble started, all those years ago.

Desmond struggled to his feet, never taking his eyes off him. "You ... abusive son of a bitch," he growled. "How dare you set foot in here!"

Kanayama was mumbling something beside him, but Desmond ignored him, fixated instead on the man who he sincerely believed was the foundation of all his life problems. Suddenly all else fell away, and there was nothing else in the world but the man in front of him.

"I know who you really are!" Desmond shouted, pointing accusingly. Gerald only stared back at him.

"Oh, don't look so damn smug!" Desmond yelled again, his voice cracking. "You showed up at my camp in the middle of the night thinking I would never figure this out, didn't you? You thought you could go through Carswell and get a job and screw around with my project and I would never figure it out! But I did! I'm not stupid! You may go by Gerald now, but I know thirty years ago you went by the name Jerry! And you claimed you worked for the Dr. Pepper Company!"

"Desmond?" Mary asked, her voice concerned, languid and fluid. "Who are you talking to?"

Desmond ignored his back-stabbing production manager and took a halting step forward. He felt every eye on him. "You said you took a break from the film business in the 1950s, and I remember that, and I know exactly what you did during that time! You traveled door to door supposedly handing out silver dollars for Dr. Peppers to lonely housewives and you tricked and intimidated them into having sex and you hit them and beat them because you knew you could get away with it! How many of those powerless women did you hurt, Jerry? How many families like mine did you destroy?"

"Dammit Desmond!" Kanayama commanded, his voice more distinct. "What the hell are you doing? You don't speak to Mr. Haile-Selassie like that!"

"Oh, his name's not Haile-Selassie," Desmond growled, never taking his eyes off the bearded Caucasian gentleman with the wire-frame glasses who never lit his cigarettes that he saw standing in front of him. "It took me a while to figure it out, but that's the son of a bitch who followed me to the desert, trying to screw up my life for the second time! Now here he is yet again, back inside my mother's house! Said he would write a script, and I trusted him, and he wrote bullshit, delaying and sabotaging my work, before he realized that I was on to him and he disappeared! Tried to make me think I had seen a ghost! I guess he hid with the Japanese, disguised by a helmet, an oxygen mask and air-conditioned coveralls so no one could recognize him!"

Feeling the pistol still in his back waistband, Desmond reached back and pulled it out, flipped off the safety and pointed it in Gerald's direction. His entourage gasped and backed up a step. A shot of pain raced down his shattered right arm as he tried to steady the pistol in his hand.

Kanayama made a noise then was gone. Desmond quickly turned his head, noticing over far to his left a larger group of men behind the trees, also with weapons drawn, watching the showdown between him and Gerald and his staff. Desmond thought they were probably waiting to get his autograph after resolving his issue with Gerald.

But good Lord, he was surrounded on all sides by strange people. And they were all backed into a corner. Gerald was backed in a corner. Everyone – the entire world – was backed into a fucking corner. Desmond felt especially backed in, but that was a price he was willing to pay. He would never get this opportunity again. And there were plenty of witnesses now, to prove how right he was.

Desmond saw Gerald glance at the group of autograph seekers on the other side of the trees, before he lifted his hands and took a step toward him.

"Mr. Desmond," he asserted, almost cheerfully, "you are talking and behaving like a crazy person. Please put that gun down so we can figure this out. I have much to discuss with you, like gentlemen. Please."

Gerald's voice sounded different, like it had a French accent. He wasn't mumbling, like he did back at the compound. Desmond put a second hand on the shaking pistol. The world was impossibly spinning but he had to keep Gerald in full, unblemished focus. Gerald stopped, like he seemed to realize he had put himself in a bad position and unwittingly made himself a perfect target. Some of the men surrounding him looked around with concern and started cocking their weapons.

"You have some nerve coming back! You broke my arm, and you wrecked my parent's marriage, and after you hurt my mom, my dad left. I love my mom and dad," Desmond choked, his voice breaking.

"I even visited you in the damn hospital after my dad tried to kill you ... yes, you and I both know it was my father who shot you that time at the bus station. My dad left us after that and I never even got a post card from him, and my mom wanted me to forgive you, but I can't – I won't."

"Desmond, no ... please, put the gun down." Desmond recognized the voice and glanced to his right. It was Schuyler. She looked like a goddess. She had been caught by one of Gerald's people and brought into the village with what looked like plastic ties around her wrists. Her camera was nowhere to be seen. Mary stood nearby watching, just as terrified. It seemed there were a hundred people standing nearby watching, all seemingly ready to either go to war or clamor for his autograph.

"Schuyler?" Desmond yelled to her, "thanks for coming. Go find my mom and tell her to stay in the kitchen while I settle this." Schuyler only stared back at him, her mouth ajar. "I don't want her in contact with this man. He hurt my arm and he will hurt her again in a second."

Desmond turned back toward Gerald. "Now thirty years later you tried to get back at what my dad did by wrecking my documentary," he railed, his voice again rising in anger. "You knew who I was, that the Afarkil project was my return to filmmaking, my big chance to prove myself. Now, luckily, I caught you back at our house before you got a chance to hurt my mom again. You are a slippery bastard, but you are always a step behind me, my friend."

"Desmond," the man in front of him began in a somewhat stern voice, "have you forgotten that I was the only voice you could trust on this project? Don't you remember what I told you? That we cannot change the natural course of things that are pre-ordained by God and nature? I warned you, about all of this, but you wouldn't listen to me."

The sun was up to full broil and illuminating the village as a war zone. All of the huts were either destroyed or damaged by flying debris, which littered the ground all around them. What was left of the

Kodanoguchi equipment truck had burned itself out. The once mighty Baobabs surrounding the village stood silent, their skeletal branches raised in lifeless anguish, almost begging this horrible event to end. One of them still cradled a smoldering upside-down jeep in its arms like a war orphan in Life magazine.

"You wouldn't listen to me."

"I can't let you get away with what you did to my family back then, and what you tried to do now ... Gerald, Jerry, silver dollar man, whatever name you go by ... the biggest mistake you ever made was coming back here, and the second was telling me I could not finish this project. But I'll show you – I'm going to finish this project after I now finish what my dad started – this is the natural course of things."

Gerald's voice was loud and precise. "Put the gun down now."

Desmond did not put the gun down. No one told him he was incapable of completing something. He pulled the trigger. He had to. Not once but six times.

And the world exploded.

EPILOGUE

I don't know how they kept all their laws straight. I think some of the crew thought we were wasting our time; that they were killing themselves with all their odd procedures and that the village would die out no matter what we did.

But my job was to document their eccentric traditions, not interfere in them. I had to make the difficult decision to only observe, and take no role in their customs, which seemed impossible under the circumstances.

Desmond sat on his bed, staring at the floor. His right arm ached like hell. It had been three months since he and his crew were taken out of the Danakil. It was a chaotic exit – he remembered believing he was back at his mom's house, being pushed and pulled in many directions as the world shattered all around him. In fact, he barely remembered what it was all about in the first place, despite constantly replaying the experience – including one episode in particular, a favorite of his:

With the Japanese director under gunpoint, I had the upper hand. "Wait, Kanayama," I ordered. As Eric and Buzz held down the whimpering man, I grabbed his coveralls at the lapels and jerked them apart. Inside, sewn to the inner lining, was a very small Mitsutoyo air-conditioning unit, not more than a few inches square, with aerated plastic tubing running inside the lining across the chest and down the extremities, happily humming along. It felt a comfortable seventy degrees inside those coveralls. I grabbed the unit and in two or three jerks ripped it from the lining.

"Now," I said with an arrogant sneer, dangling the unit in Kanayama's sobbing face, "you can just suffer along with the rest of us." I dropped the still-humming a/c unit on the ground and stomped it until

it stopped humming.
But to my horror, maggots squirted out of it as I stomped.

He both smiled and shuddered at this memory, however true it may or may not have been, but he still hurt from the experience. His right arm ached, his knee still hurt and his back was in a knot. He sat gingerly on the edge of his bed. Even the hair on his back hurt.

There was a knock on his door. Oh my God, a fan. Desmond straightened up. He was barely in any condition to meet a fan. "Come in," he called out in his strongest voice.

It was a man in a chauffeur uniform that seemed a half-size too small for him. "Mr. Tom Desmond?" he asked.

"I can give you an autograph but I have to use your pen. I don't have one of my own."

"I'm not here for an autograph. Mr. Carswell is waiting out front. He said it's time to go."

Desmond waved in acknowledgement. "I'll be right out." The man nodded and gently closed the door. Desmond glanced at the VHS box next to his bed. It was a souvenir, salvaged and presented to him by Schuyler: five seconds of Afarkil children walking through a village, and a colorless shot of an Afarkil man with a large, oblong head stopping and looking to his right. The man who neglected to tell anyone he learned English words like "ya'll" and "ain't" from a southern Baptist missionary. That tape was a prominent addition to the twenty seconds of a plane exploding shortly after takeoff that he salvaged from Pyro.

I shot a man and they said I should feel terrible about that and no one could decide if I should serve time for it or not, owing to what they claimed was the man's supposedly murderous and fearsome reputation. Many countries and organizations, even the United Nations, argued over what happened and if I actually did the region a favor by killing him. They said I had a 'profound mental illness as a mitigating factor,' whatever that is.

I definitely did not, however, run over that marketing guy in the Humvee, despite what many of my former crew members testified. He was injured in the chopper crash, and died of those injuries.

There was another knock on his door. Perhaps this was a fan wanting an autograph? Desmond perked up. "Please come in," he called out.

It was that driver again. "Um, Mr. Carswell requested you come out now," he advised ominously. "He means right away. He is legally obligated to be there from the beginning."

"Sure, I'm coming." After the driver paused then went back outside Desmond stood after two or three tries, smoothed his hair and attempted to tuck in his rumpled shirt. It probably was not a good idea to leave his producer waiting. Mr. Carswell seemed to be plenty upset about what happened on the shoot, and if he wanted to work with him again, he better get outside.

Donato pulled that gun out of the security guard's hand and guess what happened. He tried to put the barrel in his mouth and pointed it up. You're trying to kill yourself, right? I remembered the barrel was hot between my teeth. He was going to give Dick Cavett a heart attack! How hard can it ...

Wait, that's not what happened at all ... Dick Cavett wasn't in the desert. Now I'm confused.

Satisfied he looked somewhat presentable with his best face on, Desmond opened his door and walked with a limp down the hallway. He stopped at the counter and intentionally printed his name on a ledger so an autograph hound wouldn't steal it, then walked past the indifferent receptionist outside into the hot California sun toward the limousine idling in front of him. The driver stiffly opened the back right-hand door, and Desmond crawled inside, gritting his teeth and complaining to himself about how difficult it was to do something as basic as get into a limousine. It was nice and cool inside, although it smelled a little moldy. Once he was seated the driver closed the door, walked around and got in the driver's seat. The car took off.

Mr. Carswell sat directly across from Desmond, staring emotionlessly at him. The big brown leather limo seat seemed to swallow him whole. He balanced a clinking drink of some sort in his nicotine-blotted fingers, one of which was clipped with a blood oxygen sensor, wired to a small monitor lying on the seat beside him. Desmond thought Mr. Carswell's newly-sprouted grey goatee intensified the devilishness of his face. His too-long eyebrows arched unnaturally down, making him look angry, even when he wasn't. Three months after his health episode he was still thin and washed out – he looked just like a guy who suffered a quad bypass after a stroke, then spent ten days in a coma. Which he did.

He was a survivor, for sure.

He swirled his drink, took a sip and continued to stare. Desmond met his gaze for a few seconds, then finally looked down at his feet. Mr. Carswell tapped out a British cigarette, lit it and exhaled a cloud of smoke just left of Desmond's face. He choked back a cough, not wanting to show weakness.

"You never met my former accountant, Marvin Waltz," Mr. Carswell finally spoke, his voice weak and tired. "I hired him away from a celebrity law firm in the mid-1960s, Turtletaub and Turtletaub. He was a financial genius – for every dollar bill the studio brought in, he found a way to spend one side and invest the other. I owe a lot to him for that."

Mr. Carswell paused, took a drag on his cigarette and looked back at Desmond. "Marvin talked me into a lot of good decisions, but he failed to talk me out of hiring you. He knew better than to bring a washed-up junkie on board a high-profile project, I know. He acted like he never heard of you. It is the one thing I wished he would have talked me out of."

Mr. Carswell stared at Desmond, without smiling or even

blinking. Desmond avoided his steely gaze. He wanted to address the "washed-up junkie" comment but chose to save that argument for another day.

Carswell leaned forward. "Desmond ...? You honest to God had no idea you were killing the most powerful and hated man in Ethiopia? Possibly in all of Africa? You thought he was an elderly scriptwriter? Inside your mother's living room? Please explain."

Desmond paused – according to Schuyler, the one time her camera worked perfectly it caught him going insane and shooting a man multiple times, but not the man he claimed it was. But in the ensuing chaos somebody confiscated the camera and the tape went missing. That tape would have been proof positive who he really shot dead – the sole piece of documentation – and it was being held somewhere by someone to discredit his version of the events. With no physical proof of who he really shot, he had no dog in the fight. But he knew who he shot. He was positive. And no one would change his mind.

"I was ... confused from the explosion and the shooting," he answered in a low voice without looking up. The interior of the limo was tired, and wearing badly. The long, gaudy vehicle bounced through some potholes down some anonymous West Hollywood Street. "There were unresolved issues."

Mr. Carswell took an extremely long pull on his tarry cigarette, held the smoke in his charred lungs for several seconds, then blew it out toward the cracked, padded ceiling. "Yea, that's what you were coached to say in your defense, I get it, but I want to know ..."

"I learned I can't depend on anybody, okay?" Desmond interrupted. "This crew failed to grasp my innovative vision of what the documentary needed to accomplish and the unique style I created to achieve it." His courage returning, the words seemed to tumble out of his mouth as he looked up at his boss, meeting his gaze head-on. "Saving the Afarkil clan from extinction was a responsibility I took very seriously. But my crew was careless and failed to follow my direction. They made many missteps. And the desert was brutal. It was a ..."

"You depended on those Eritrean Liberation Army guys who got you and what was left of your half-wit crew out of the Danakil to Asmara alive, didn't you?" Mr. Carswell interrupted in as loud a voice he could muster. "Both the Ethiopian and the Djibouti governments wanted your head on a stick, so thank God they dragged your sorry ass into Eritrea so you could get the hell off that continent without losing any vital body parts."

"A mole in Haile-Selassie's entourage gave them his location, that's the only reason they showed up, armed to the teeth, saving your clueless white asses," he continued angrily. "They had been planning to assassinate him for months. You were fucking standing in the middle of a long-simmering political gang war in that desert and you somehow not only manage to shoot dead the most hated man in Africa but safely stumble your way out to safety in a hail of gunfire. Thank your Gods, you are the fucking luckiest man in the world."

"And where did that goddamn bus even come from?" Mr. Carswell asked, "Out of nowhere, just when the shit hits, a bus pulls up. It was like the most unlikely chain of events just came together for the benefit of a nobody named Tom Desmond."

Desmond resumed staring down as the limo thumped and bumped on worn shocks. Mr. Carswell's words made little sense. He did not remember those events as he described. "...it was ... a harsh and unforgiving environment."

Mr. Carswell shook his head in amazed frustration as the end of his cigarette glowed in the darkening interior of the limousine. He blew two matching opaque plumes from his nostrils, like pissed-off jet exhaust. He never took his eyes off Desmond. "Harsh and unforgiving indeed. A Federal Court judge who believes in unconventional sentencing guidelines was willing to forgive my role in this clusterfuck in return for taking you and the rest of your crew to see this 'harsh and unforgiving indictment of man's inhumanity to man' as the L.A. Times film reviewer called it. This is now my sixth viewing. And it just gets harder and harder to watch, I assure you."

Mr. Carswell took a sip of his drink, took one last pull on his cigarette then ground it out a little too enthusiastically in the ashtray under the window to his left. "It has been interesting, though, to see how all of your former crew reacts to it. Your camerawoman? Would not stop sobbing. Said she wants nothing to do with movies anymore, and was going back to school after she gets off the anti-anxiety and bulimia medication. Gonna be a nurse, she says. Some nurse – she got Donato hooked on Percodans and vodka.

"I was hoping to hook up with her but I don't need to get involved with another fucking emotional train wreck. Christ, I was with Mary, after all."

Desmond looked up at him expressionless.

"The two punks, Ricky? And Eric?" Carswell continued. "They had no real reaction. They mostly stared at the floor. The Bitzer kid wouldn't stop kissing my ass long enough to watch, but I guess I deserve that honor since he was my idea to send as an interpreter."

Desmond looked confused. "His name is Bitzer?"

Carswell paused. "Watching it with Mary was the worst – the single most uncomfortable thing I have ever had to do. We're former lovers but we didn't say one word to each other. We picked her up at her job at a Barnes & Noble in Santa Monica and she never even looked at me."

"How did Mr. Donato react?"

"You don't remember, do you? Two weeks back in the states Mr. Donato elected to permanently check out of a hotel room in Tupelo, Mississippi. He washed down over one hundred Percodan tablets with two liters of vodka. Even his iron guts couldn't tolerate that. I heard they found vomit on the fucking ceiling."

"Oh yea. It's good to know he gave up the gin," Desmond observed as he stared out the window for a minute. "Look, Mr. Carswell, I'm sorry that judge put you in this position, it wasn't your fault ..."

"Your cook was exempt. He was the only innocent person in this whole sorry experience."

"It is very true," Desmond insisted, "I could have made the most-watched documentary of all time had I first unit status, functional equipment and a more competent crew. This wasn't your or my fault."

Carswell sarcastically laughed one time and leaned forward again. "You brain dead fuck," he hissed, his eyes widened to a psychotic stare. "I have worked with some dumbasses over the years but nobody even comes close to you, Tom Desmond. You talk about your crew being incompetent – but I wonder how does a stupid fuck like you stumble through life with your shit always smelling like roses? It took salt and uranium miners generations to eradicate the Afarkil society but you do it in under a week, and walk away from it. I found out Gabriel Haile-Selassie got a hundred death threats a year from skilled assassins from all over the world, but a clueless American moron takes him out on his first visit. It's fucking uncanny."

Desmond stared at the words foaming from Mr. Carswell's mouth with a casual, detached interest.

"You begged me for work for a year, two years, actually, so I hire you for a harmless second unit job in the middle of a desert on a whole other continent. I told Marvin even Tom Desmond could not fuck up taking pictures of sand, but damn, was I wrong. Then I laid in a fucking coma while you were busy destroying the very civilization you were supposed to be saving and unknowingly altering the political climate of an entire continent. I guess you would be a brilliant political strategist if you weren't so goddamn stupid."

Mr. Carswell paused to light yet another cigarette with an angry, shaking hand. "You know, by the way, most of Kanayama's villager footage had to be recreated because you fucking blew it up in that truck. He was one pissed-off Nip."

Desmond perked up. "Hey, I remember Gerald told me that he destroyed all of Robert Flaherty's footage of Nanook of the North when he dropped a cigarette in the film can. I assumed that was why he never lit his cigarettes. Small world."

Mr. Carswell only stared. "Yea… anyway, then here I am – while

I blissfully snooze, hooked up like a gomer to life support with a ventilator jammed down my gullet, a foley up my dick and a poop tube shoved to my neck, I lose the biggest opportunity of my career to Blatt and Preston over at fucking Cannon, who salvages it for a tenth of the original cost. My partner – God bless him – has to put my business under receivership before he comes into my hospital room and leaves his resignation note on my chest."

"And today," Mr. Carswell continued, "while we walk in circles on our elbows with our thumbs up our asses, a BBC reporter releases a doc about the Ethiopian famine and it goes worldwide to great acclaim. And I'm reduced to hauling the most worthless man in Los Angeles under court order to see this ... fucking celluloid bear trap to the groin. Jesus H. Christ."

The limousine at that point pulled to a stop, stopping Mr. Carswell's tirade. "Ah shit, here we go one last time, Thank God," he groused. The driver hopped out, walked around and tugged twice on the door before it opened. Mr. Carswell got out first, followed slowly by Desmond. They briefly stood on the sidewalk, under a former silent movie palace on North Fairfax Avenue called the Visualite. Squinting in the hot, bright southern California sun, Desmond glanced up at the name of the movie on the overhead marquee before following Mr. Carswell inside. It was a late afternoon Monday matinee, and crowds were thin.

Not wishing to be recognized, Desmond held his head down, not making eye contact with a couple patrons as he and Mr. Carswell walked through the lobby, the thick miasma of buttery popcorn and Coke syrup lingering heavily in the air. Mr. Carswell bought two tickets, and a young usher in a black pullover shirt nodded at them, tore their tickets and held the door as they entered the huge, 1940s-era air-conditioned theater. They walked only one or two rows down the aisle and took two seats way in the back in the corner, close to the door. Desmond saw about twenty patrons scattered about the theater.

Sitting and leaning back in the threadbare red velvet chair, he stared at the giant blank screen in front of him and all the memories flooded back: all the movies he created, all the edits, every take, every word of dialogue; it was all still there. But it wasn't organized, the memories were a jumble. Which movie came first? King Size Peggy? What was the name of the other one? Which movie had the accident?

He was once called by all the trade papers the most promising young director to step behind a movie camera since Alfred Hitchcock, right? Weren't his first two films in the top-grossing movies of the 1960s? Didn't he have two Oscar nominations under his belt? Didn't that usher holding the door for them know that? What kind of clueless kids did they hire at theaters who didn't know enough about film history to know who Tom Desmond was?

Desmond suddenly sat up and looked around at the patrons in the theater, and the ones still trickling in. A few were single men carrying a newspaper. Did any of them recognize him? How did he fall off the radar, anyway? He thought that if those people knew who sat in the back of this theater with them there would probably be a rush for autographs, delaying the start of the film.

"Excuse me, aren't you Tom Desmond?" they would ask as they gathered around, followed by "We love your movies!"

But then the inevitable, worrisome concerns would arise. "Where have you been?" they would ask, "How come we don't see your movies anymore? Why did you stop directing? Are you planning a comeback?"

Or the worst one: "I thought you were dead."

Desmond sat back in his seat and smiled. "Comeback" was an ugly word in the entertainment industry, but not as ugly as "dead." But all that was about to change. Five nights ago, in this very theater, was the American premiere of the documentary about to start in a few short minutes. He had read the review in a copy of the Los Angeles Times left lying in the day room. The reviewer wrote it was "a harsh and unforgiving example of man's inhumanity to man."

He knew he should have trademarked that expression.

Desmond had begged Mr. Carswell to take him to the premier but the court order prevented it – he could not go out after 5:00 p.m. But this was his return to the big screen! How dare a ridiculous court order keep him away! But no matter; in a few moments everyone would turn in recognition to the man sitting in the back of the theater, thinking "That's him! Over there! That's the guy up on the screen! That's the guy in the movie!" Then they would know, and they would respect him again.

The theater finally darkened and the movie started with no previews. Desmond wondered if the other patrons would be able to still recognize him with the lights so low. The scene opened with a long, sweeping low aerial shot of the familiar, beautiful and deadly Danakil Desert. The music, by a Philip Glass knockoff, started slowly then quickly began a swirling crescendo. The flying camera panned right against the silhouette of a dead, skeletal Baobab tree as the title faded in.

Cannon Films Presents

A Blatt and Preston Production

NAKED SAVAGES:

The Unintended Consequences of Man's Inhumanity to Man

Obsessing on his own perceptions of the events about to unfold on the screen, Desmond saw but could not acknowledge the next line – it was obtuse and foreign:

A Film by Yukio Kanayama

A quote scrolled behind the music. It was superimposed over a still shot of the abandoned village, littered with debris after the explosion. In the foreground were two destroyed huts and the destroyed Japanese equipment truck, with the dead Baobab trees in the background.

Is it not enough that a culture has been decimated by the greed of capitalism and the ignorance of white supremacy?
So why does the white man also come today, to destroy a village and a way of life, then drive a people from their homes for purely selfish reasons?
They are a simple, honest people. What did they do to incur the world's wrath?

"I'm sure I may have many types of skin cancer by now," Desmond thought as he half-heartedly watched the screen and picked at a mole on his arm. "It was a very harsh and unforgiving environment."

Suddenly Desmond could smell Mr. Carswell beside him. He had a distinctive, old school affluent man scent, with notes of dirty dollar bills, expensive yet flowery cologne, work sweat, Vitalis hair product, rich meals at supper clubs and steak houses, small-batch bourbon and hard-to-find British cigarettes. It was a power smell, and he reveled in it.

The scroll continued to the rising crescendo of the music over another still of Donato's unused replacement village, highlighting the hut facades, one of which had fallen over face down, exposing the x-bracing on the back. The ingenious cooking apparatus appeared barely standing. Far in the background were thousands of oil drums scattered all over the ground. It looked like a weather-beaten and abandoned Hollywood set of an oil production company disaster.

This is not just about the life of a struggling society but the willful destruction of it by generations of careless, murdering misfits. Recently, a film crew went into the Danakil to document the re-

emerging lifestyle of the Afarkils and nearly succeeded, through sheer incompetence and willful ignorance of the culture, in destroying that society in their misguided attempt to save it.

Several of the men in coats carrying folded newspapers got up and angrily left the theater. Desmond and Mr. Carswell watched them parade out.

"You see 'naked' in the title you think it's a stroke flick, you sorry assholes," Mr. Carswell announced loudly to them as they walked past.

Desmond watched them leave. "They're leaving angry. I wish that Asian marketing woman didn't leave angry that day," he whispered too loudly to Mr. Carswell, who never acknowledged the remark as he slumped in his seat, staring at the screen with his arms folded. "I hate it when someone leaves with a negative impression of me. I used to not care, but now I do."

He looked directly at him. "I'm a changed man, Mr. Carswell."

The next quote was over a shot of a destroyed Humvee with no windshield or driver side door, parked near the destroyed village. All four tires were flat. An obvious human body, wrapped haphazardly in a sheet and carelessly tied to the roof, hung almost upside down off the side. An exposed, lifeless dangling hand brushed the sand.

My task then became not only documenting the deliberate destruction of the Afarkil people down through history, but also by that modern film crew today, telling prematurely what was almost the posthumous story of their society – a story I was not expecting nor prepared to tell.

In the dim light Desmond examined the blackened nail on his right index finger, a visible on-set injury he wore as a badge of honor. "I set out in the desert to make the ultimate documentary," he stated out loud as he stared at the nail. "I was singular of purpose and driven to fulfill my initiative, but there were exterior forces that thwarted my progress. I fell victim to incompetent scriptwriters and unskilled technical personnel. I was like a symphony conductor ..."

Mr. Carswell suddenly exhaled and leaned over close to Desmond, who – desperate for his attention – stopped and leaned back into him, ready to soak in his wisdom. Though at times explosively confrontational, he knew Mr. Carswell also could be measured in his theories and criticism of filmmaking, and Desmond wanted to savor every word.

"Shut your cake hole and watch!" He hissed. "I paid twelve bucks! Good God, it's like taking a fucking four-year-old to a movie."

A startling, high-contrast close-up of Desmond's frantic, furious, grizzled face jumped off the screen. Mr. Carswell moaned and looked away. It was an awkward, embarrassing still, obviously taken while Desmond was yelling at Kanayama to leave their compound or when he encountered Gerald at the village.

A quote scrolled up over top of it.

... A former American filmmaker of some renown believed he was a 'white savior,' whose job was to rescue the Afarkil society by bringing their plight to the attention of the world. My job is to show his barefaced incompetence.
He failed.
I did not.

-Yukio Kanayama

Desmond stared in honor at the image. There he was. He had returned to the big screen.

One hour into the awkward, incriminating movie, Mr. Carswell looked at his watch and again leaned over. "My time is up. Let's get out of here before anybody sees me with you."

Agreeing that leaving was a good idea, since the crush of recognition would be a disruption, Desmond shakily stood, trying to un-kink his back, before he and his boss discreetly walked in the dark toward the door, which was held open by the same teenager who held it when they entered. Desmond nodded to the young man, who maybe seemed to recognize him but not really. Desmond figured Mr. Carswell ordered the theater staff to ignore them, again so there would be no disruptions.

As they exited the theater the limousine driver was in front, closing the hood. He opened and held the rear passenger door. It was a warm, pleasant southern California early evening. Mr. Carswell got in, followed by Desmond. He immediately popped two pills under his tongue, then lit a cigarette once he was seated. A double bourbon had already been prepared, and waited in the cup holder.

"That Japanese director should be thankful," Desmond explained. "He only got that movie made because of his air-conditioned coveralls."

"He's not very thankful that all his celebrity and rock star endorsements pulled out when the story of your incompetence hit the trade papers," Mr. Carswell responded angrily. "They all switched their checkbooks over to Geldof and that big Live Aid benefit coming next July. Kanayama only got a half-hearted endorsement from Steve Lawrence or Eydie Gorme or something."

"But you, on the other hand, should be thankful to Kanayama for a whole lot of things. Those pregnant women, for example," Mr. Carswell continued. "You went in that maternity hut, strutted around at your discovery, then walked out. Kanayama walked in and recognized preeclampsia in one of the women. He talked all of them – in their native dialect, by the way – into going to Addis Ababa, and they had healthy babies there. And, that was the only thing that saved them from a helicopter crash that I still can't wrap my head around. I guess we'll never know what that was about."

"That's good news about the babies," Desmond recalled, not registering Mr. Carswell's snip at him. "That guarantees the survival of the tribe. I'm sorry, the clan. Society."

"Yes, the Afarkils will survive after all, no fucking thanks to you," Mr. Carswell retorted, taking an irate sip of his drink. "A small group of them, still willing to hang on to the old ways, have voluntarily settled at the northern Sudanese border, where they are safe, and have a consistent food and water supply. The rest of them elected to remain in Addis Ababa. But you know, there are still so many unanswered questions."

Desmond was surprised – he thought everything came out in the trial. "What questions?"

"Like I think you know what really happened to Brad Steele. Your team testified his injuries appeared consistent with being run over by a heavy vehicle. I hope one day you come clean on that." Mr. Carswell stared out the window for a few seconds lost in thought as they passed the Toddle House restaurant before continuing.

"It was an act of God that Kanayama found Steele's assistant wandering in the desert just as he was leaving. She survived that chopper crash with just scratches. Unbelievable. Too bad though about Haile-Selassie's pilot. And Melvin Flohr."

Desmond drew a blank. "What happened to the pilot? And who's Melvin Flohr?"

"Flohr? He was your damn security officer! Didn't you take the time to learn his name?"

"We called him by a nickname," Desmond recalled after a short pause. "I don't remember, it was based on his haircut, I think. Crewcut, or flattop or something."

"The pilot was thrown from the copter and killed," Mr. Carswell continued impatiently. "Kanayama found the body and had it sent back to his home in southern Ethiopia. Paid the funeral bills. He claimed he never saw Steele when he found the crash. Christ, Desmond we've told you this a thousand times, you really don't remember shit, do you?"

The two passengers remained silent for several bumpy miles. Desmond remembered it was in late 1980 when he received a letter at his mother's house in Gurnee from Reliance Film Group. He had sent out over 50 inquiry letters to studios reminding them of his former accomplishments and informing them of his decision to return to directing.

Mr. Carswell was the only producer to respond, and Desmond recalled quite clearly the language of the letter: "Reliance may consider the opportunity to work with you on any suitable project that may arise in the near future." Encouraged, Desmond borrowed a couple thousand dollars from his mom, gave her a kiss and moved back to West Hollywood. He took odd jobs, read and edited television scripts for pocket change and worked at Woolworth's playing an almost three-year waiting game.

Mr. Carswell suddenly interrupted his thoughts. "Tell you what Desmond, since this is our last meeting, I'll buy you dinner." He hand-cranked down the window separating them from the driver. "Roy?" he asked the man, "Go through a drive-thru window at one of those fast food places."

He turned and addressed Desmond directly. "I'm going to treat Mr. Desmond here to a Double Whopper."

After the fast food stop the limo finally parked in a handicapped spot in front of Gateways Hospital as Desmond emptied the remaining few cold fries from the paper container directly into his mouth. The driver once again came around and opened the door.

"Listen good, Desmond," Mr. Carswell ordered. "I have fulfilled the last term of the order. I have now taken you and every one of your retarded crew members to see Kanayama's film, so our relationship ends today. You realize I won't have anything to do with you or any of your half-wits anymore. This chapter is over. Now get out of my car."

Desmond paused before he winked at Mr. Carswell and got out. "Yea, I figured you would say that," he replied as a phone somewhere started ringing, "I know how political this town can be. But I'll be ready to go back to work whenever you say the word."

Desmond groaned as he got out of the limo. He looked at the hospital and turned back toward his producer. "I just wish I could have gotten a better place to live."

"Be grateful," Mr. Carswell explained angrily as he flipped open a cellular car phone and yanked out the antenna, "A voluntary manslaughter conviction in federal court generally gets a prison term. The prosecutors did you a favor by agreeing to compulsory institutionalization instead of jail. You're up for review in three years, so suck it up, asshole.

"And take your damn trash with you!" Mr. Carswell ordered as an afterthought. "Fucking California flies will have maggots in my car in a heartbeat."

Desmond paused, as if something just occurred to him.

"You know I'm not scared of maggots anymore," he noted as he mashed up his fast food bag, catching only a quick glimpse of Mr. Carswell taking his phone call just as Roy the driver closed the door.

"Yea? No, nothing important ..." were the last words he heard his producer say.

Desmond walked painfully through the patient entrance into the sterile lobby, barely acknowledging the security personnel and the indifferent front desk clerk. He knew they all knew who he was, and were probably told not to engage him, again to avoid a media crush.

He walked down the long tile hallway, made a turn and walked to his room, number 15A. He unlocked his door and tossed his key on the dresser. He had some time to kill before they turned on the day room television so he lay down on his bed.

After a few minutes there was a knock on the door.

And now it starts, Desmond thought, as he struggled back to his feet and checked his hair. The first wave of fans, eager to meet me and ask for my autograph. Now they all know who I am.

"Please come in."

A nurse entered, pushing a rolling metal cart with several pill cups and a dozen or more paper cups of water. "Good evening, Tom. How was your first unsupervised outing?"

"Great, I went to watch a movie with a friend of mine," Desmond explained, sitting back down on the edge of his bed. "Actually, he's my producer. He and I are going to start making movies again. You may have heard of him, his name is Wallace Carswell."

"Well, of course everyone has heard of Wallace Carswell," the nurse replied without looking up as she studied her clipboard. "But before you start making movies with your friend you have to take your meds." She handed Desmond two cups with two pills each and a cup of water. Desmond swallowed the four tablets and chased them with a swallow of water and a shudder. He never liked the water in this place; he thought it tasted like eggs.

The nurse logged the date and time on her clipboard. "Have you urinated today sweetie?" She asked.

"Yep." She checked it off.

"Any bowel movements?"

"Yep. One this morning. Firm." He took notice of the nurse's crisp white scrubs and white walking shoes. She had powerful facial features and a strong black female voice. He made a circle with his right hand and looked at her profile through the opening. She would have been perfect as one of the Afarkil women – perhaps the mother of the loveable twin scamps? Desmond would remember to jot that down in his notebook after she left.

"Have you taken any prescription or over-the-counter medications other than the ones I just gave you?" She looked up. "What are you doing?"

He dropped his hand. "Nothing. Do you happen to have twins?"

"No personal questions, now. You know that. Did you take any drugs or medication of any kind today, honey?"

"No ma'am."

"Did you consume any alcohol today?"

"Nope."

She asked him five or six more questions relating to his physical health, including if he had any sexual activity. Answering no to them all, she replaced the clipboard back under the cart. "Did you swallow the pills?"

"Yep."

"Let's take a look." Desmond opened his mouth wide and moved his tongue back and forth to prove to the nurse he had indeed swallowed them.

"Okay, you don't have any shoe strings now, do you dear?"

"Oh, right." Desmond picked up his shoes and noticed the strings were already gone, in accordance with regulations. That was odd; did the nurse remove them? Good grief, he didn't go to the movie theater without shoe strings, did he? How unprofessional! What would people think?

"I have a note here that says your mother called the front desk phone while you were out," the nurse added, lifting a page. "She said to call back when you feel like it."

"I'll call her tomorrow. I may have good news by then."

"Okay, I hope you have a pleasant evening, Tom. The television in the day room will be on from 7:30 until 10:00 tonight, but you must be back in here no later than ten minutes after ten. So don't get involved in some movie, understand, baby doll? It becomes a problem when you don't cooperate."

"Sure. And I guess you want my autograph before you go."

"Honey, you gave it to me when you first came here, remember?" The nurse smiled and patted the scrubs pocket over her heart. "I carry it right here."

She left the room as Desmond lay back and folded his arms behind his head. He glanced at the two VHS tapes by his bed.

As God is my witness, I was miraculously able to bring closure to the worst episodes in my life, then heroically get out alive through a hail of gunfire to tell about it. What happened to Gerald, or Jerry, or whatever name he used, was a long time coming, and I was the only one who could right that wrong, and I did because of my unique, perceptive abilities. Who would have guessed that I was placed in that desert under the auspices of making a movie to right a wrong 30 years old, almost to the day?

My experiences there were profoundly life-changing. I was an enormous success in that respect, and I think it is a story worth telling.

Someone should make a movie about it.

ABOUT THE AUTHOR

Dale M. Brumfield is an anti-death penalty advocate, award-winning journalist, sometime adjunct professor, author and cultural archaeologist. Dale received his MFA in fiction from Virginia Commonwealth University in 2015, and writes for numerous publications nationwide. He and his wife Susan have three adult children, and currently live near Doswell, Virginia.

Thanks Zac Valdez, Ward Tefft, all my Richmond and Virginia supporters, my patient wife Susan, and the greatest kids in the world, Hunter, Jackson and Hollis.

Photo by Heinrich Brumfield near Cape Town, South Africa, 2017